SILENT BUT DEADLY

SILENT BUT DEADLY

ANOTHER LIŌ COLLECTION

BY MARK TATULLI

**Andrews McMeel
Publishing, LLC**

Kansas City

LIŌ is distributed internationally by Universal Press Syndicate.

 For information, write Andrews McMeel Publishing, LLC, an Andrews McMeel Universal company, 1130 Walnut Street, Kansas City, Missouri 64106.

ISBN-13: 978-0-7407-7742-4
ISBN-10: 0-7407-7742-4

Library of Congress Control Number: 2008923477

08 09 10 11 12 WKT 10 9 8 7 6 5 4 3 2 1

www.andrewsmcmeel.com

TO MY THREE
LITTLE MONSTERS...

DEAN LEXA AND TORI

LOVE ALWAYS —
DAD

Foreword

So you have this book in your hands. Odds are, it's not by accident that you've picked it up, because you already know *LIŌ*. In fact, you don't just know it, you love it. It's one of your favorite comic strips. This made me wonder why such a book would need a foreword. I can't imagine that anyone who's a fan of *LIŌ* would even bother reading a foreword. What could I possibly tell you that you don't already know about the strip? You're going to skip right over this and go right to the cartoons, right? You can't even answer that question because you're not reading this, you're reading the cartoons! Hey, I don't blame you.

So why am I spending my valuable time writing this? Hmmm . . . Well, maybe someone has given this book to you as a gift and you've never seen the strip before because your local paper doesn't carry it (which means the editor is a moron and should be fired immediately). OK, I can see that, but that would be a pretty small percentage of people holding this book in their hands. But if that's your case, let me just tell you that *LIŌ* is brilliant. It's not the usual comic strip fare . . . which is one of the reasons it's brilliant. *LIŌ* is original and unique, and fits into my definition of greatness in art.

I've noticed over several decades of observation that if a movie, television show, book, or comic strip can be easily summed up and understood in one simple sentence, then it has no depth or intelligence behind it. Conversely, if it can't be adequately described in a capsulated form, where it has to be seen to be understood, then this puts it in the highest level of its art form. *LIŌ* is definitely a case of the latter. The best way I could describe the essence of *LIŌ* is that it's sweetly dark. You'll have to read it to know what I mean by that. So if you've never seen *LIŌ* before, sit back, open your mind, and have a great time.

Now, for the majority of you who are already devoted fans, I guess the only reason you're still reading this is that you're hoping to gain new insight about the mind behind *LIŌ*, what Mark Tatulli is really like, and what led him to this. Or perhaps you're hoping for some juicy nuggets that you won't find in his usual bio material. Frankly, I've never quite understood such prurient interest. Isn't it enough that he works his butt off creating a feature you love to read every day? Does it really matter that he worked his way through medical school as an "exotic dancer" and later gave up a lucrative career as a research scientist to become a cartoonist? OK, OK . . . for those of you who are hoping for some actual inside info, something that isn't public knowledge, here it is:

Through his creation of *LIŌ*, Mark Tatulli has received the highest compliment given to a cartoonist. It's a compliment that comes from within the cartooning community. It's not an award handed out at some lavish ceremony. It's something uttered privately, if uttered out loud at all, by nearly every professional cartoonist after first seeing his creation: "I wish I had thought of that!"

Another hallmark of brilliance. But you already know that.

—Wiley Miller, creator of *Non Sequitur*

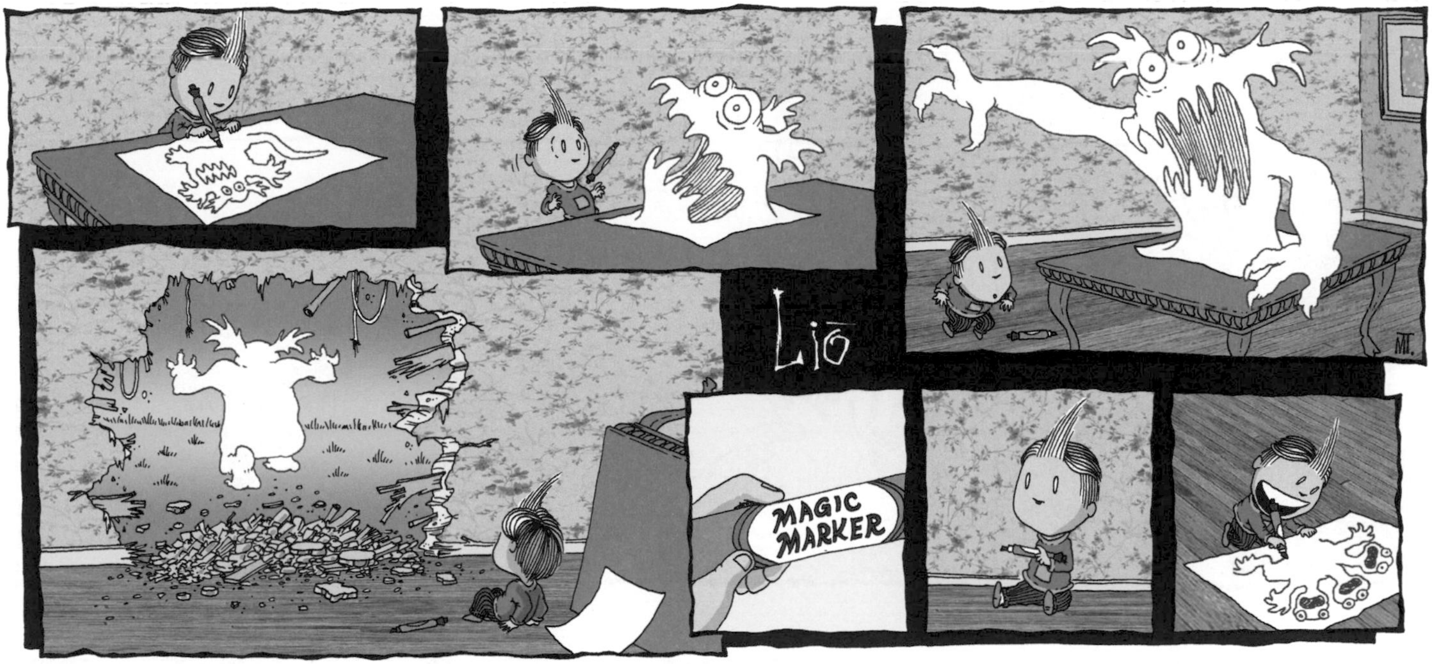
Liō
MAGIC MARKER
MT.

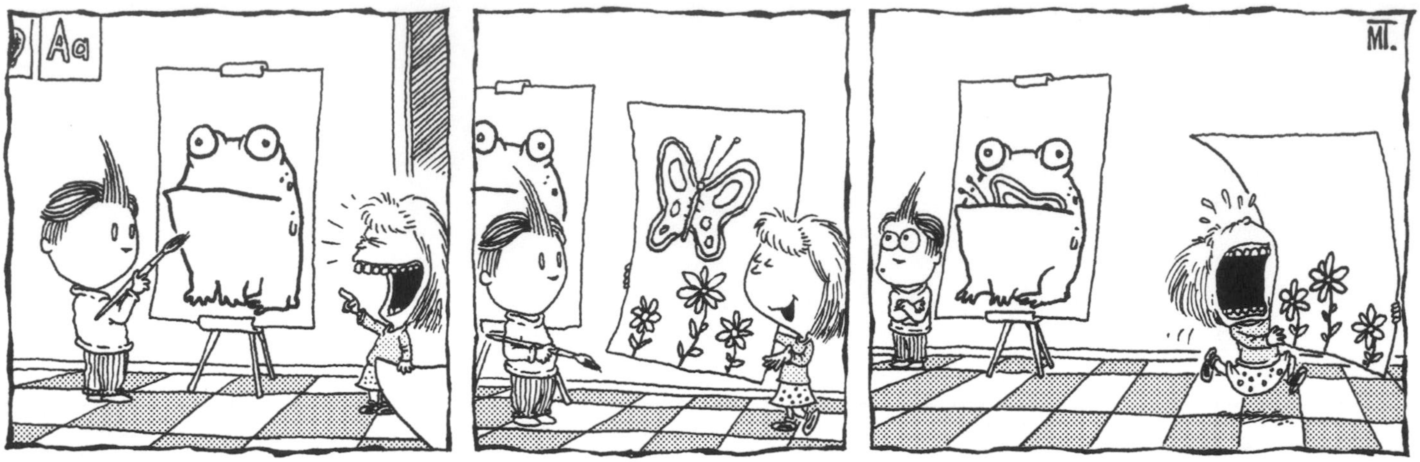
Aa
MT.

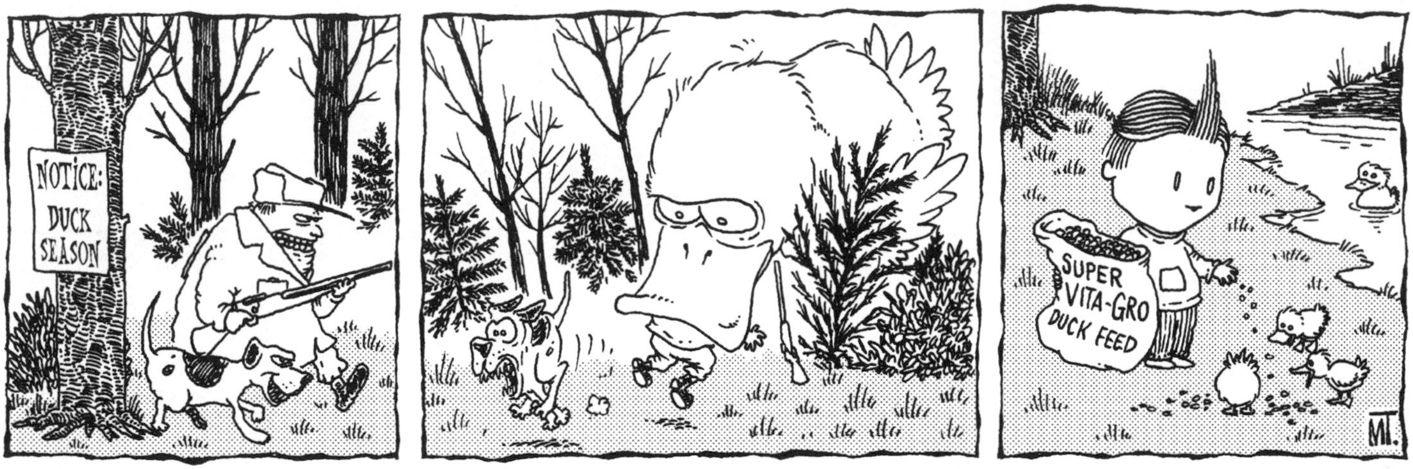
NOTICE:
DUCK SEASON
SUPER VITA-GRO DUCK FEED
MT.

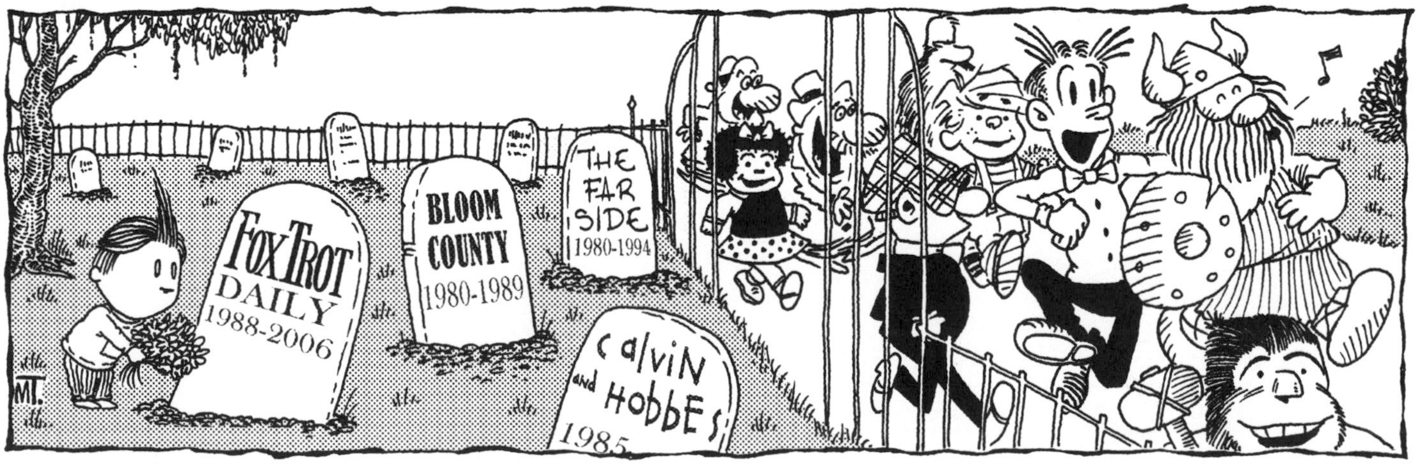
MT.
FOXTROT DAILY 1988-2006
BLOOM COUNTY 1980-1989
THE FAR SIDE 1980-1994
CALVIN and HOBBES 1985

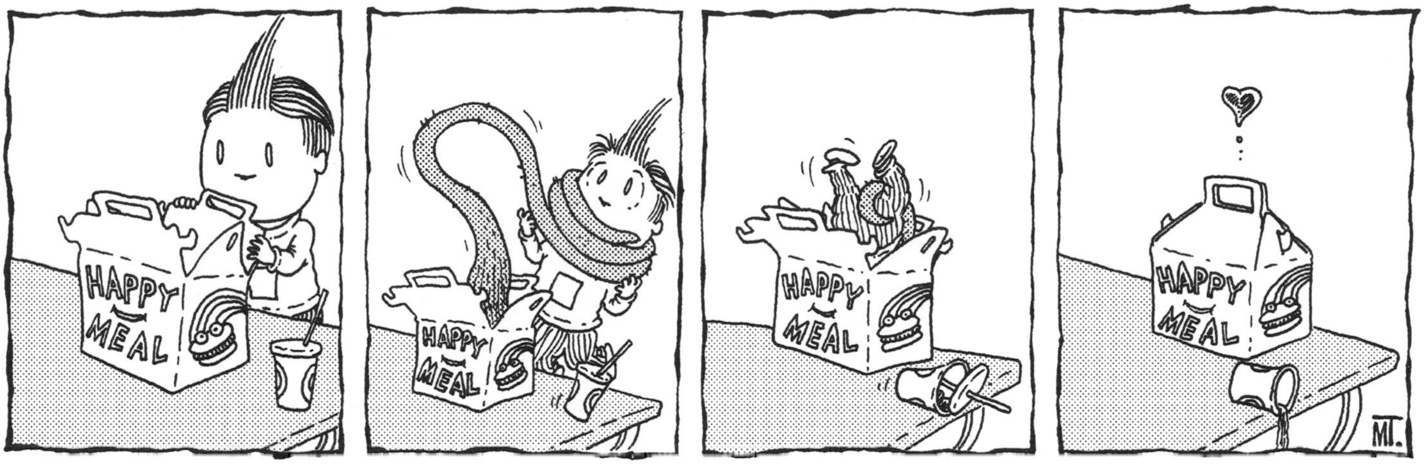
HAPPY MEAL
HAPPY MEAL
HAPPY MEAL
HAPPY MEAL
MT.

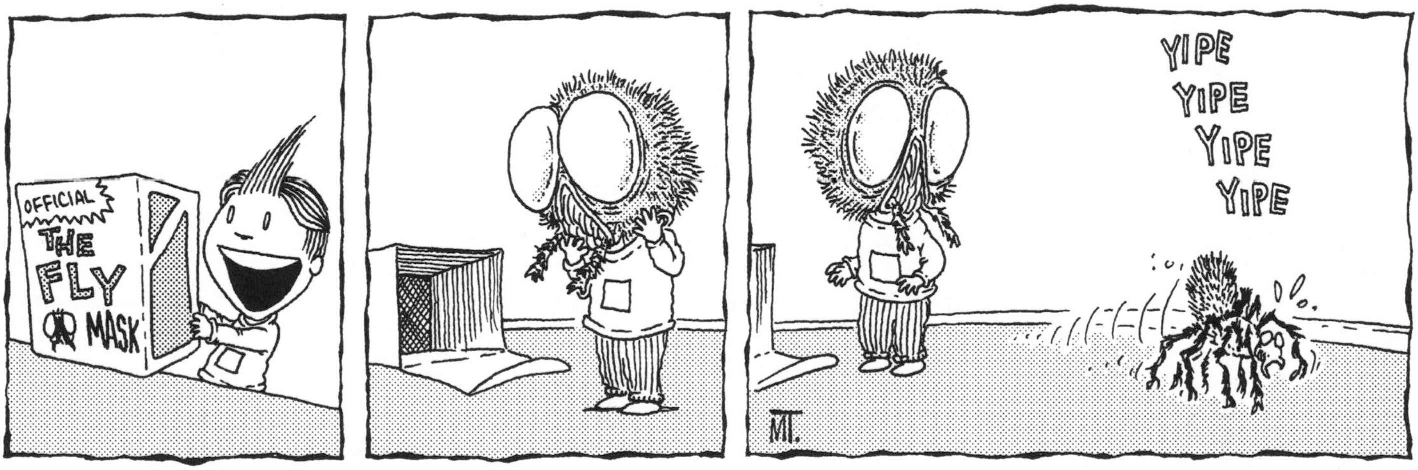
OFFICIAL THE FLY MASK
YIPE
YIPE
YIPE
YIPE
MT.

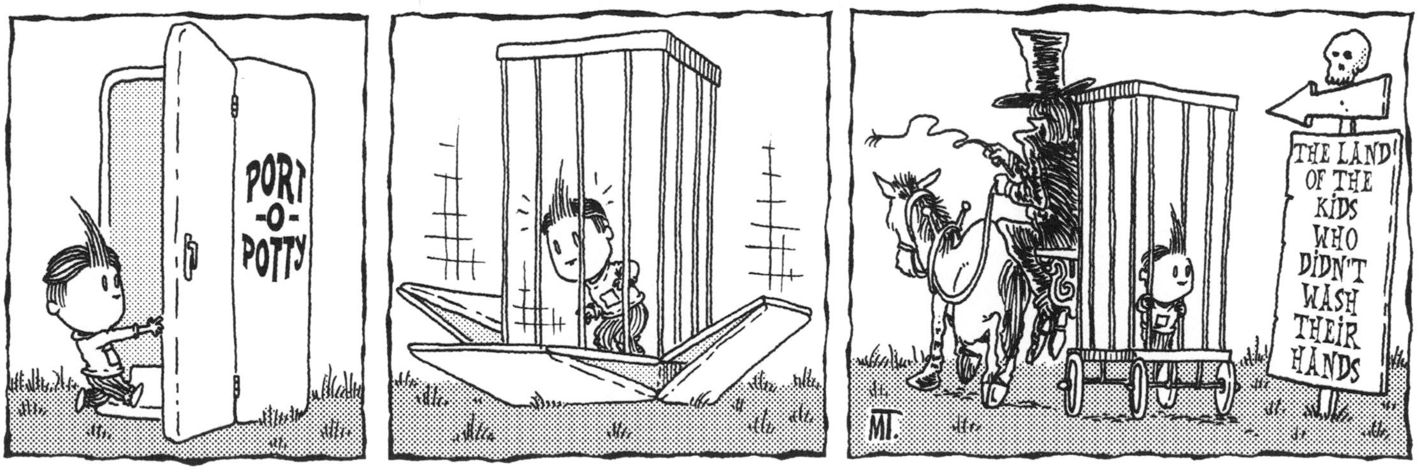
PORT -O- POTTY
THE LAND OF THE KIDS WHO DIDN'T WASH THEIR HANDS
MT.

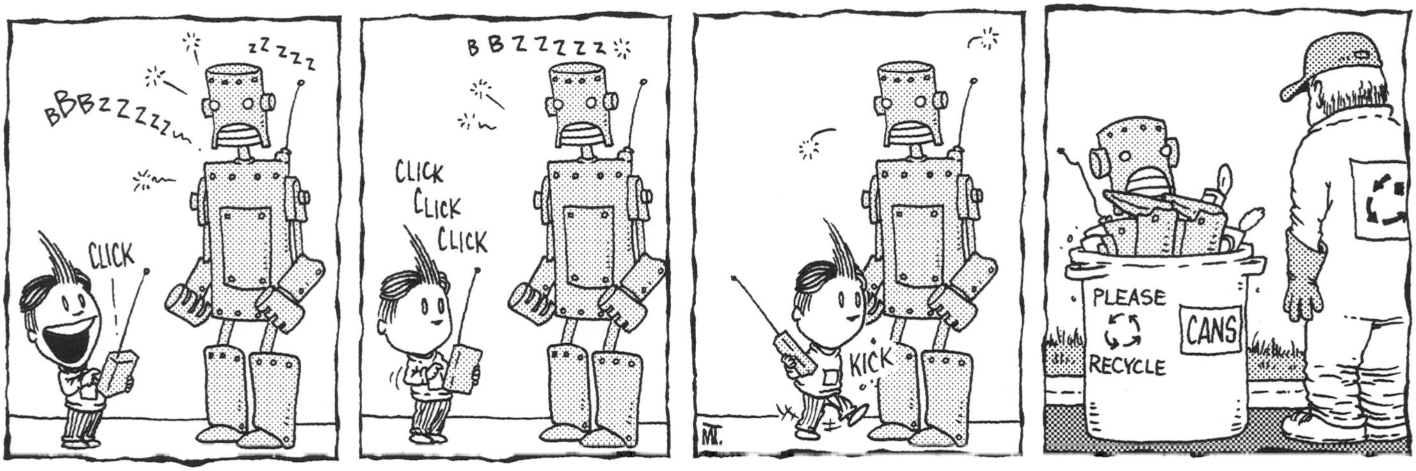
zZZZZ
BBBZZZZZZm
CLICK
BBZZZZZZ
CLICK
CLICK
CLICK
KICK
PLEASE
RECYCLE
CANS

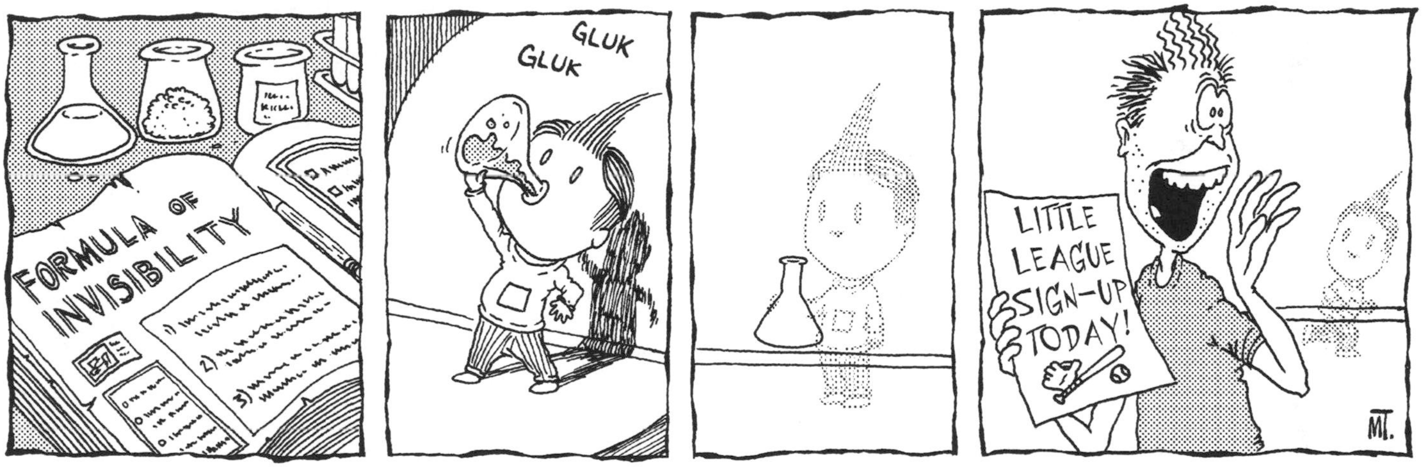
FORMULA OF INVISIBILITY
GLUK
GLUK
LITTLE LEAGUE SIGN-UP TODAY!

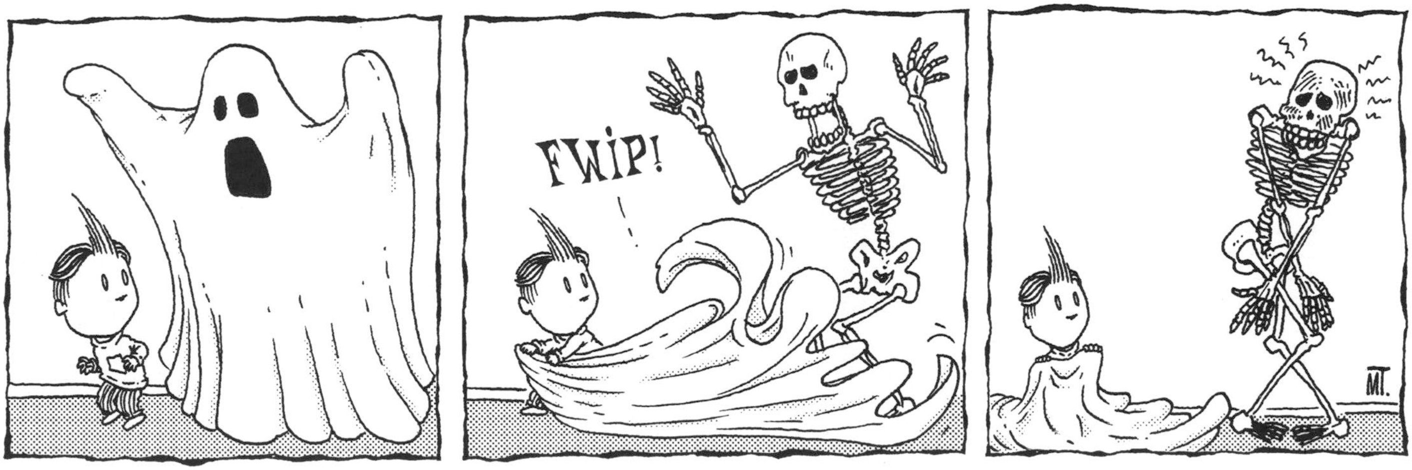
FWIP!

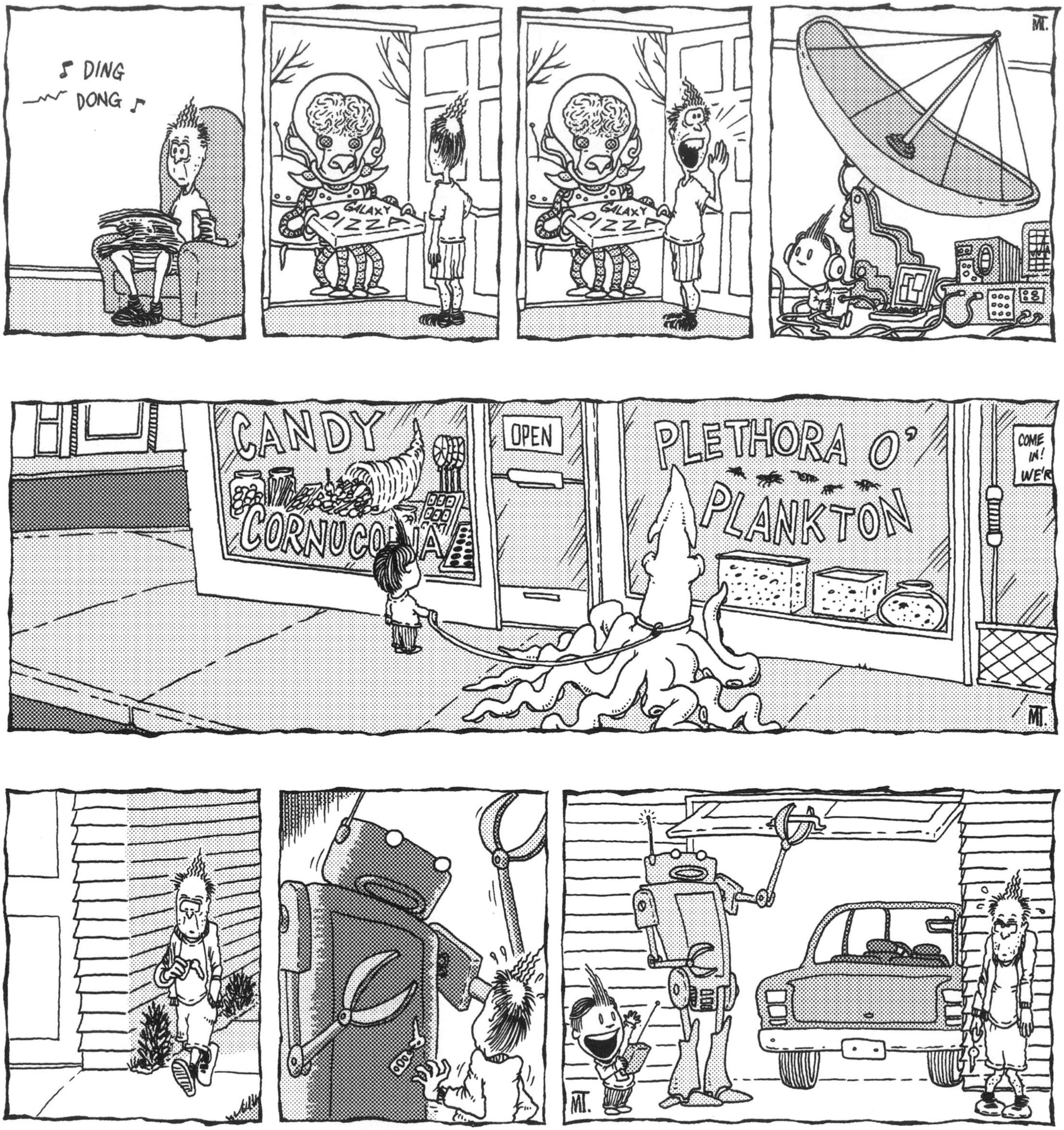

DING
DONG
GALAXY PIZZA
GALAXY PIZZA
MT.
CANDY
OPEN
PLETHORA O' PLANKTON
COME IN! WE'R
MT.
MT.

Lio

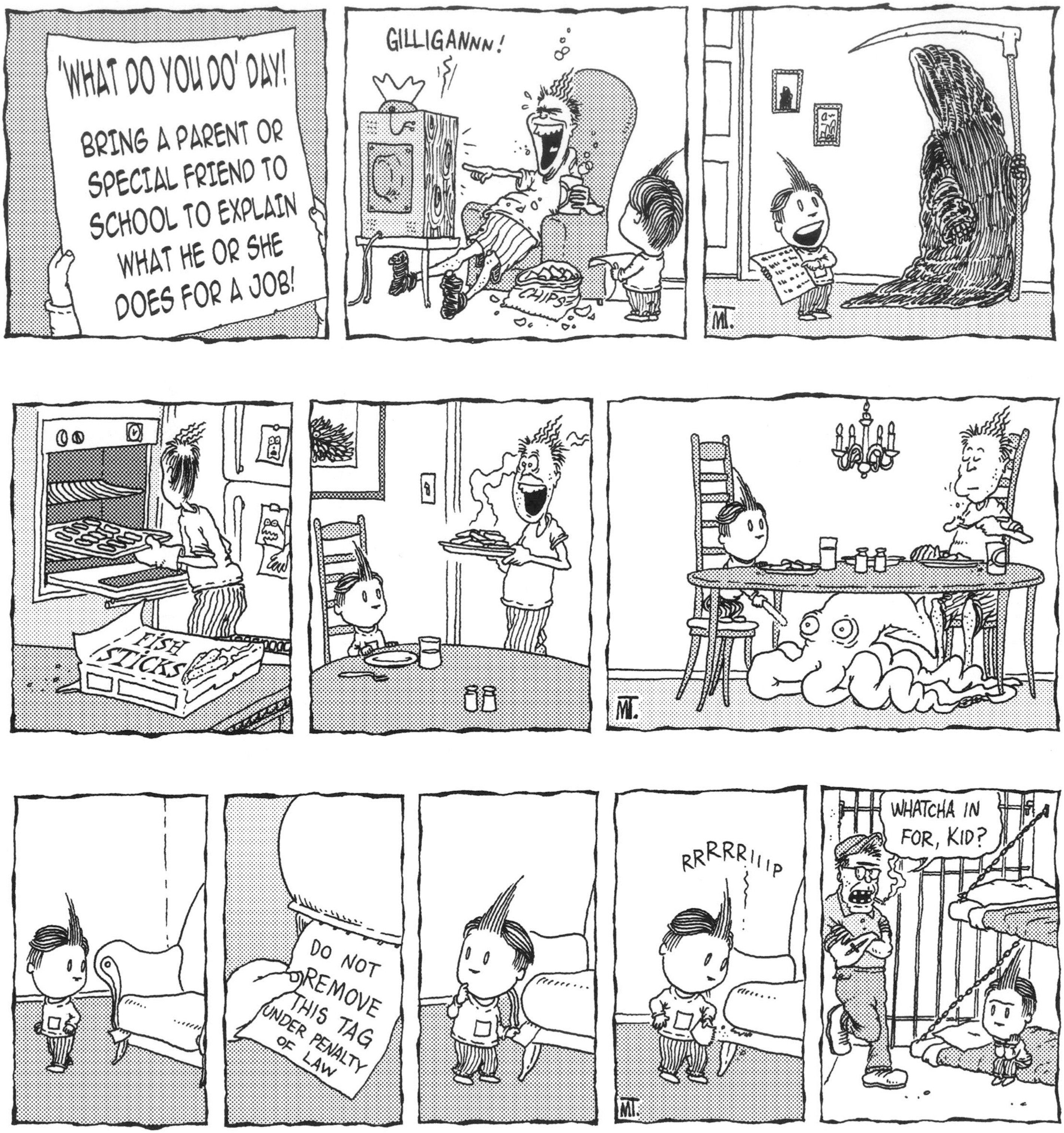

'WHAT DO YOU DO' DAY!
BRING A PARENT OR SPECIAL FRIEND TO SCHOOL TO EXPLAIN WHAT HE OR SHE DOES FOR A JOB!
GILLIGANNN!
CHIPS
FISH STICKS
DO NOT REMOVE THIS TAG UNDER PENALTY OF LAW
RRRRRIIIP
WHATCHA IN FOR, KID?

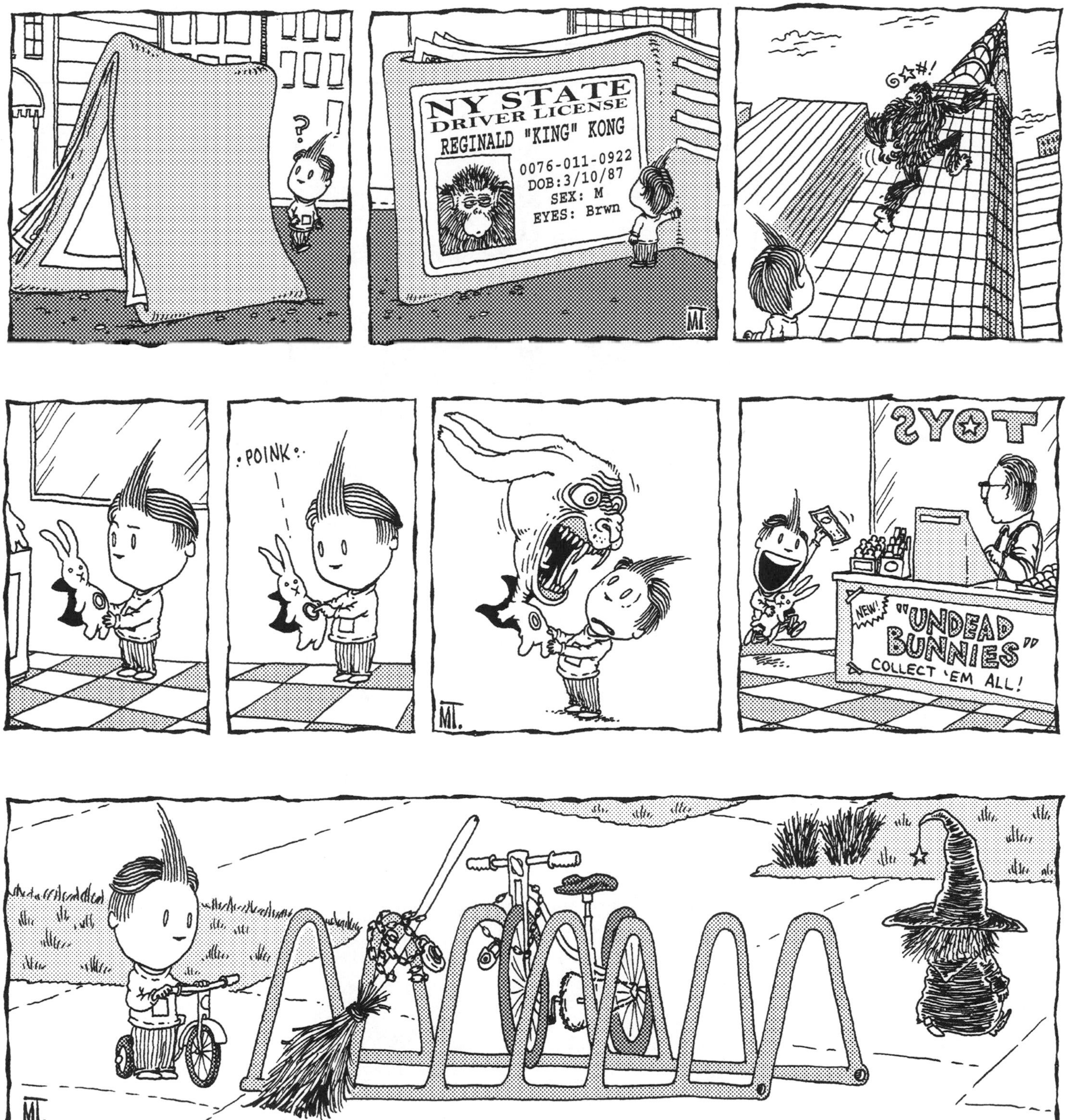
?
!
NY STATE
DRIVER LICENSE
REGINALD "KING" KONG
0076-011-0922
DOB:3/10/87
SEX: M
EYES: Brwn
POINK
TOYS
NEW!
"UNDEAD BUNNIES"
COLLECT 'EM ALL!

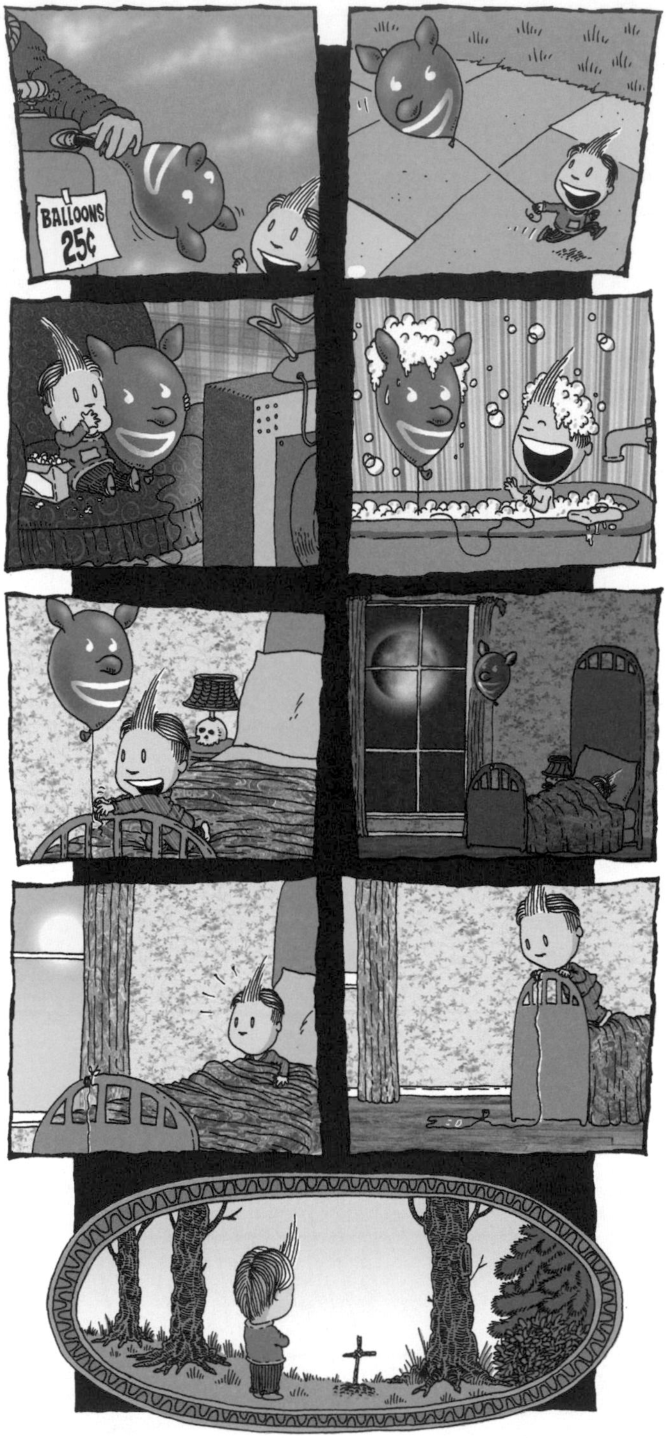
BALLOONS
25¢

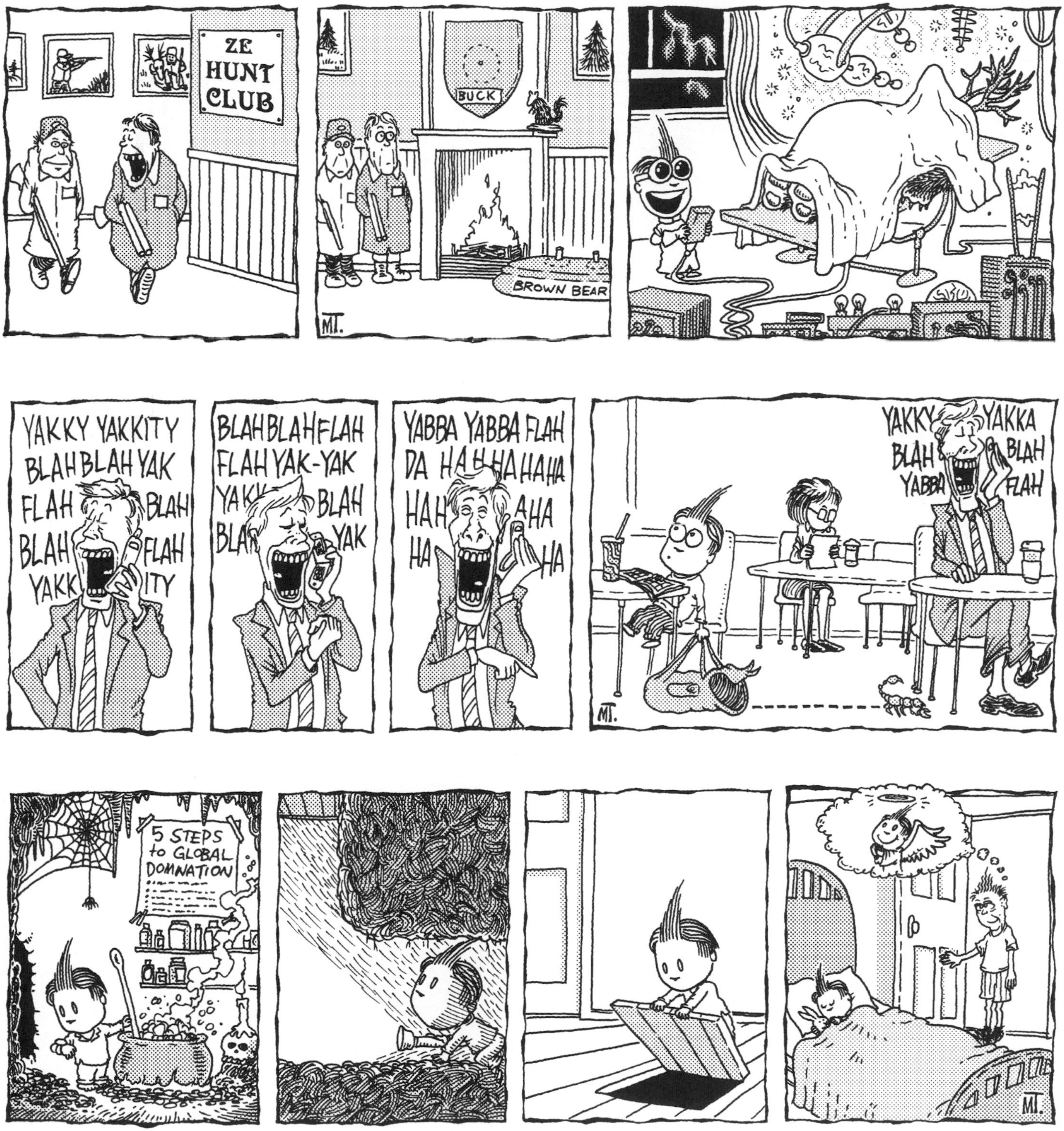
ZE HUNT CLUB
BUCK
BROWN BEAR
YAKKY YAKKITY
BLAH BLAH YAK
FLAH BLAH
BLAH FLAH
YAKK ITY
BLAH BLAH FLAH
FLAH YAK-YAK
BLAH
YAK
YABBA YABBA FLAH
DA HA HA HA HA
HAH AHA
HA HA
YAKKY YAKKA
BLAH BLAH
YABBA FLAH
5 STEPS to GLOBAL DOMINATION

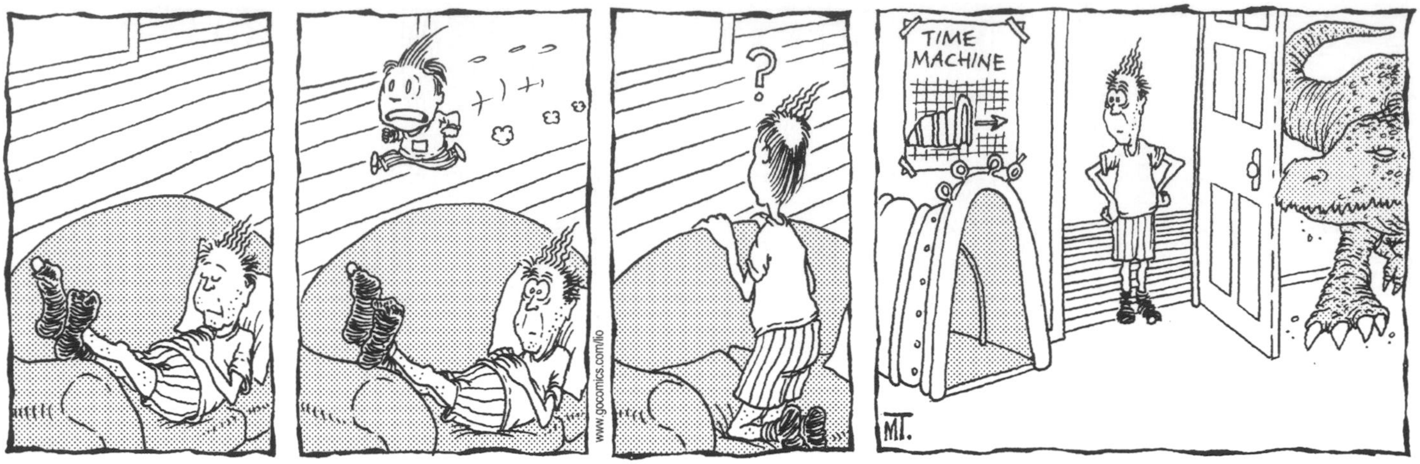
www.gocomics.com/lio
TIME MACHINE
MT.

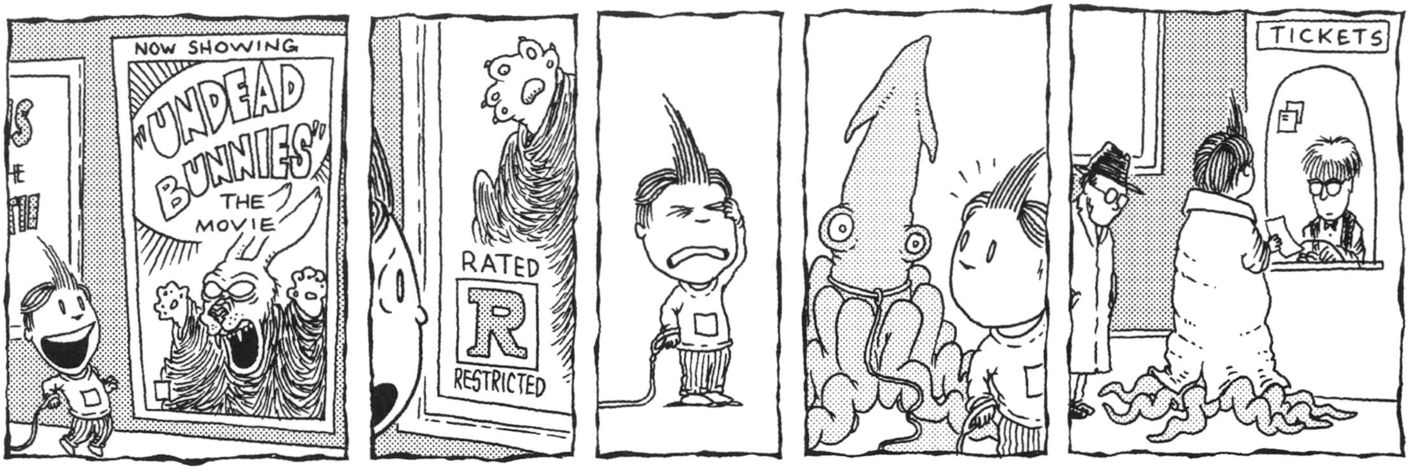
NOW SHOWING
"UNDEAD BUNNIES" THE MOVIE
RATED
R
RESTRICTED
TICKETS

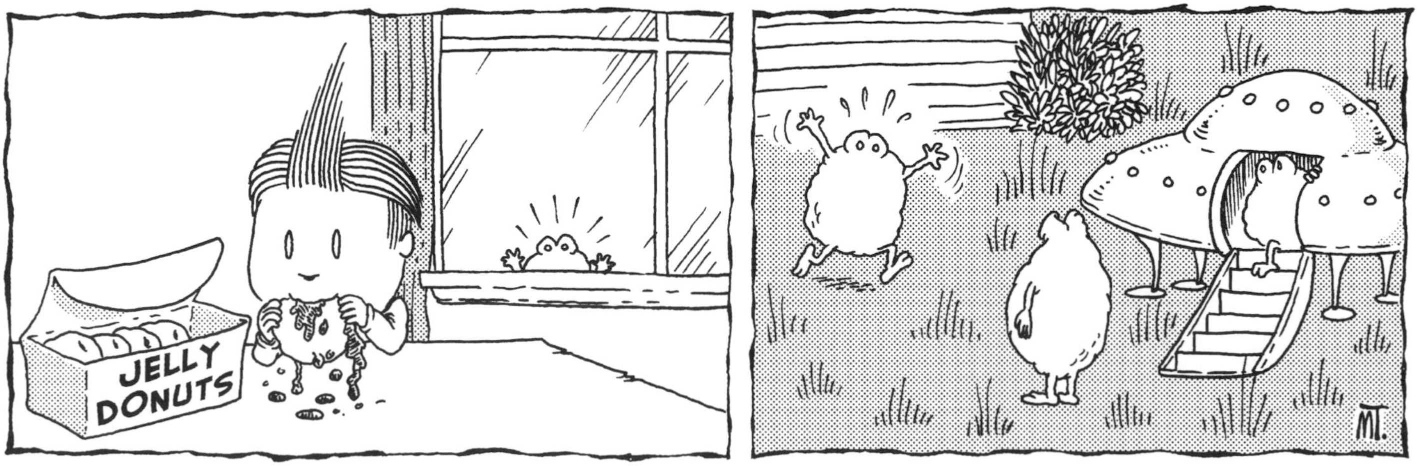
JELLY DONUTS
MT.

FOR WORSER OR FOR BEST
By Joann Lynstone
OUR MARRIAGE IS A SHAM!
THANK GOD YOU SAID IT! I'VE ABOUT HAD IT WITH YOU AND YOUR STUPID TRAIN SET!
OH, WE'RE FINALLY SPEAKING OUR MINDS? THEN LET ME JUST SAY THERE IS NO WAY I'M ENDING UP WITH THIS GOOF-BALL AND HIS WALLPAPER-BRUSH MUSTACHE!
WELL, THE TRUTH IS OUT! THEN I CAN FINALLY DITCH THIS CHAIR, DUMP YOU GOODY-GOODIES AND GO BLOW SOME DOUGH ON HOT DANCIN' CHICKS!
?
?
?
?
-- BLOW SOME DOUGH ON HOT DANCIN' CHICKS!
CUE CARDS
PRODUCTION STATION
MOM: AND WHEN ARE THOSE TWO DOGS GONNA CROAK ALREADY?!
MT.

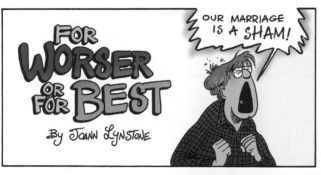

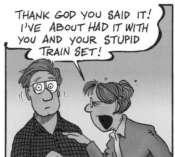

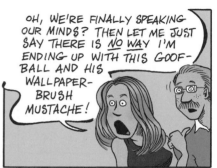

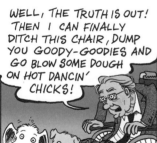

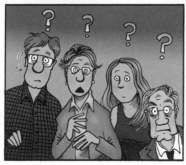

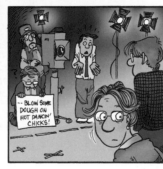

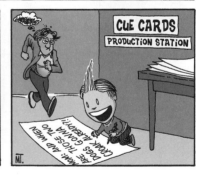

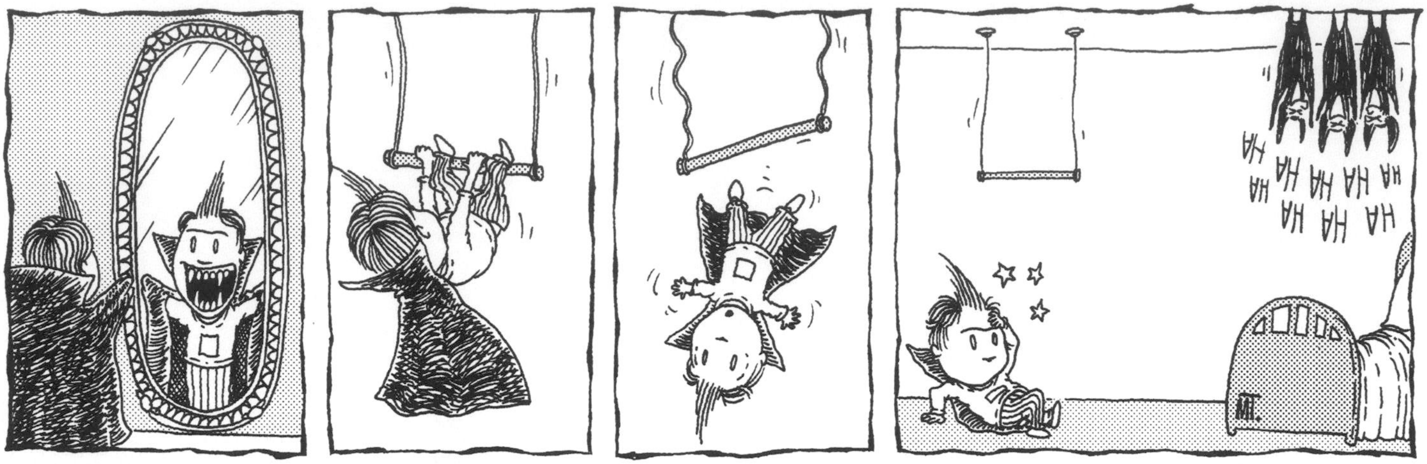
HA HA HA
HA HA HA HA HA
HA
MT.

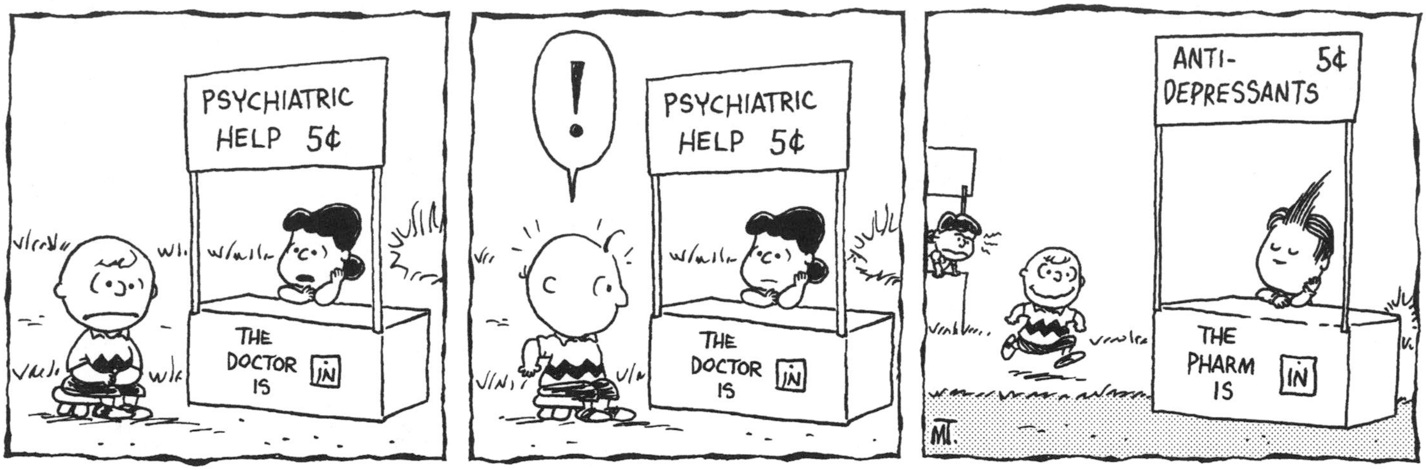
PSYCHIATRIC HELP 5¢
THE DOCTOR IS IN
!
PSYCHIATRIC HELP 5¢
THE DOCTOR IS IN
ANTI-DEPRESSANTS 5¢
THE PHARM IS IN
MT.

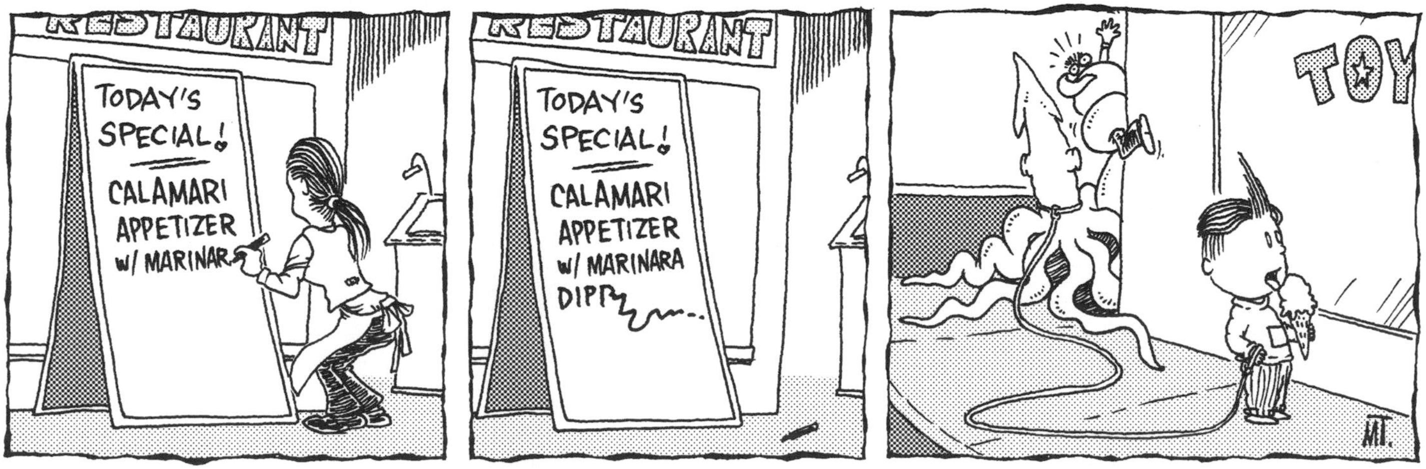
RESTAURANT
TODAY'S SPECIAL!
CALAMARI APPETIZER W/ MARINAR
RESTAURANT
TODAY'S SPECIAL!
CALAMARI APPETIZER W/ MARINARA DIPP
TOY
MT.

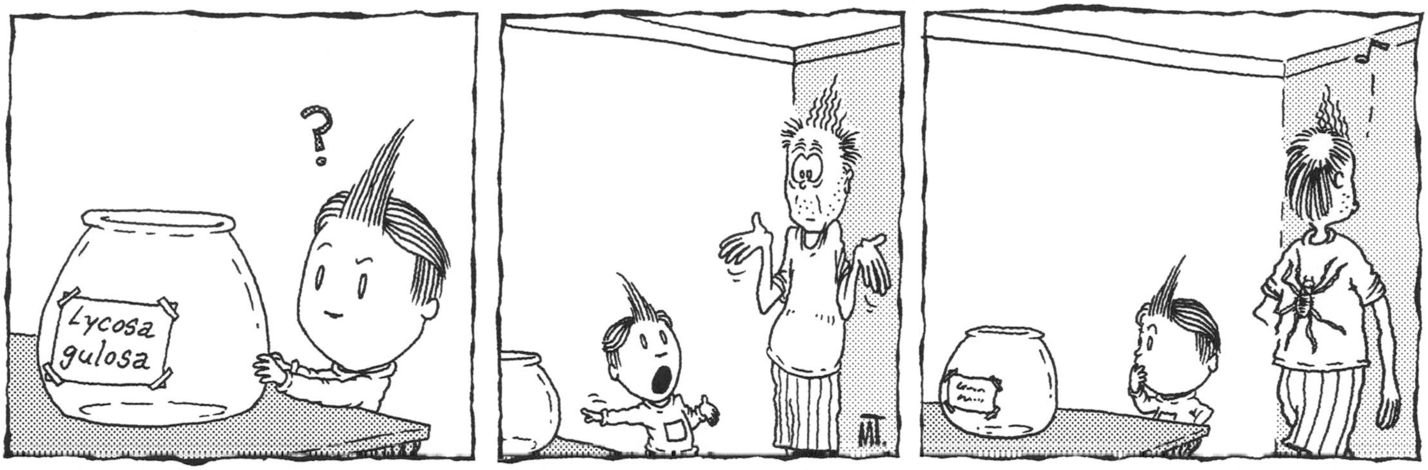
?
Lycosa gulosa

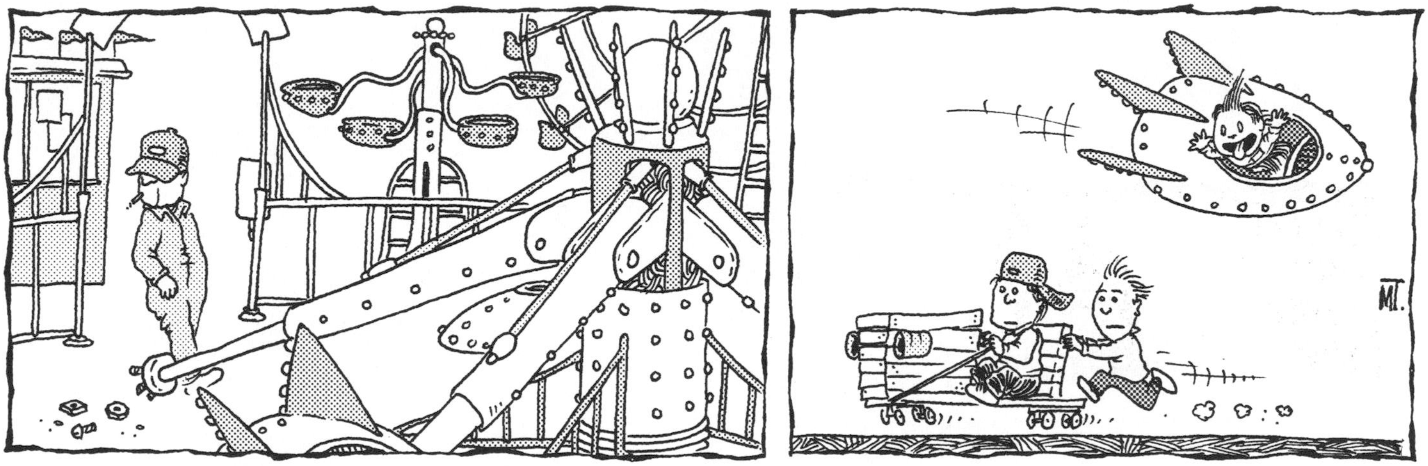

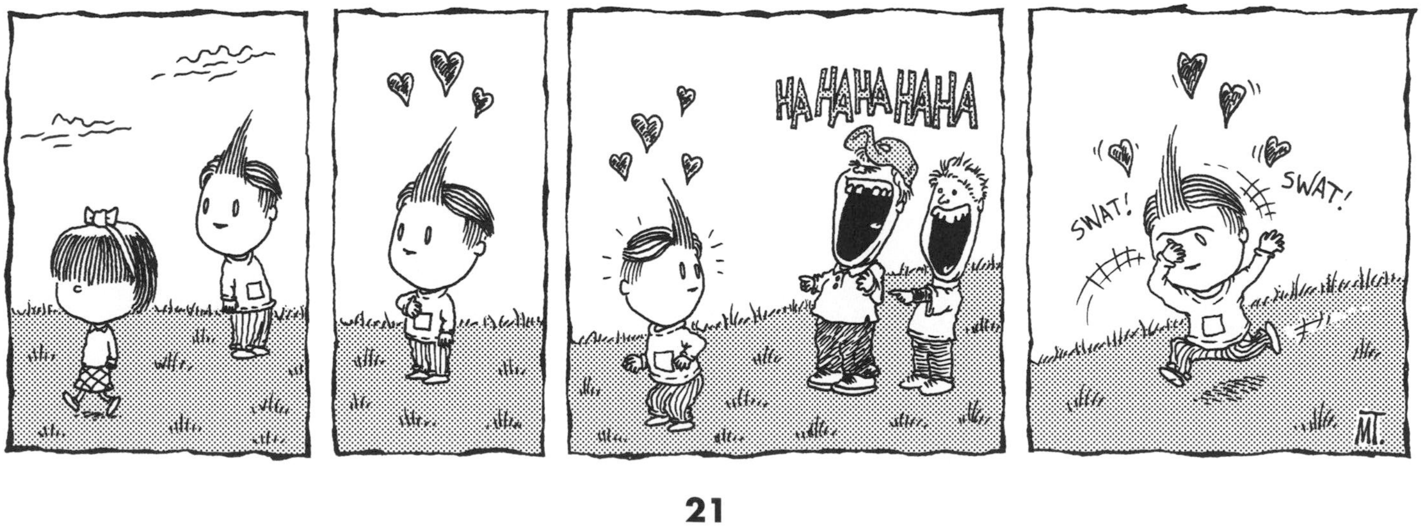
HA HAHA HAHA
SWAT!
SWAT!

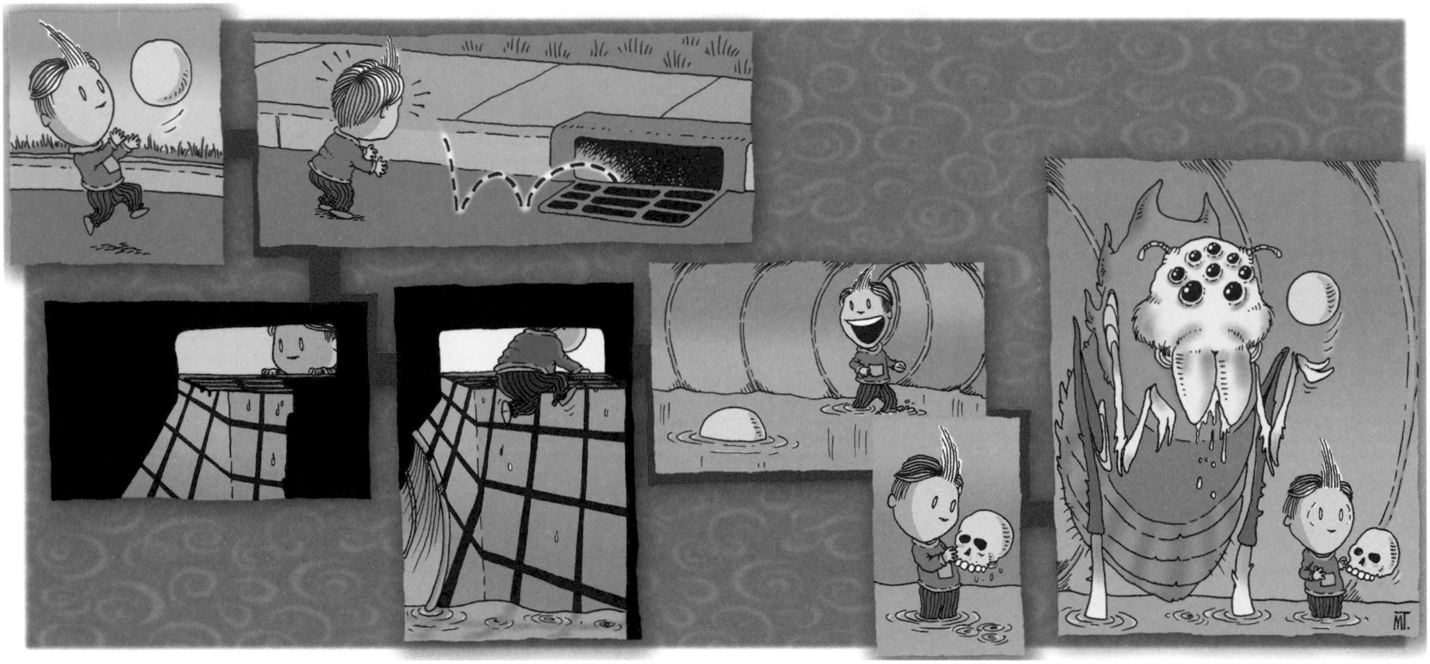
MT.

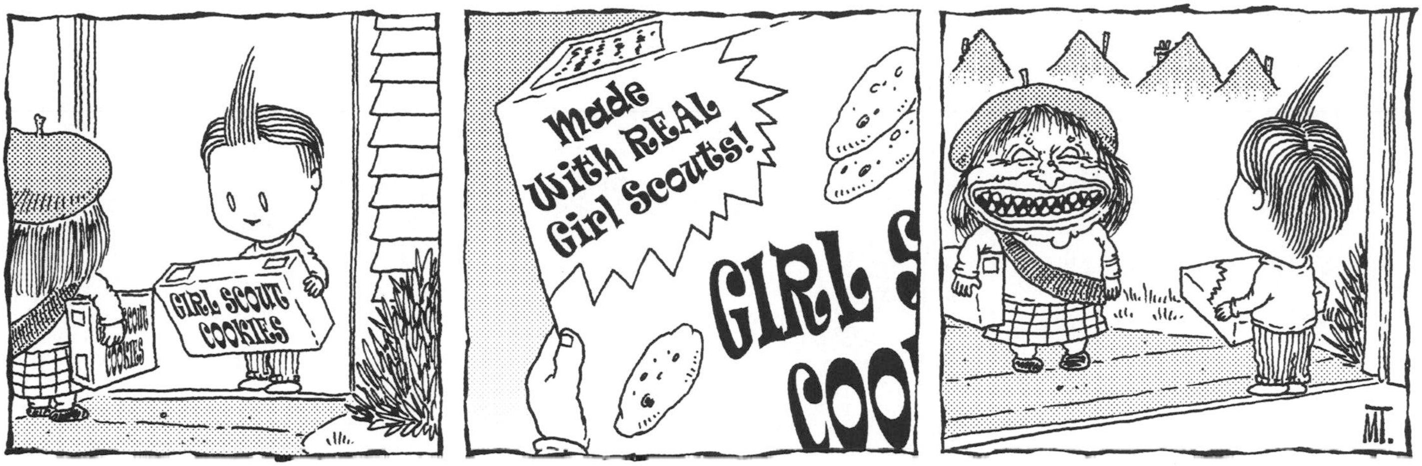
GIRL SCOUT COOKIES
SCOUT COOKIES
Made With REAL Girl Scouts!
MT.

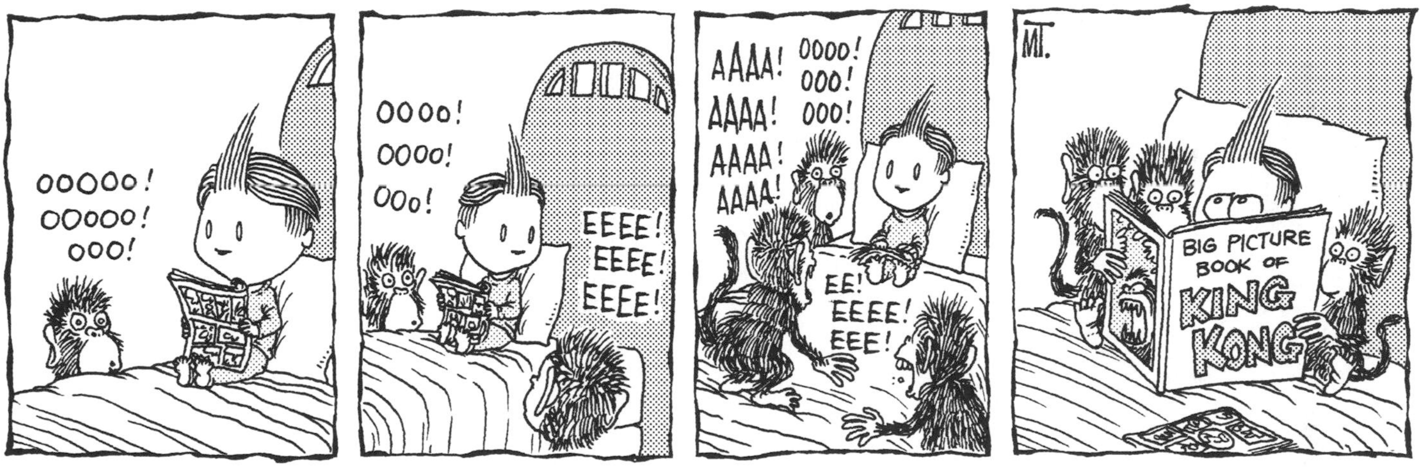
OOOOO!
OOOOO!
OOO!
OOOo!
OOOo!
OOo!
EEEE!
EEEE!
EEEE!
AAAA!
AAAA!
AAAA!
AAAA!
OOOO!
OOO!
OOO!
EE!
EEEE!
EEE!
MT.
BIG PICTURE BOOK OF KING KONG

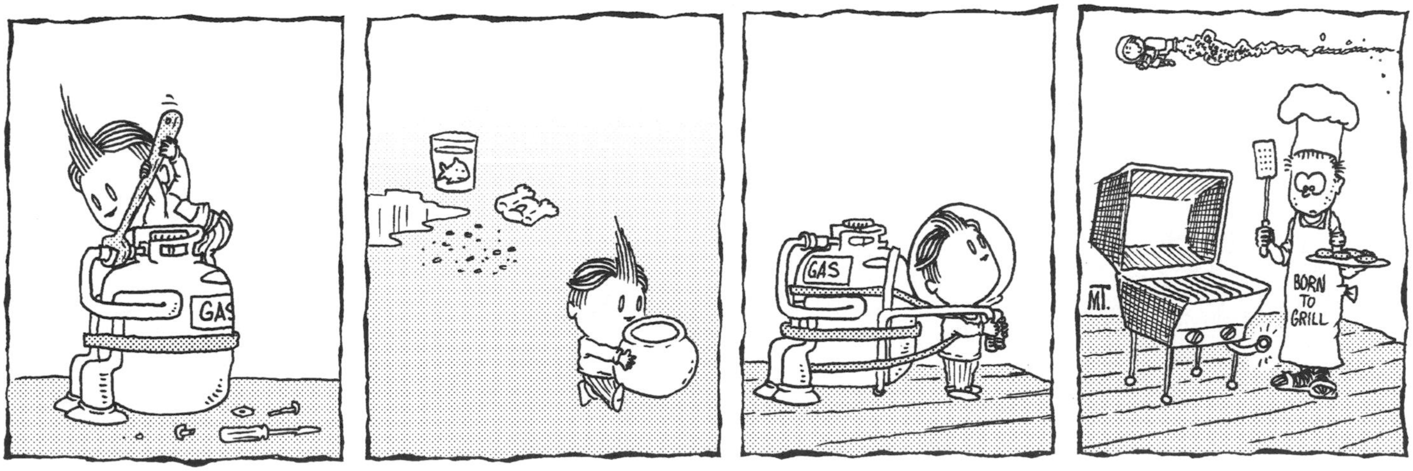
GAS
GAS
MT.
BORN TO GRILL

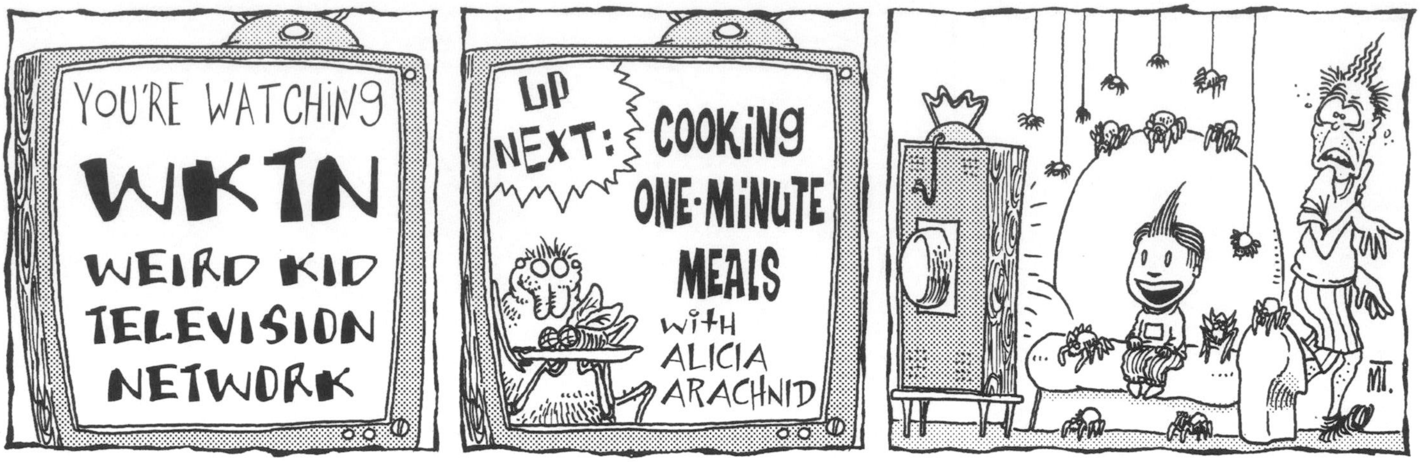
YOU'RE WATCHING
WKTN
WEIRD KID
TELEVISION
NETWORK
UP NEXT:
COOKING
ONE-MINUTE
MEALS
WITH
ALICIA
ARACHNID
MT.

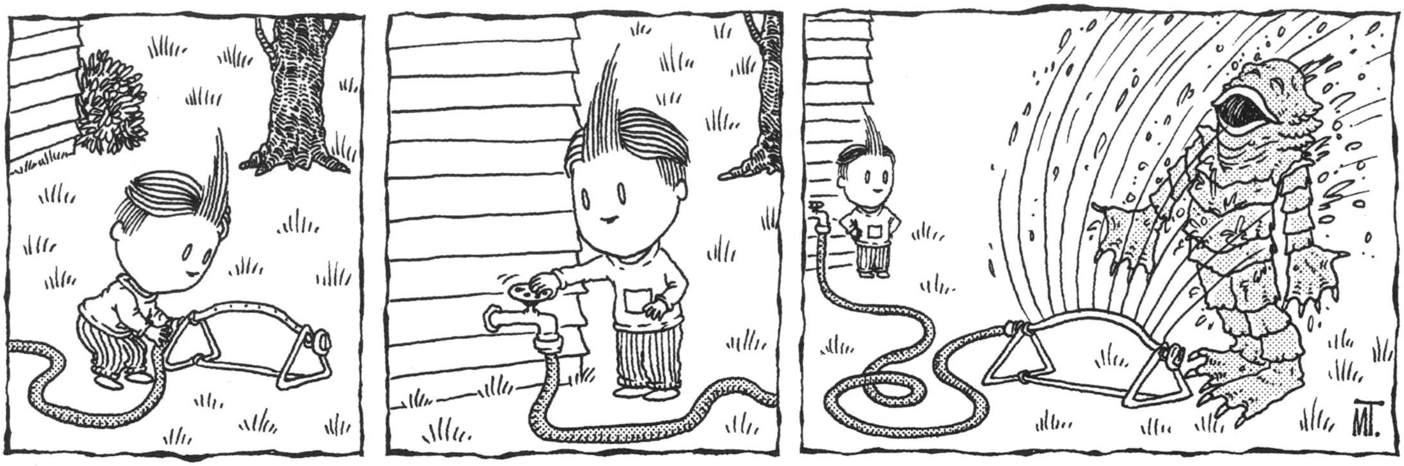
MT.

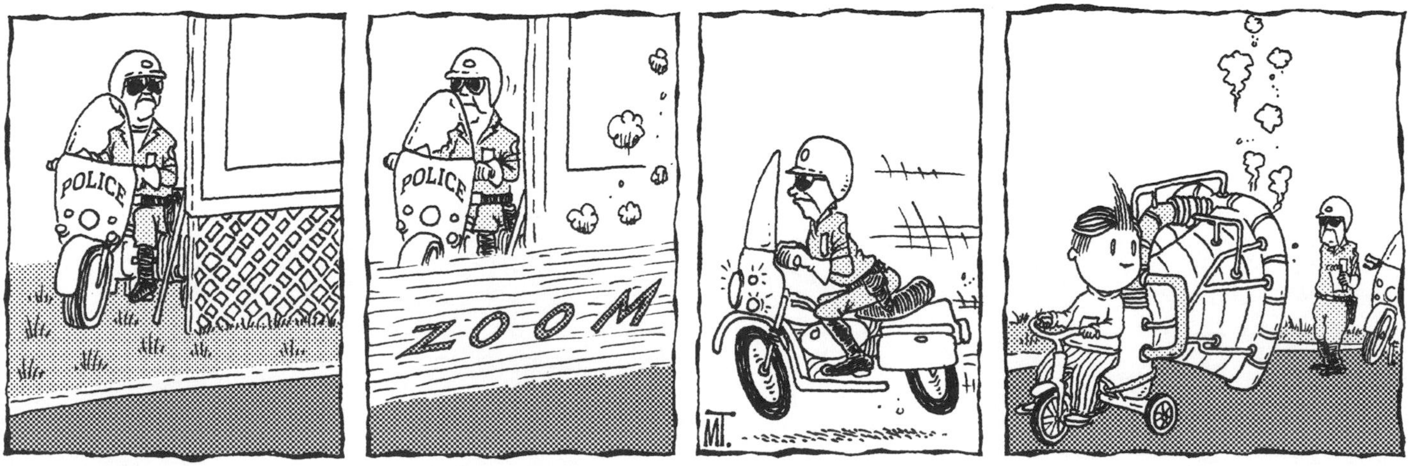
POLICE
POLICE
ZOOM
MT.

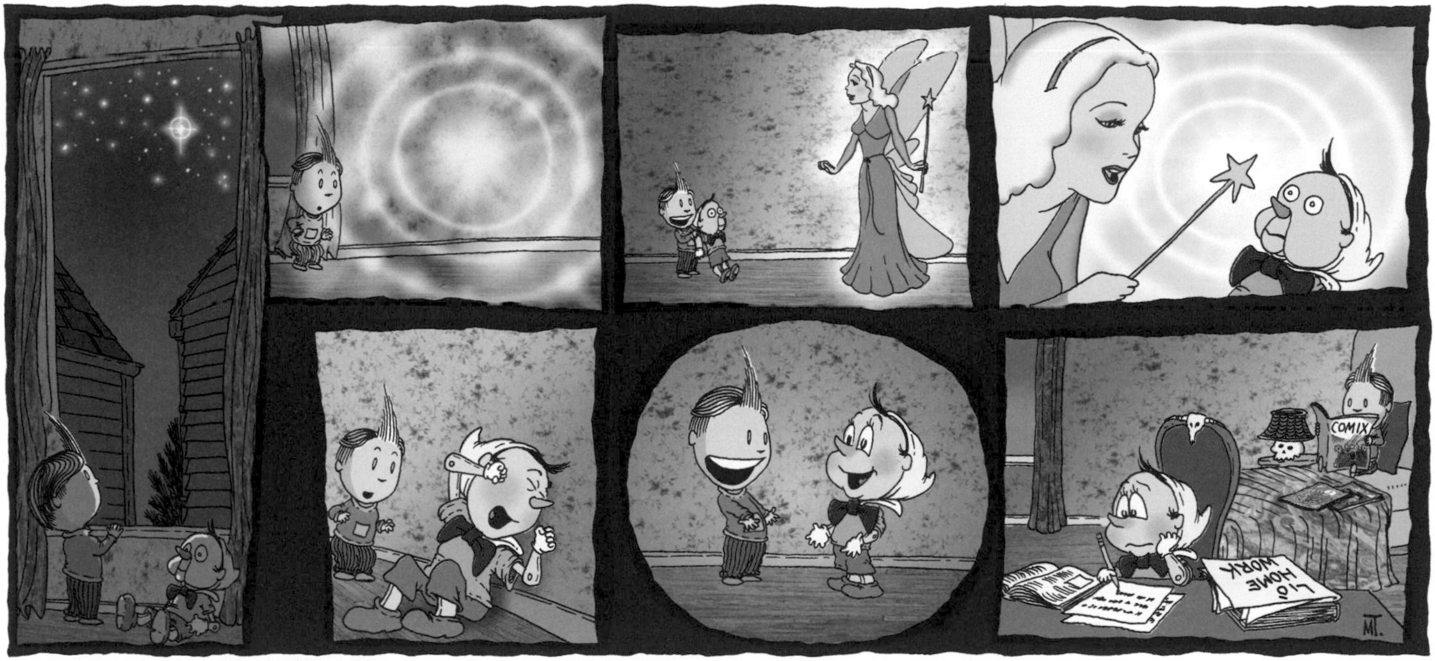
COMIX
HOME
WORK
MT.

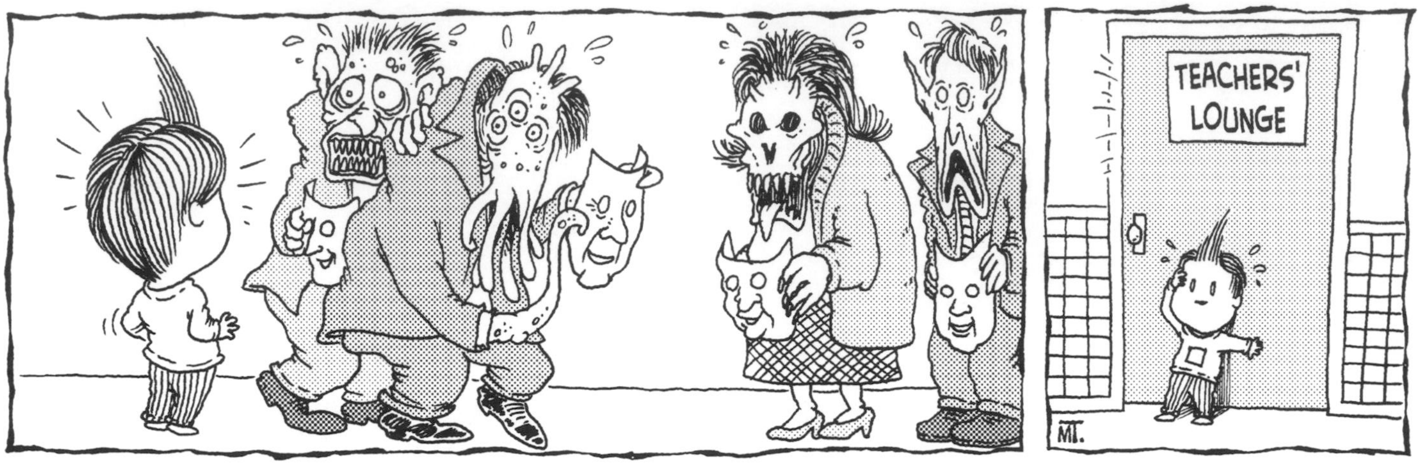
TEACHERS' LOUNGE

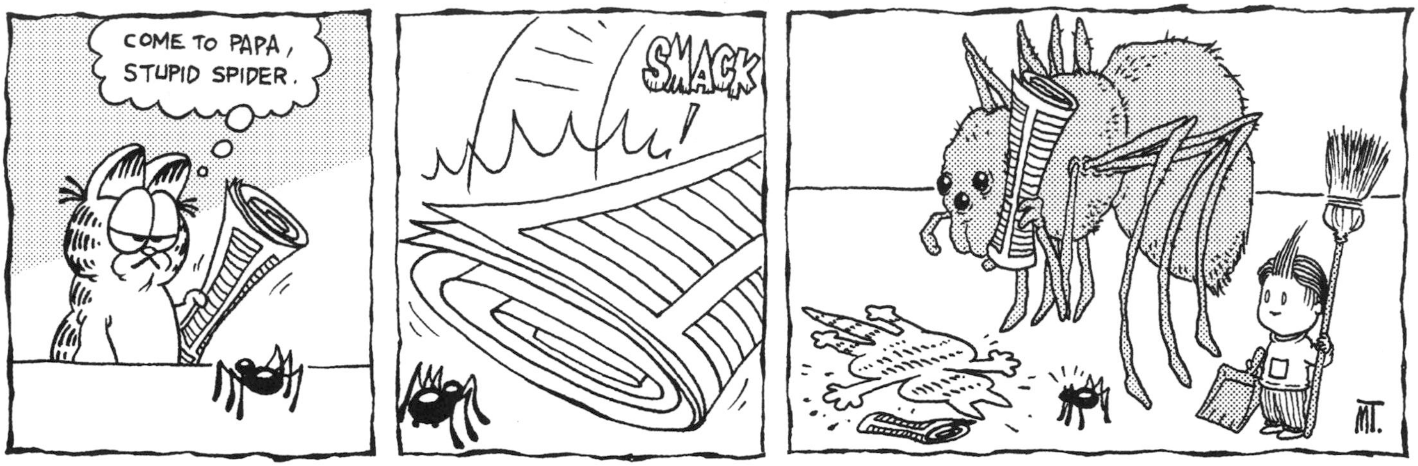
COME TO PAPA, STUPID SPIDER.
SMACK!

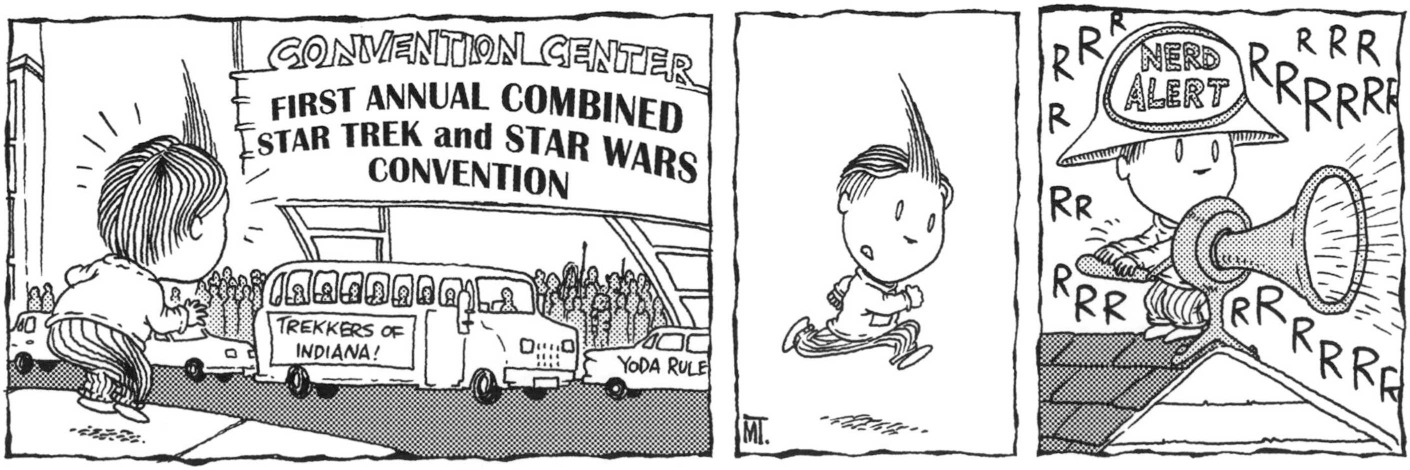
CONVENTION CENTER
FIRST ANNUAL COMBINED STAR TREK and STAR WARS CONVENTION
TREKKERS OF INDIANA!
YODA RULE
NERD ALERT

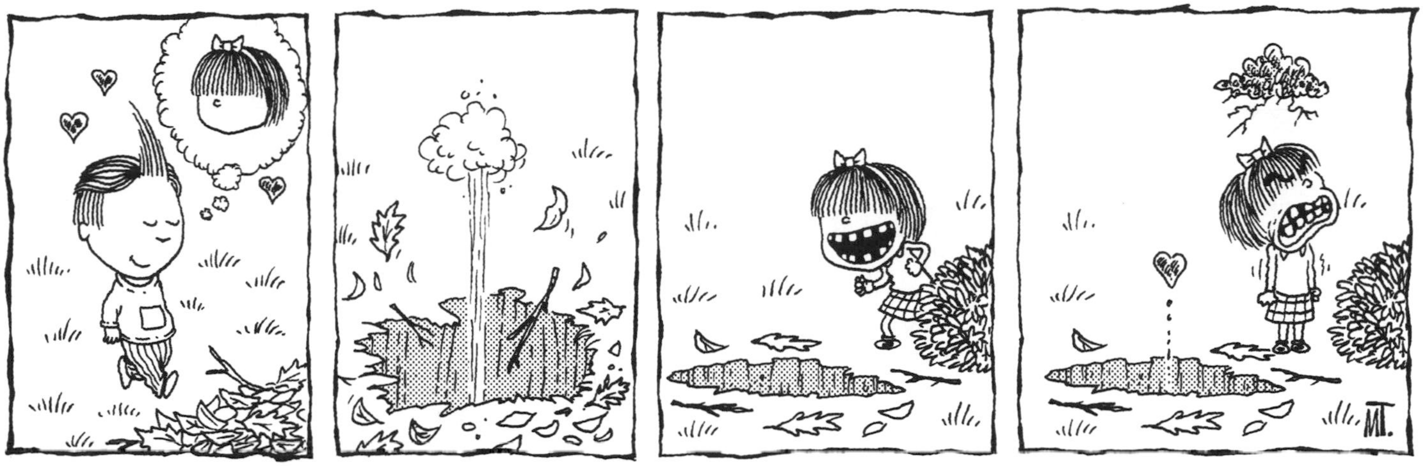

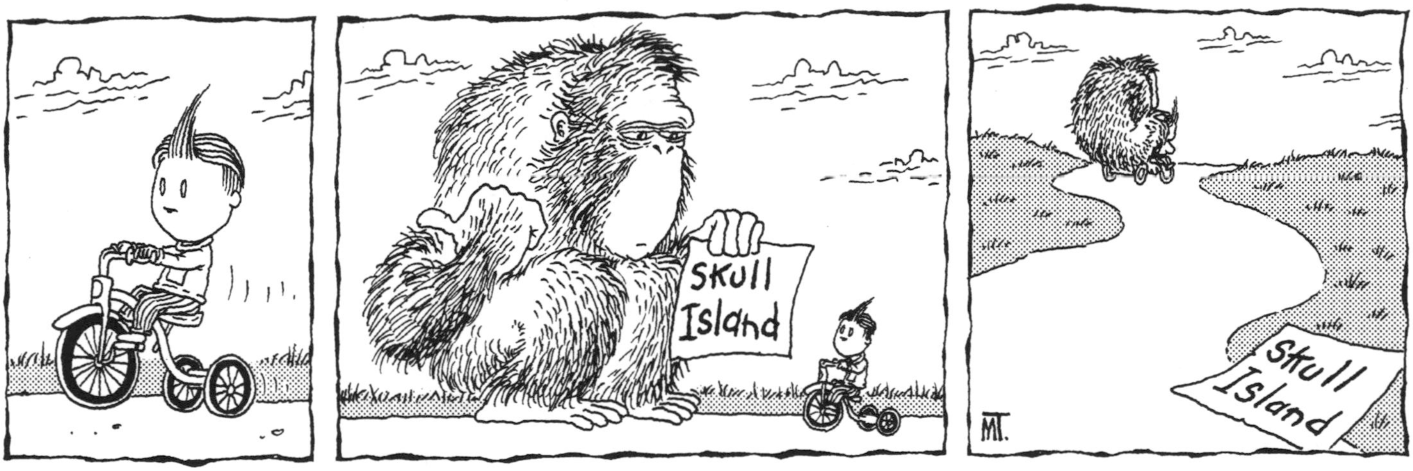
Skull Island
Skull Island

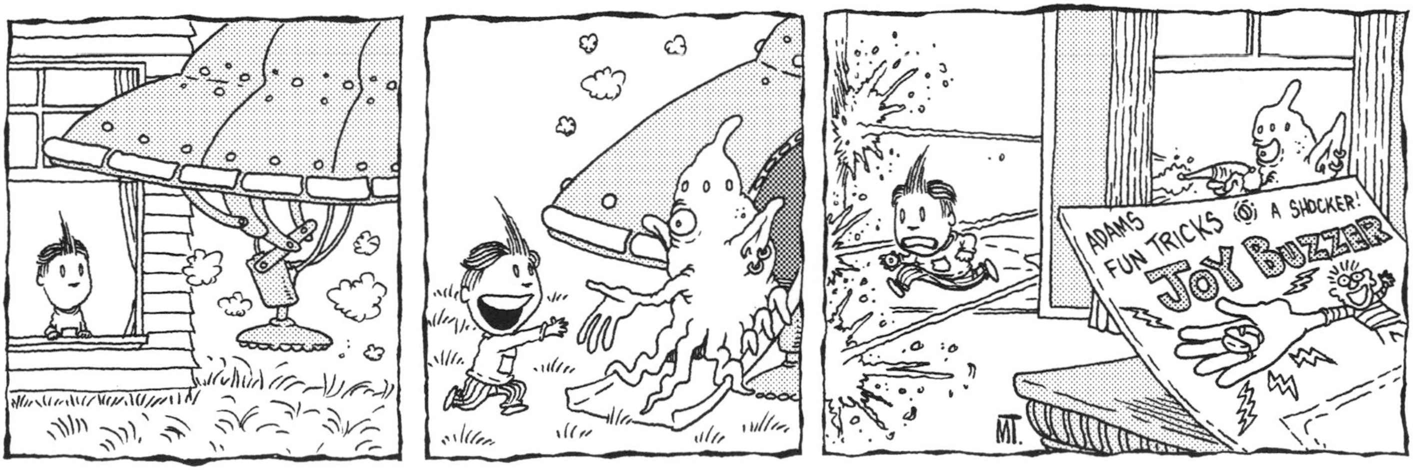
ADAMS
FUN TRICKS
A SHOCKER!
JOY BUZZER

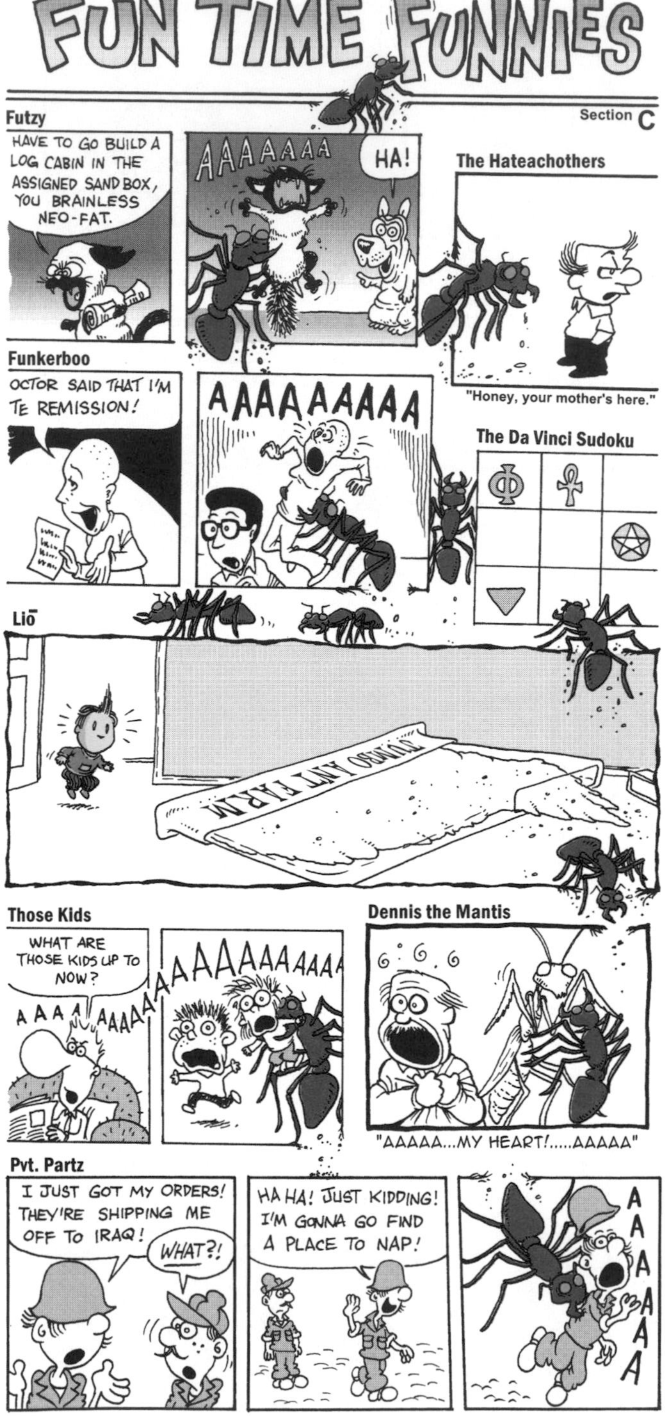
FUN TIME FUNNIES
Section C
Futzy
HAVE TO GO BUILD A LOG CABIN IN THE ASSIGNED SAND BOX, YOU BRAINLESS NEO-FAT.
AAAAAAA
HA!
The Hateachothers
"Honey, your mother's here."
Funkerboo
OCTOR SAID THAT I'M TE REMISSION!
AAAAAAAAA
The Da Vinci Sudoku
Liō
JUMBO ANT FARM
Those Kids
WHAT ARE THOSE KIDS UP TO NOW?
A A A A AAAAA
AAAAAAAAAAA
Dennis the Mantis
"AAAAA...MY HEART!.....AAAAA"
Pvt. Partz
I JUST GOT MY ORDERS! THEY'RE SHIPPING ME OFF TO IRAQ!
WHAT?!
HA HA! JUST KIDDING! I'M GONNA GO FIND A PLACE TO NAP!
AAAAAAAA

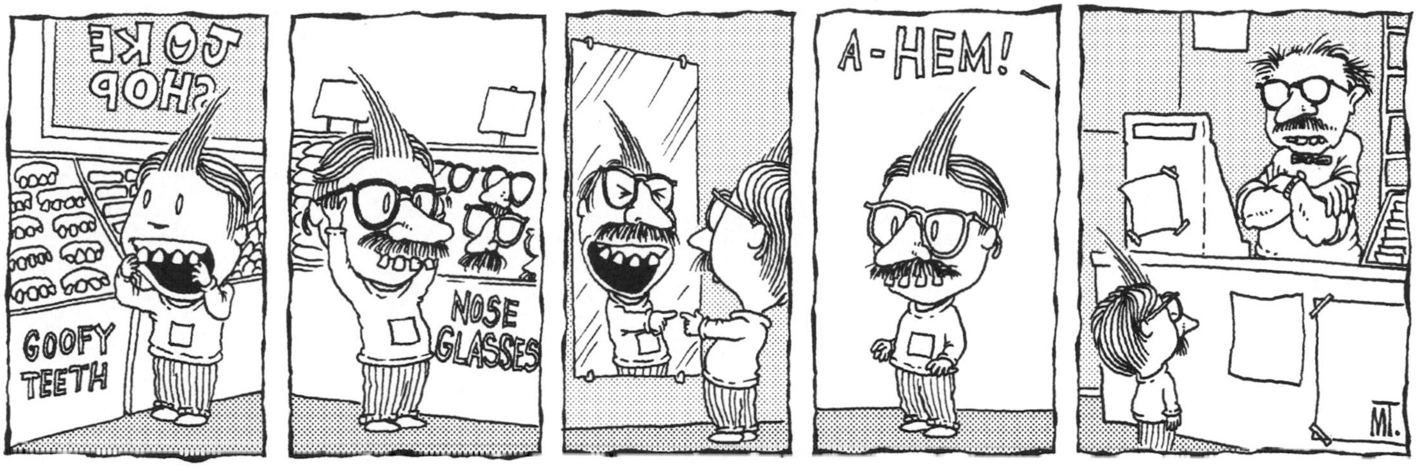
JOKE SHOP
GOOFY TEETH
NOSE GLASSES
A-HEM!

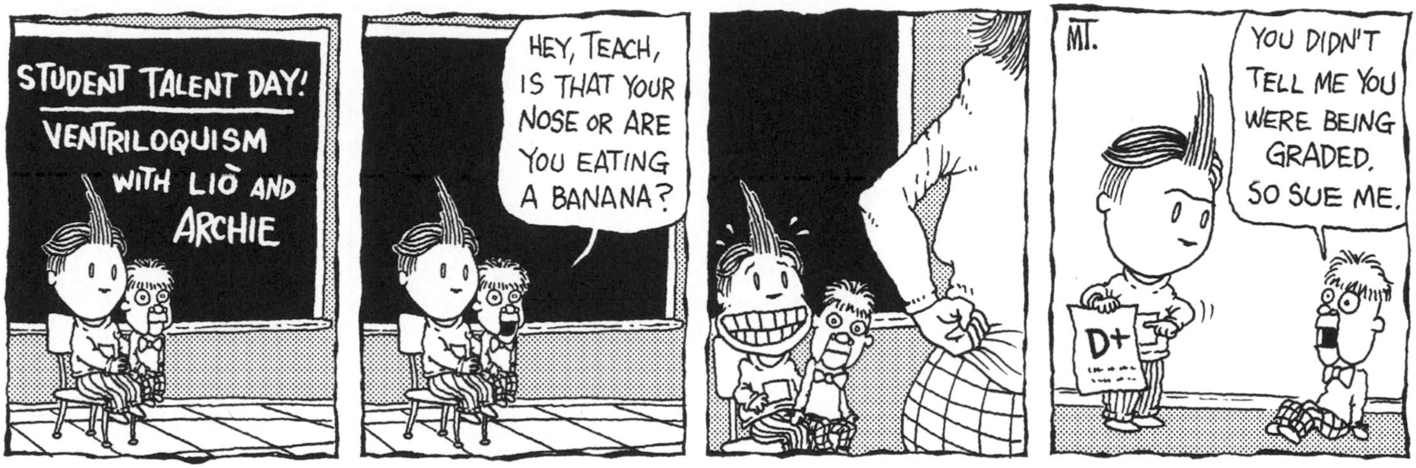
STUDENT TALENT DAY!
VENTRILOQUISM WITH LIÒ AND ARCHIE
HEY, TEACH, IS THAT YOUR NOSE OR ARE YOU EATING A BANANA?
D+
YOU DIDN'T TELL ME YOU WERE BEING GRADED. SO SUE ME.

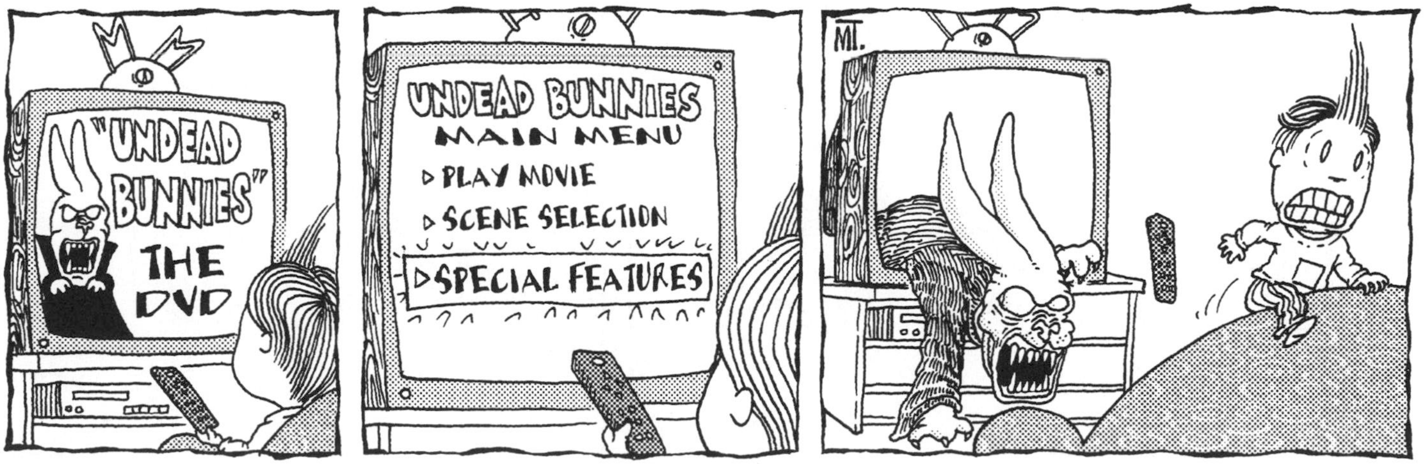
"UNDEAD BUNNIES" THE DVD
UNDEAD BUNNIES
MAIN MENU
▷ PLAY MOVIE
▷ SCENE SELECTION
▷ SPECIAL FEATURES

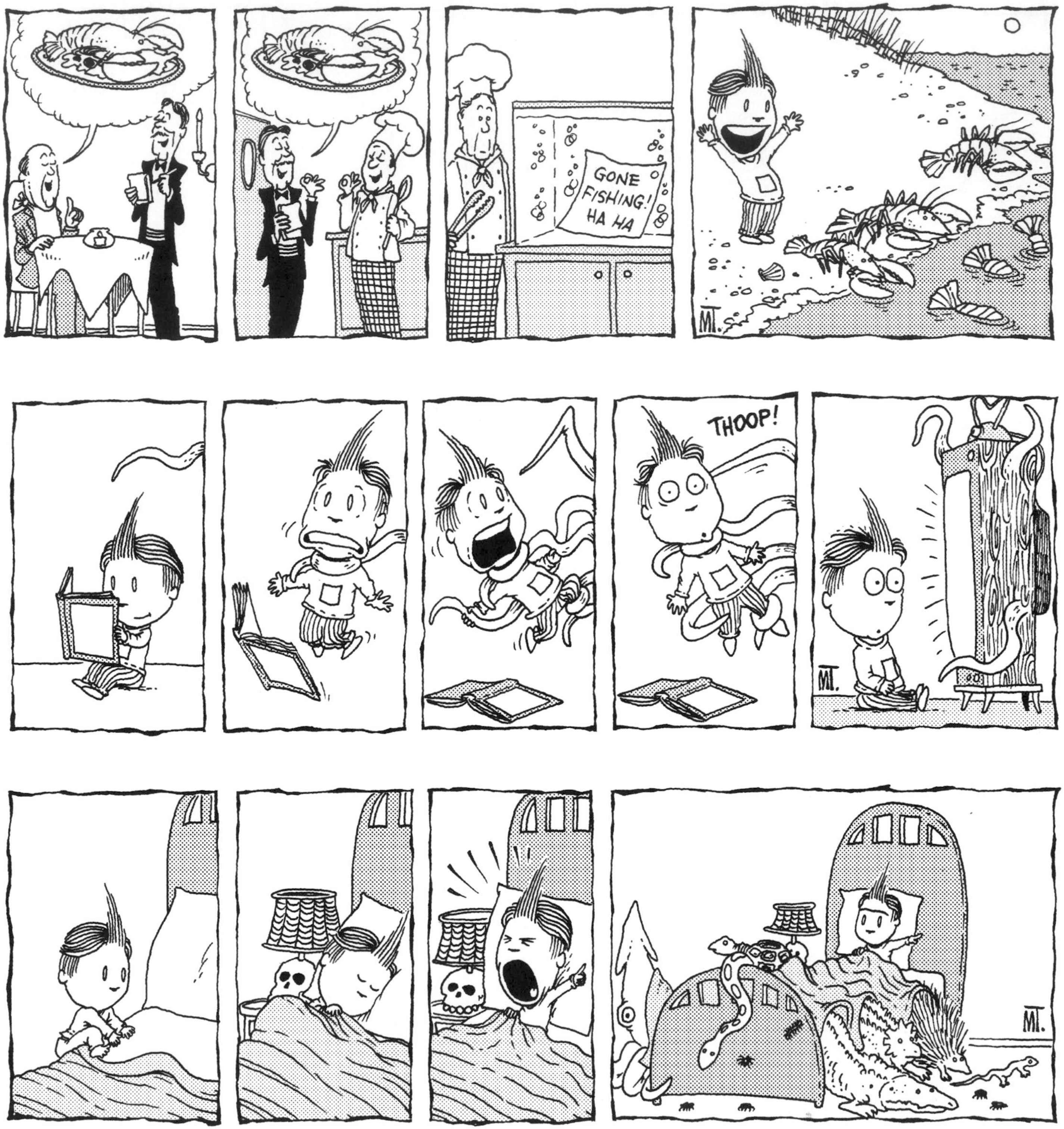
GONE FISHING! HA HA
THOOP!

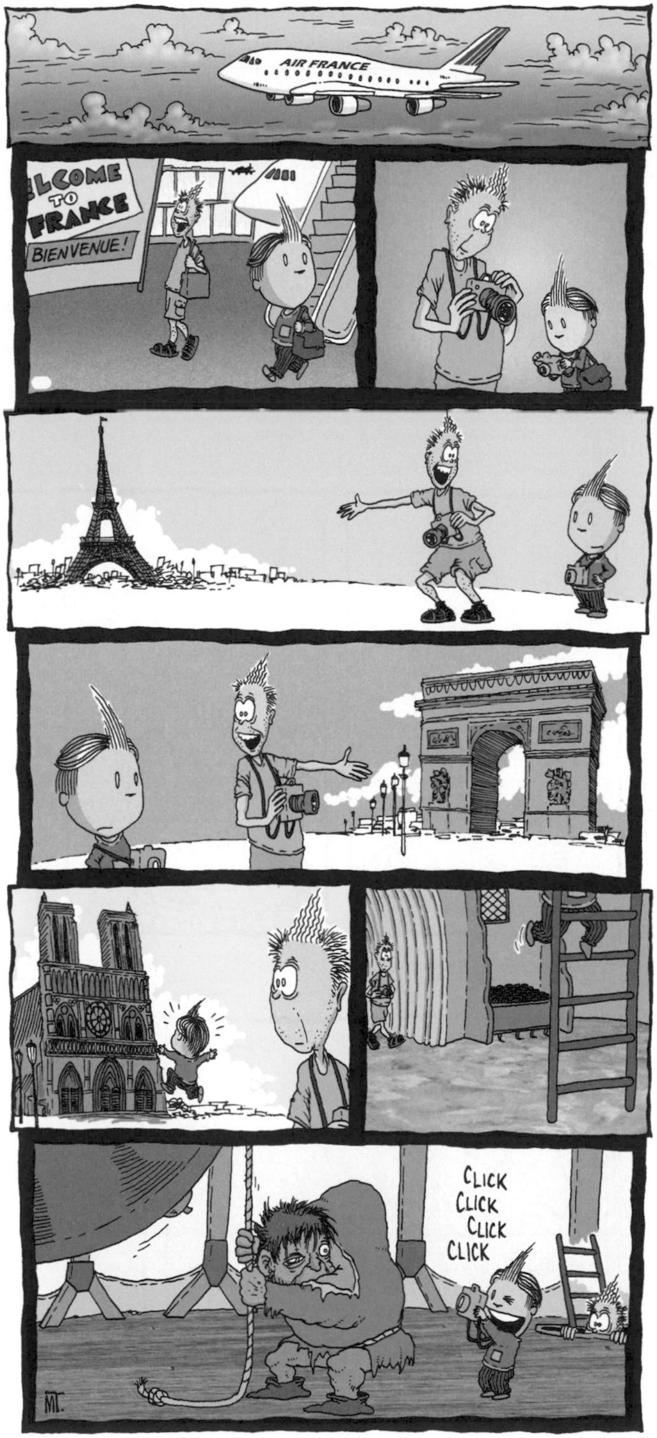
AIR FRANCE
ELCOME
TO
FRANCE
BIENVENUE!
CLICK
CLICK
CLICK
CLICK

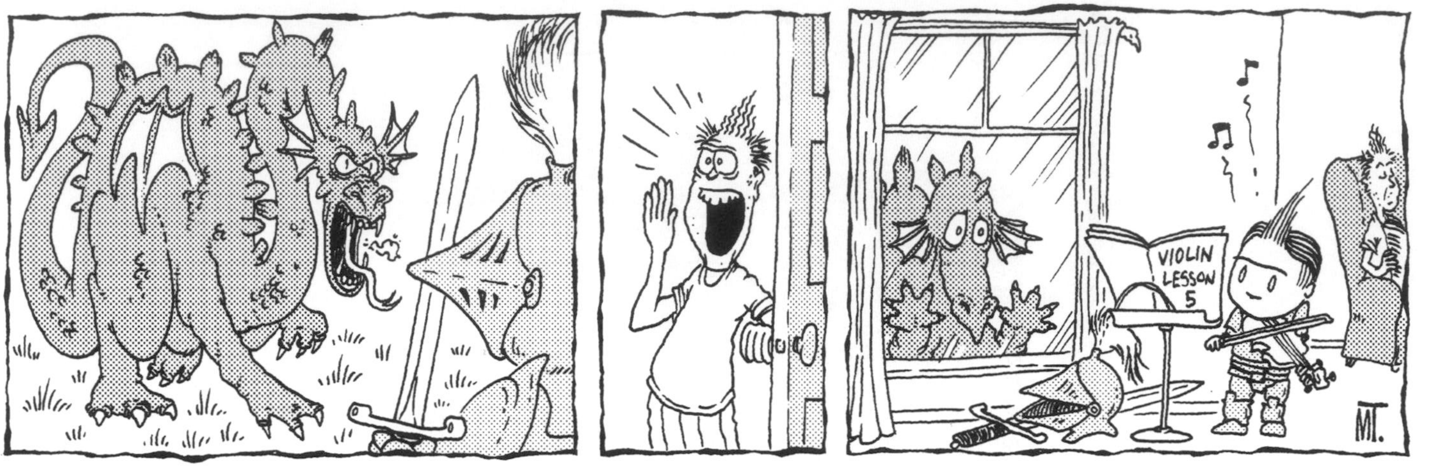
VIOLIN LESSON 5

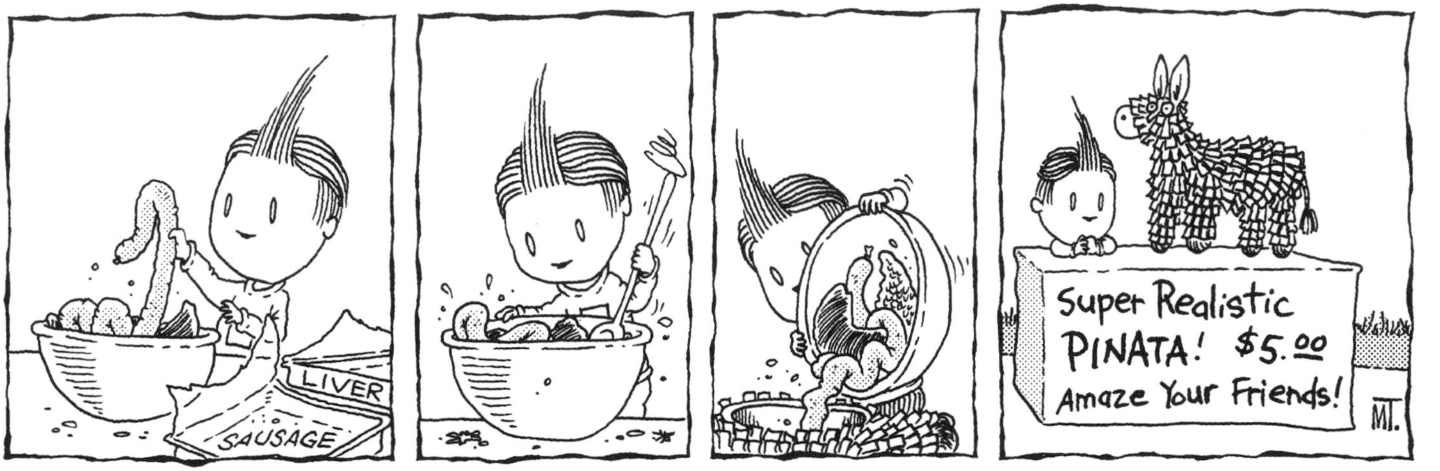
SAUSAGE
LIVER
Super Realistic
PINATA! $5.00
Amaze Your Friends!

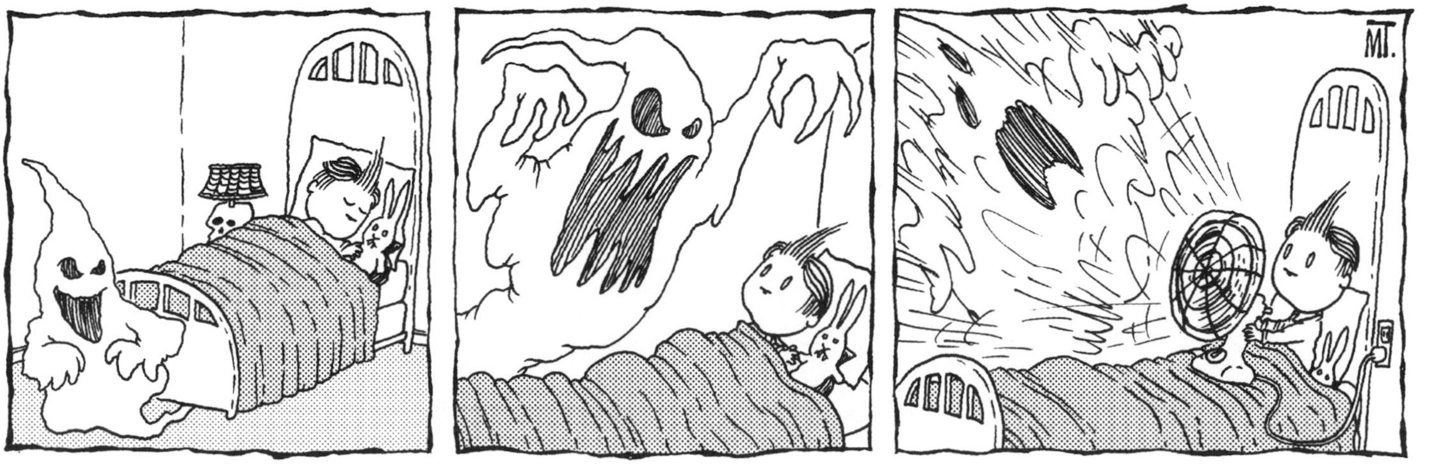

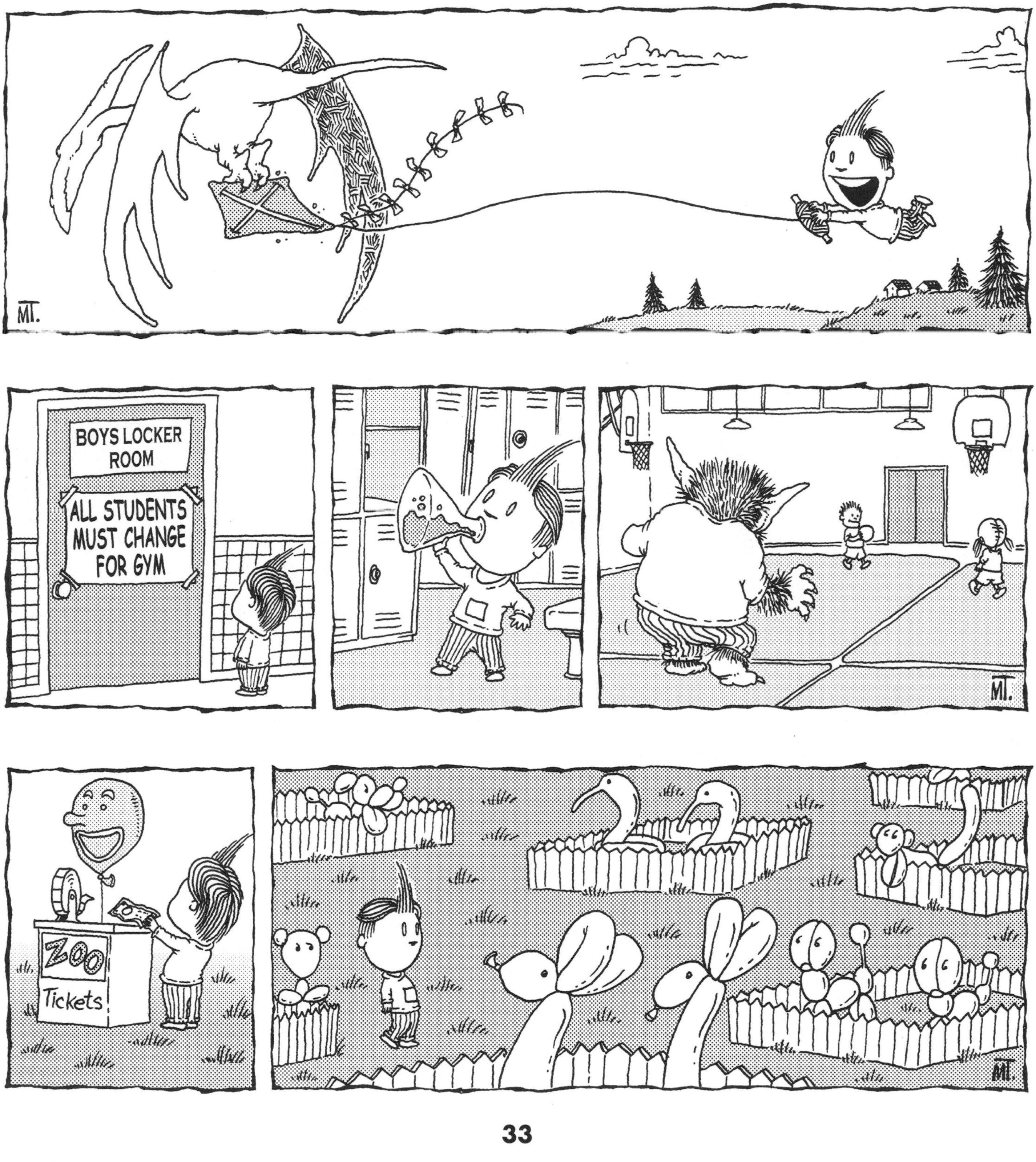
BOYS LOCKER ROOM
ALL STUDENTS MUST CHANGE FOR GYM
ZOO
Tickets

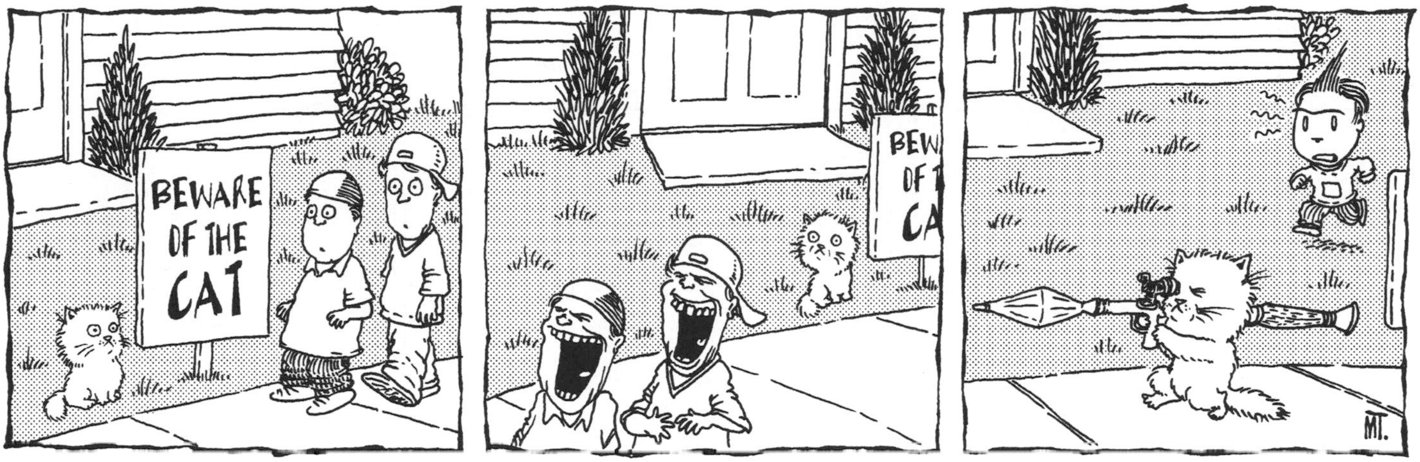
BEWARE OF THE CAT

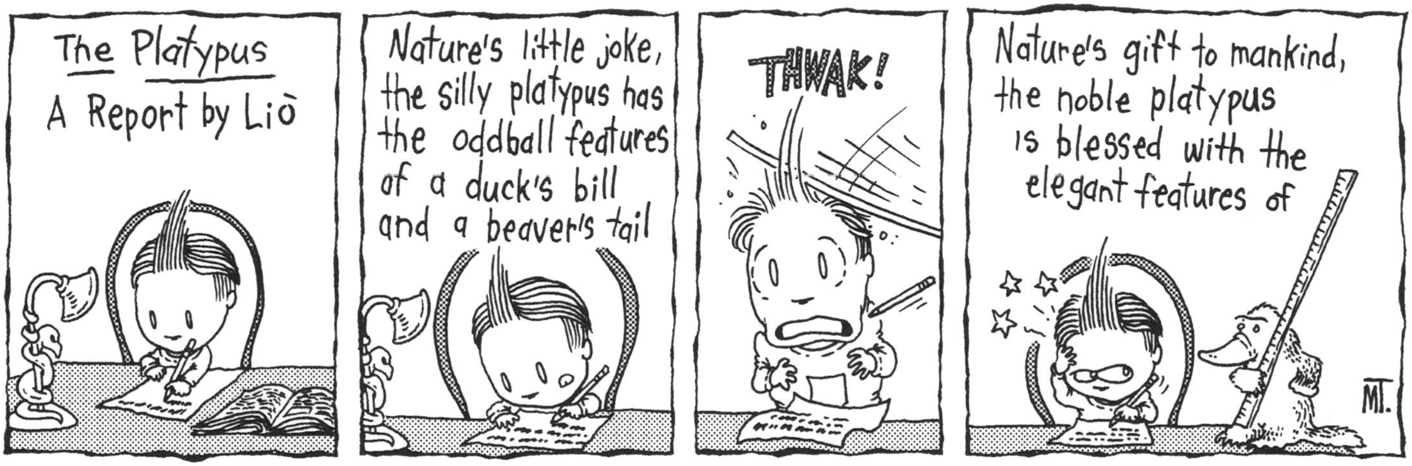
The Platypus
A Report by Liō
Nature's little joke, the silly platypus has the oddball features of a duck's bill and a beaver's tail
THWAK!
Nature's gift to mankind, the noble platypus is blessed with the elegant features of

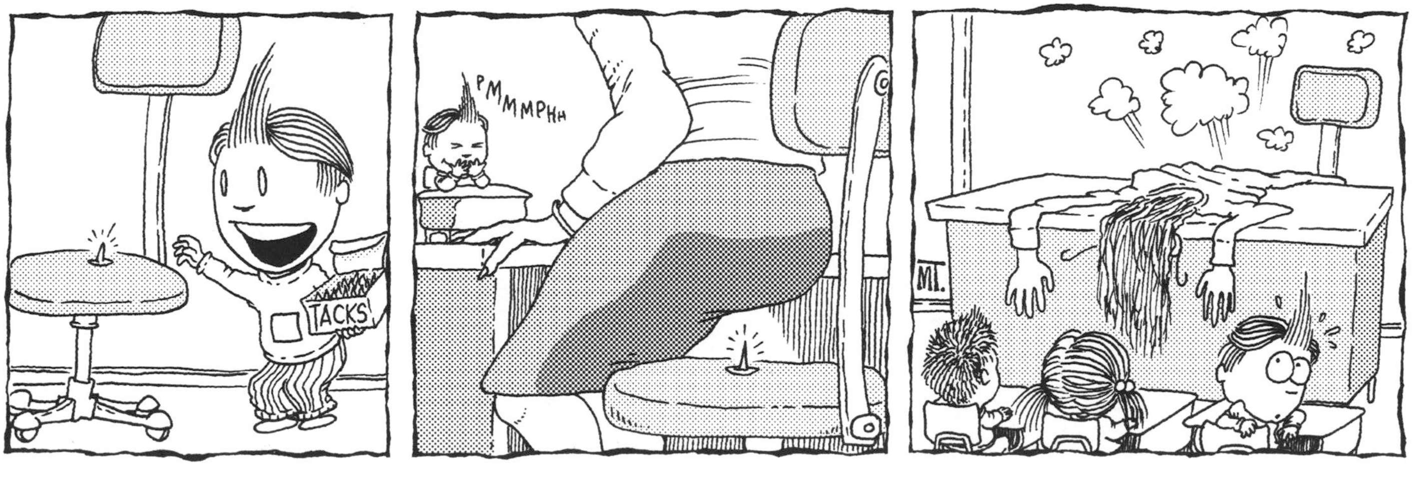
TACKS
PMMMPHH

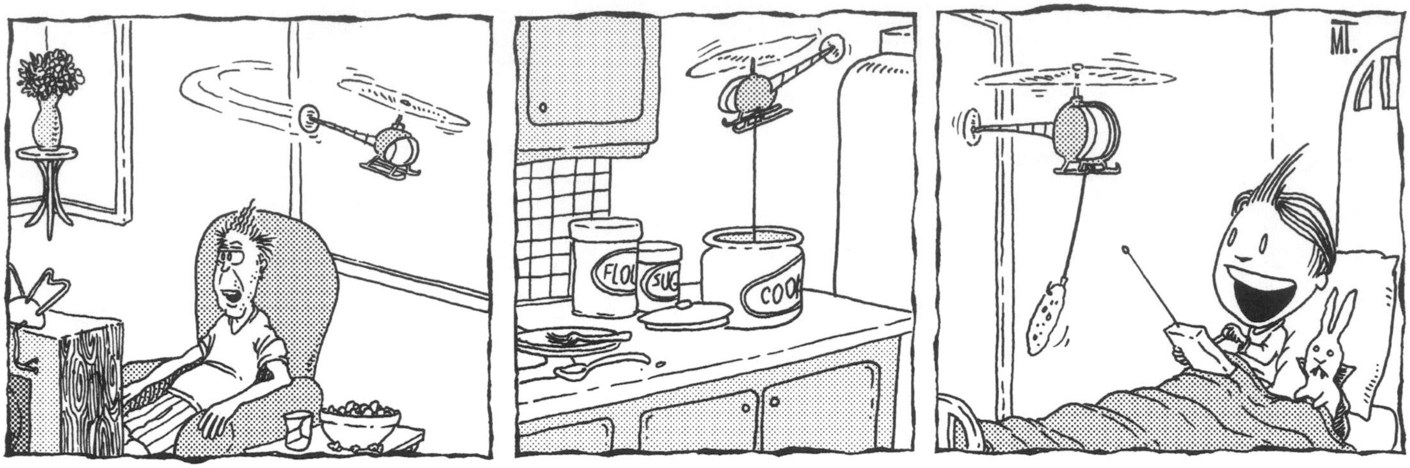

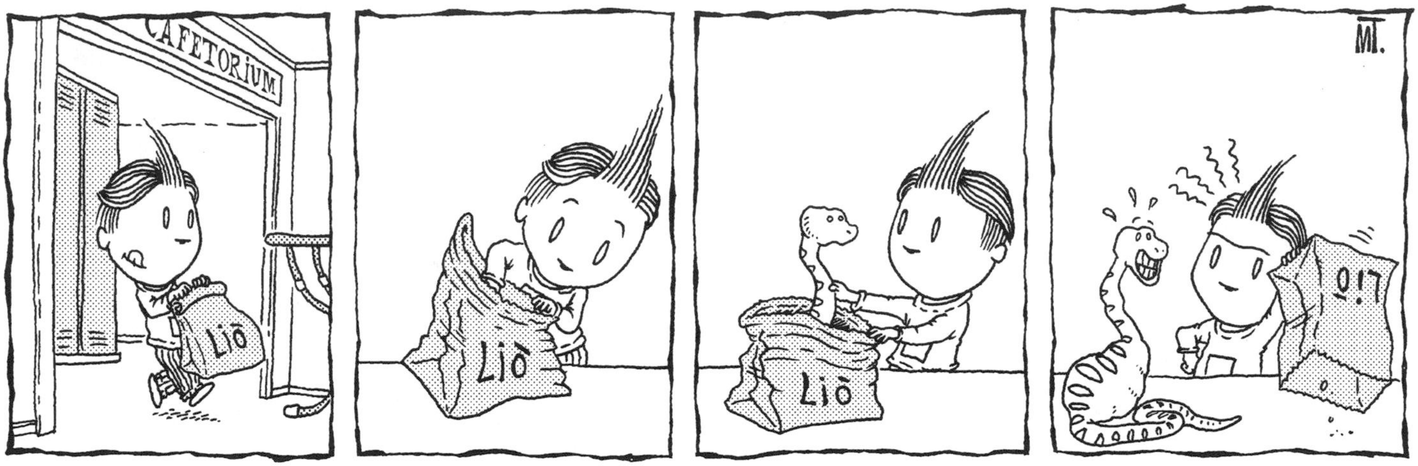
CAFETORIUM
Liò
Liò
Liò
O!?

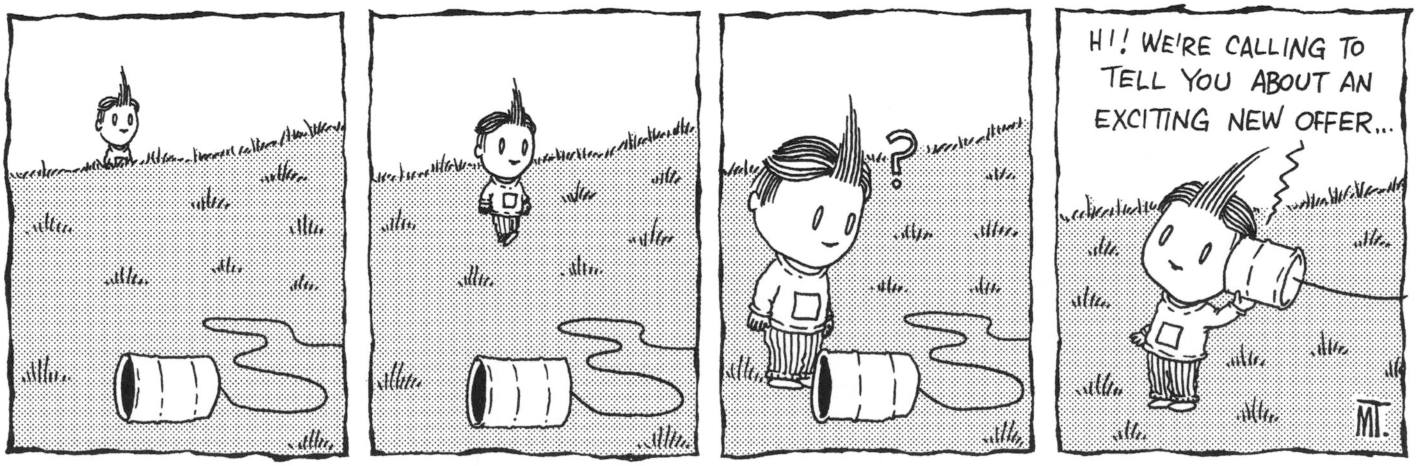
HI! WE'RE CALLING TO TELL YOU ABOUT AN EXCITING NEW OFFER...

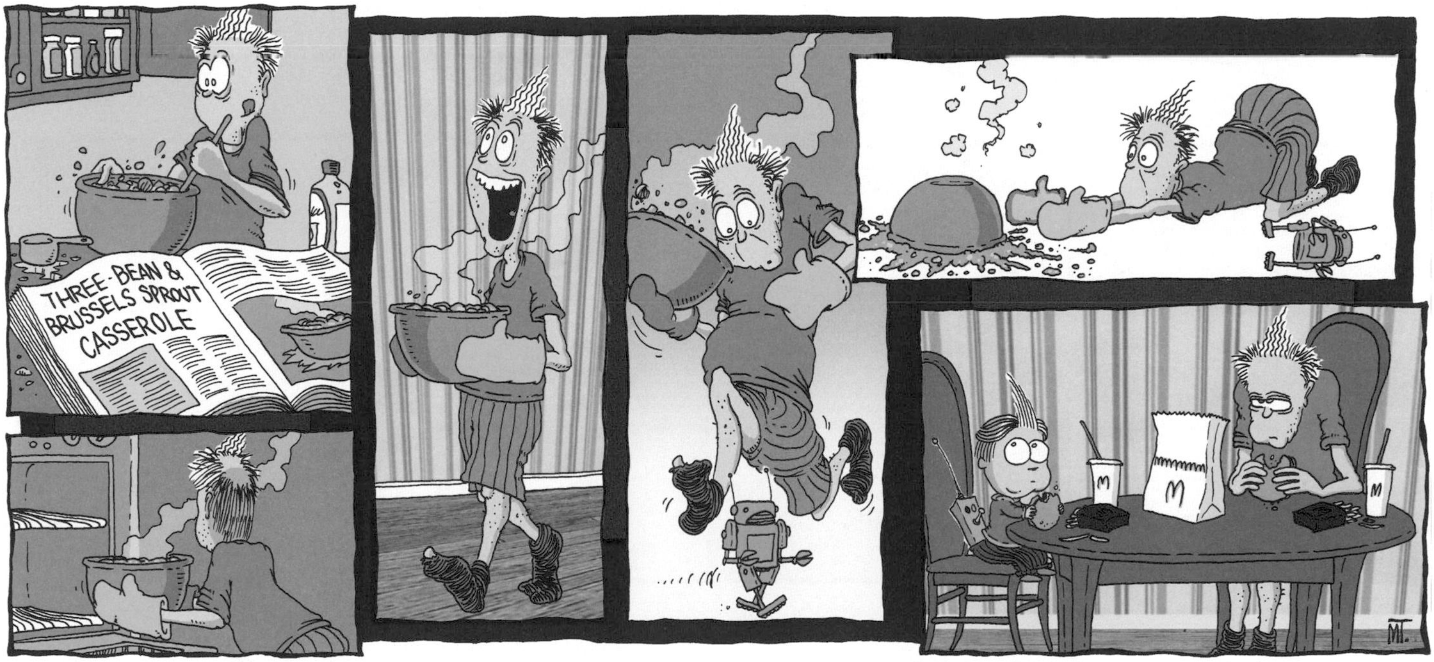

THREE-BEAN &
BRUSSELS SPROUT
CASSEROLE

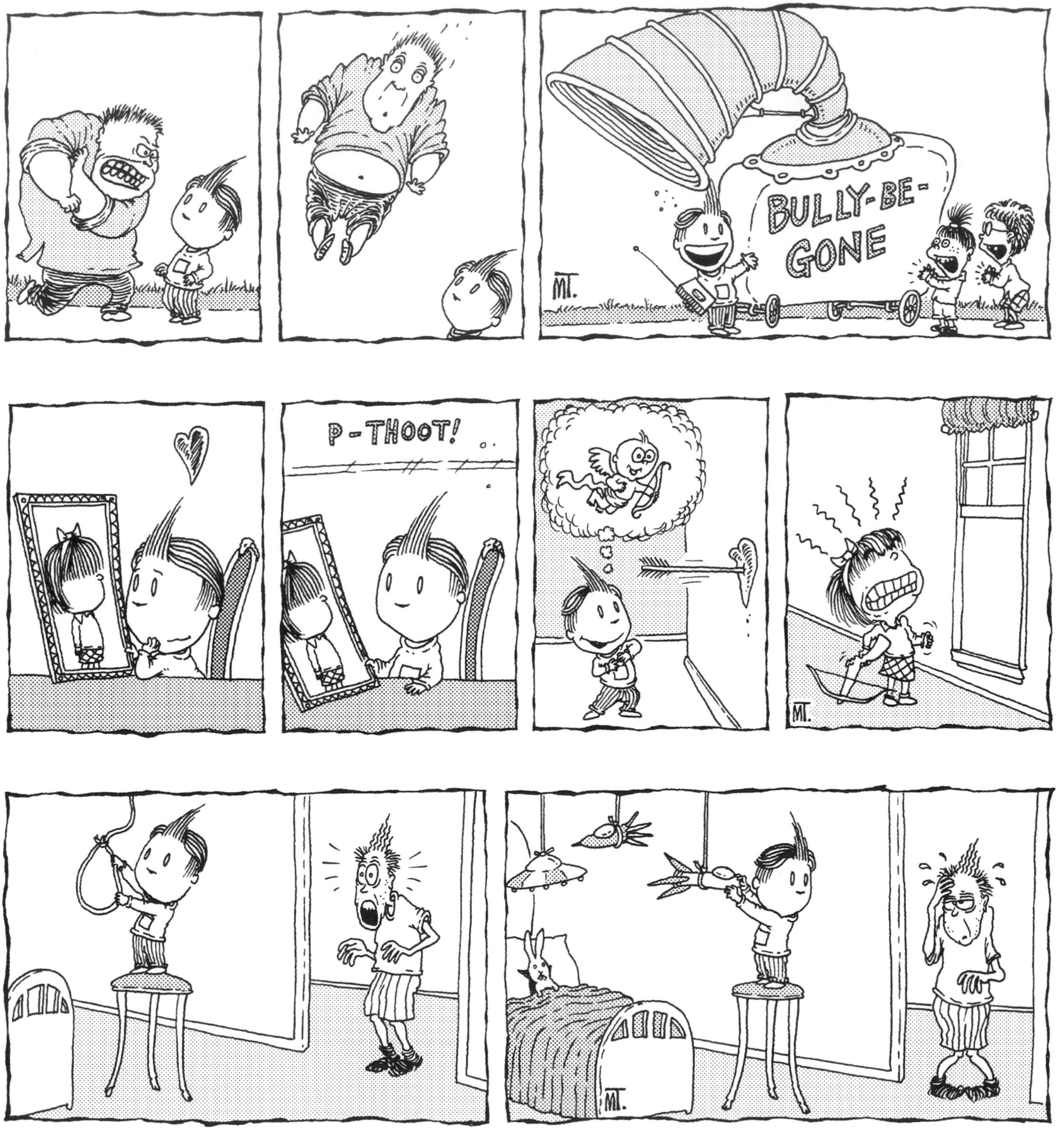
BULLY-BE-GONE
P-THOOT!

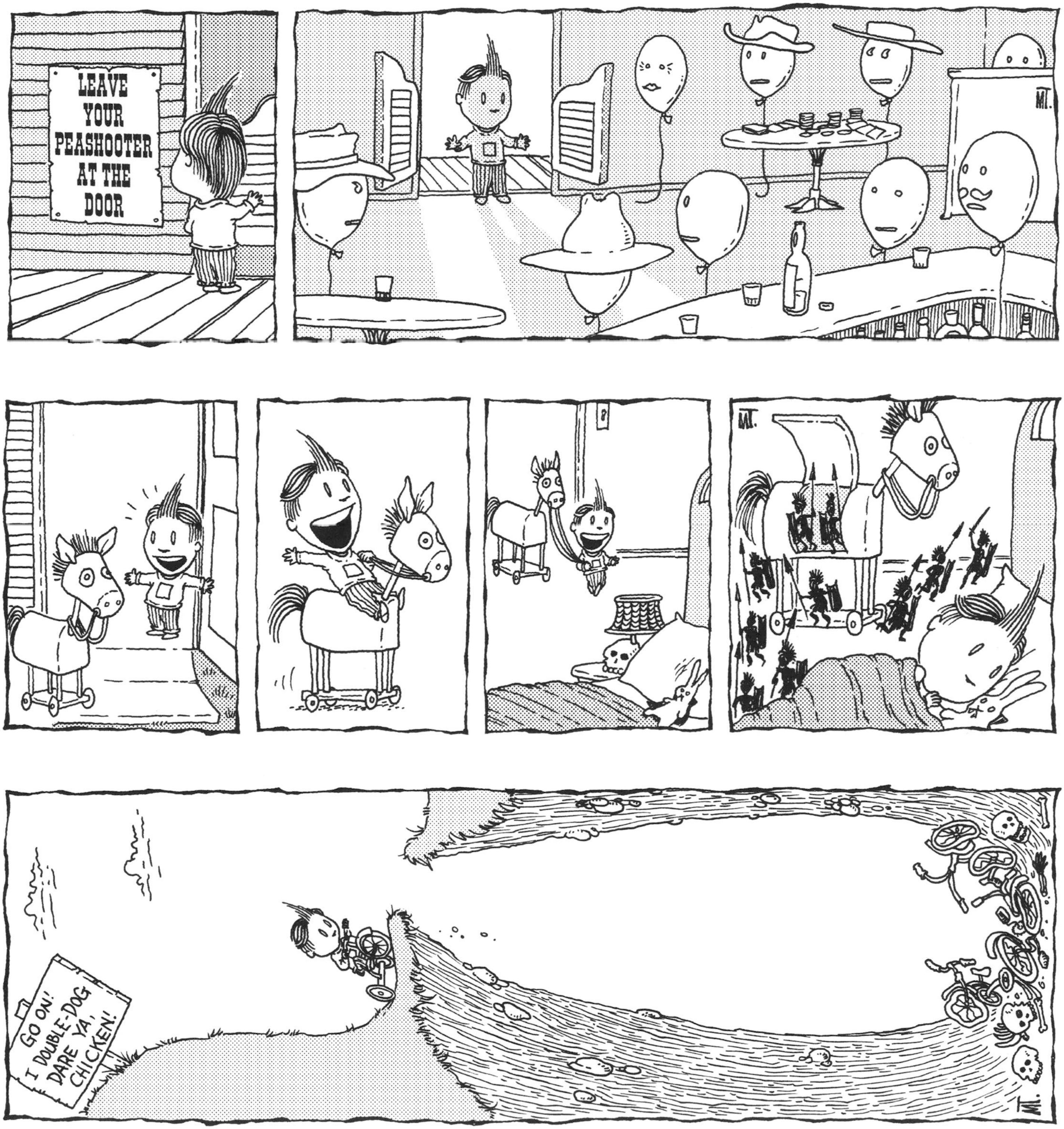
LEAVE YOUR PEASHOOTER AT THE DOOR
GO ON! I DOUBLE-DOG DARE YA, CHICKEN!

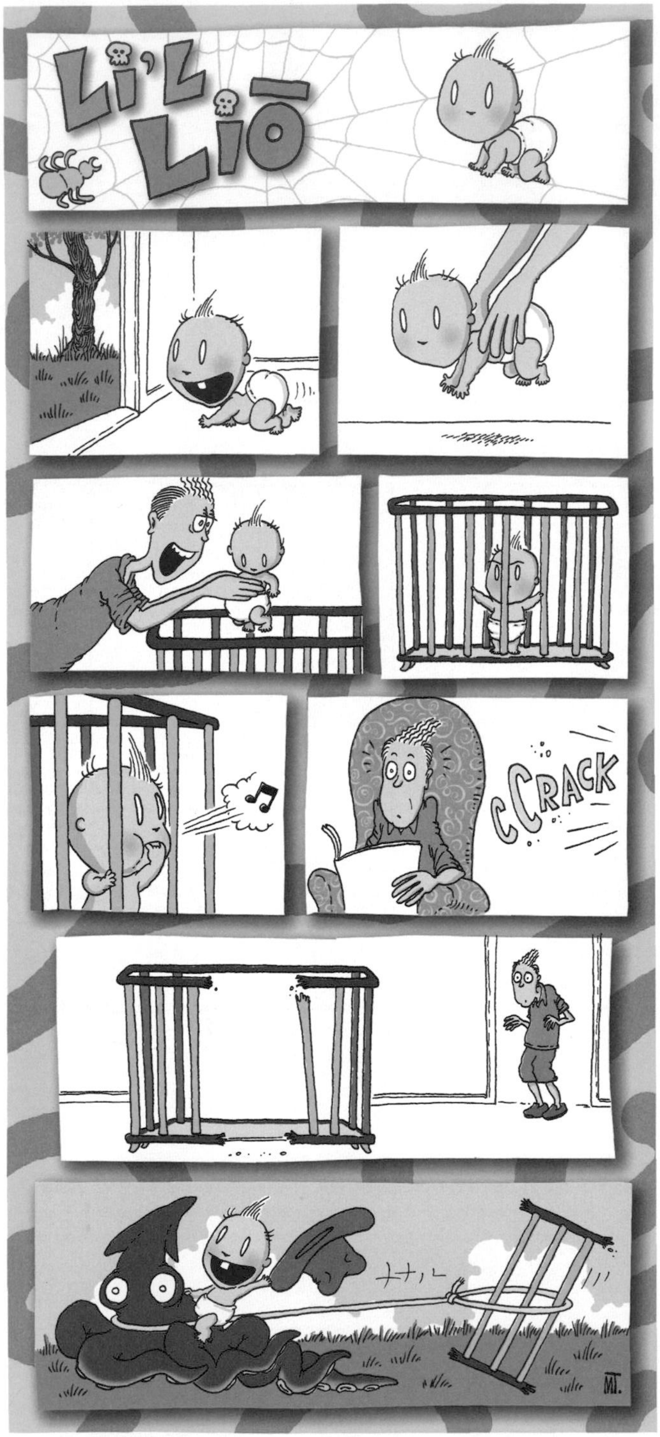
LI'L LIŌ
CCRACK

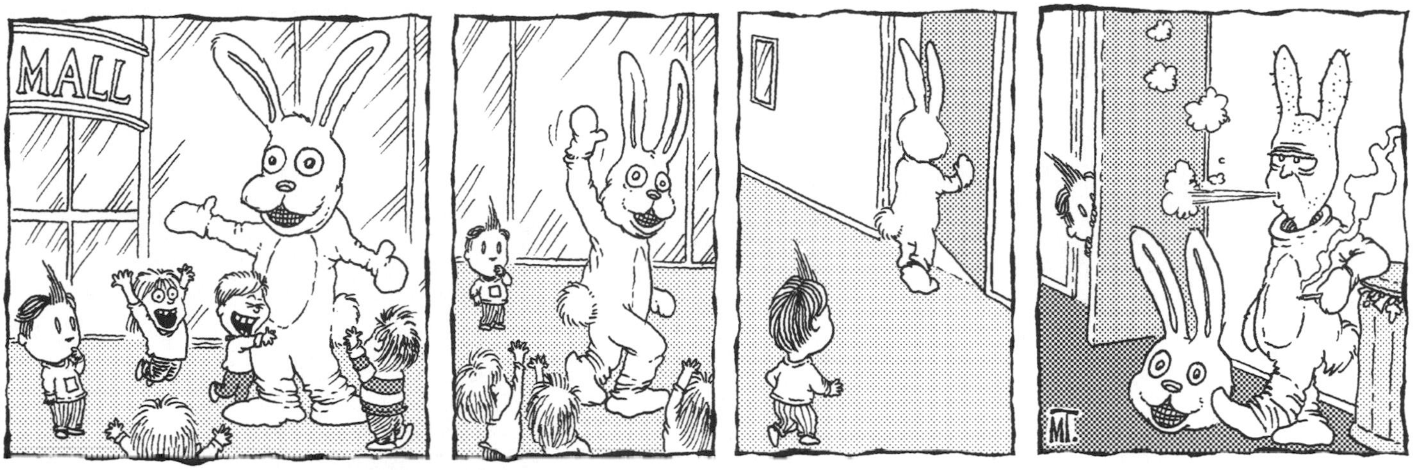
MALL
MT.

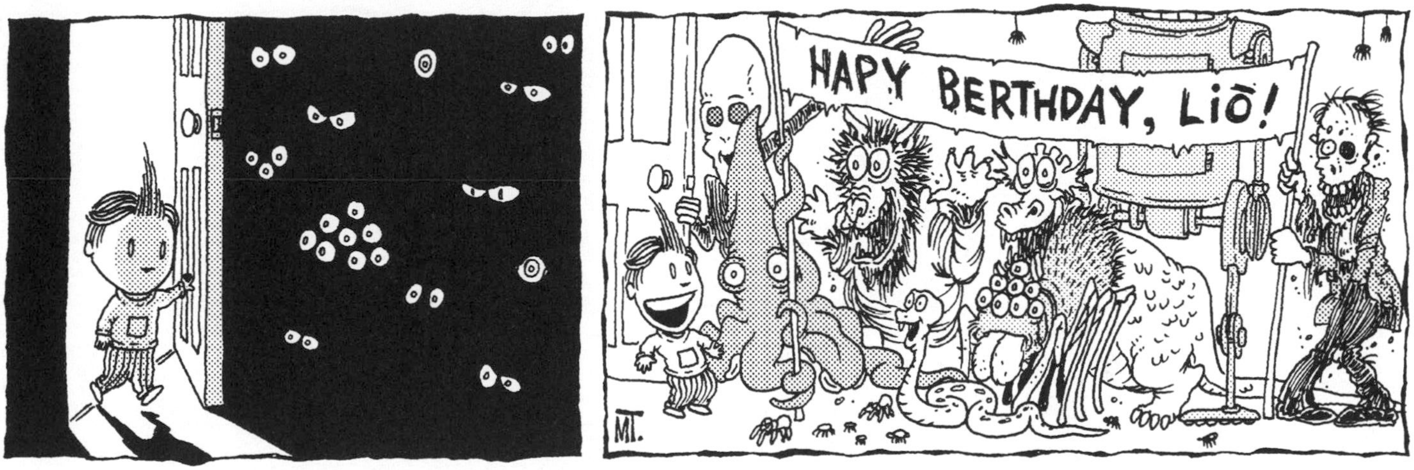
MT.
HAPY BERTHDAY, LIŌ!

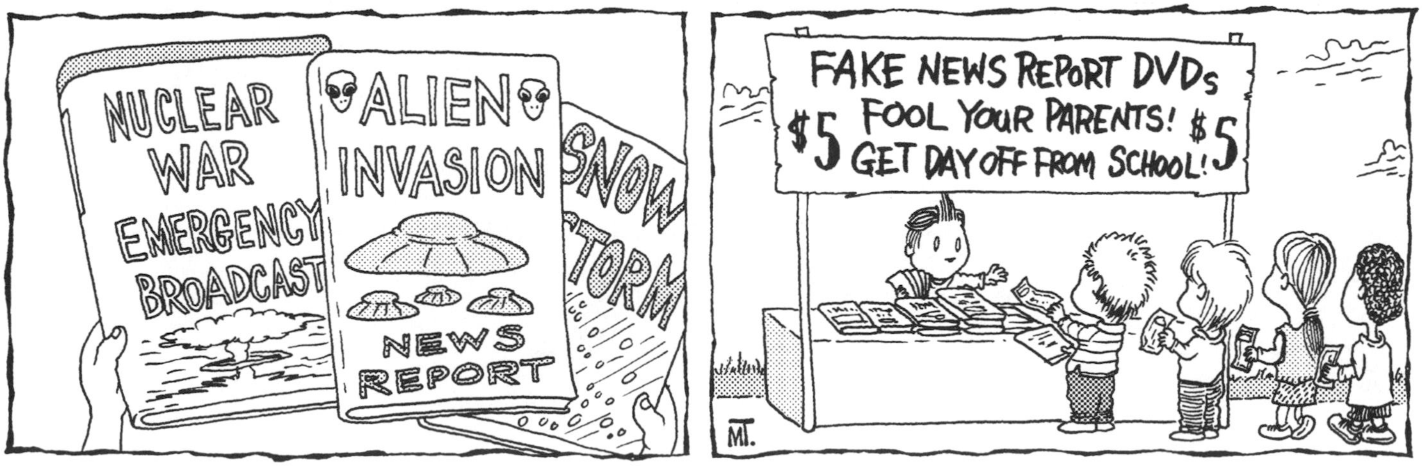
NUCLEAR WAR EMERGENCY BROADCAST
ALIEN INVASION
NEWS REPORT
SNOW STORM
FAKE NEWS REPORT DVDs
$5 FOOL YOUR PARENTS! $5
GET DAY OFF FROM SCHOOL!
MT.

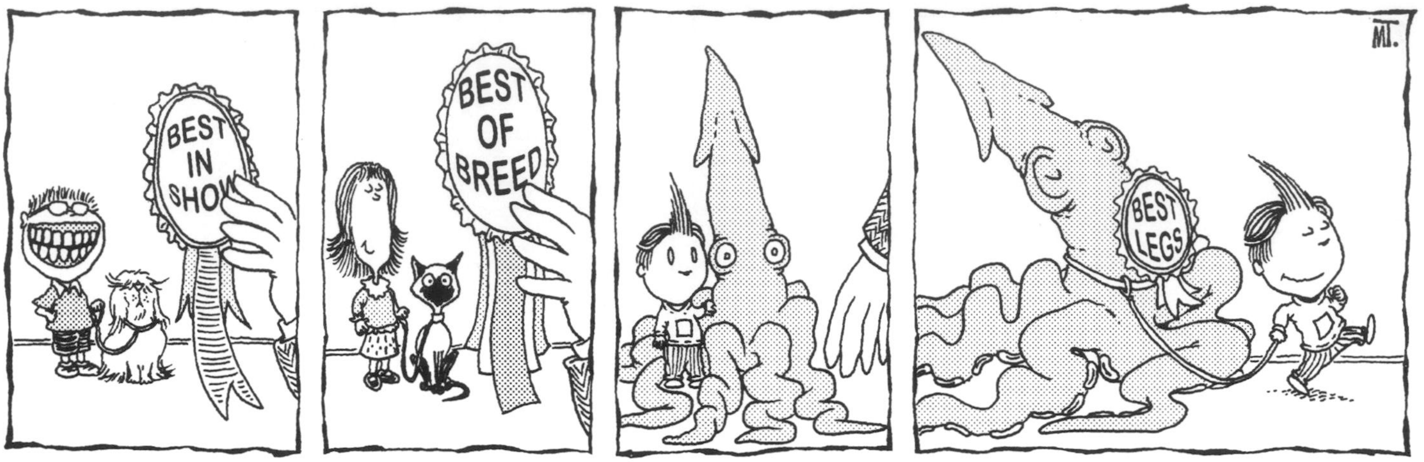
BEST IN SHOW
BEST OF BREED
BEST LEGS
MT.

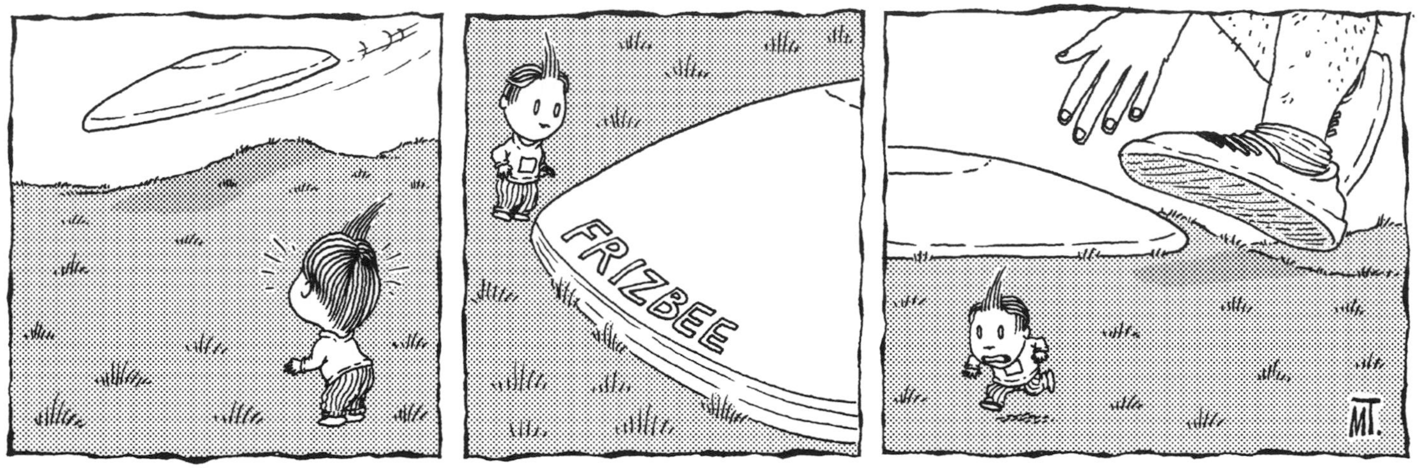
FRIZBEE
MT.

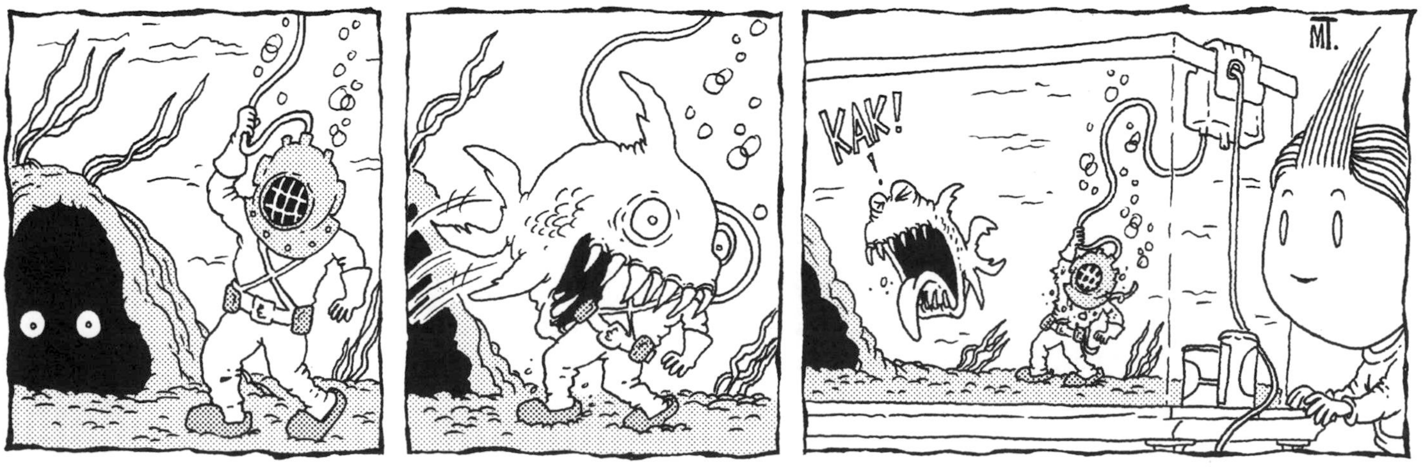
KAK!
MT.

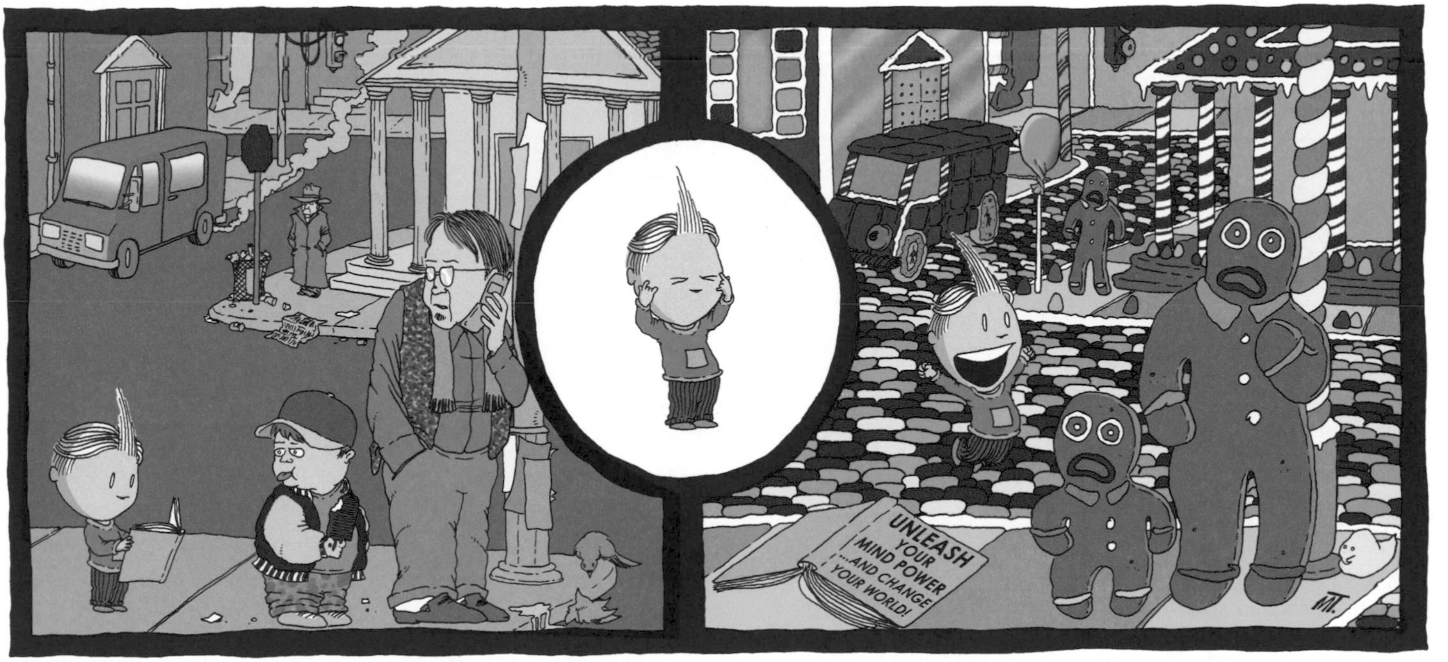
UNLEASH
YOUR
MIND POWER
...AND CHANGE
YOUR WORLD!
MT.

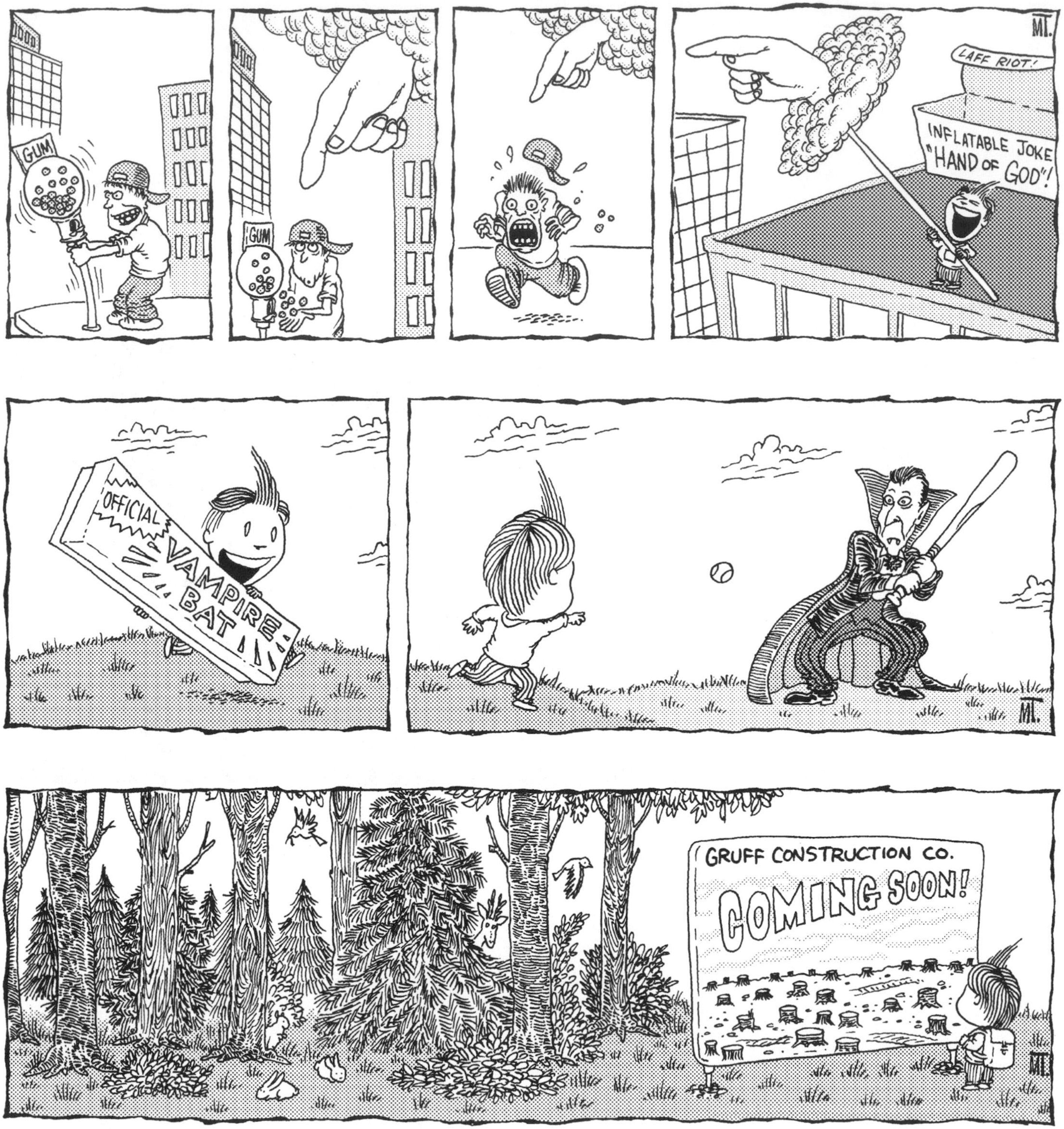
GUM
GUM
MT.
LAFF RIOT!
INFLATABLE JOKE "HAND OF GOD"!
OFFICIAL
VAMPIRE BAT
MT.
GRUFF CONSTRUCTION CO.
COMING SOON!
MT.

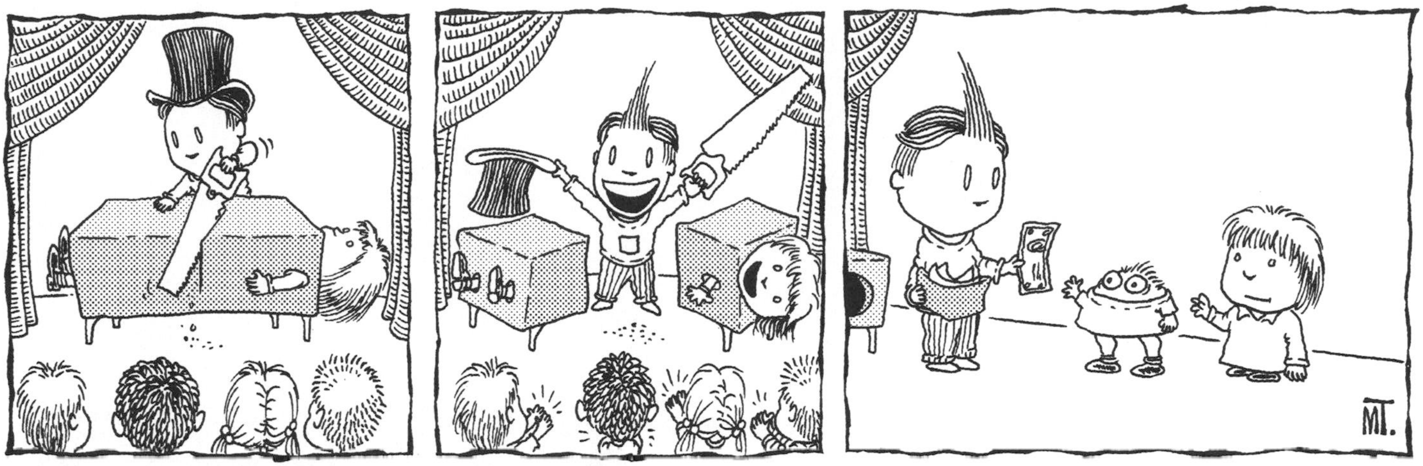
MT.

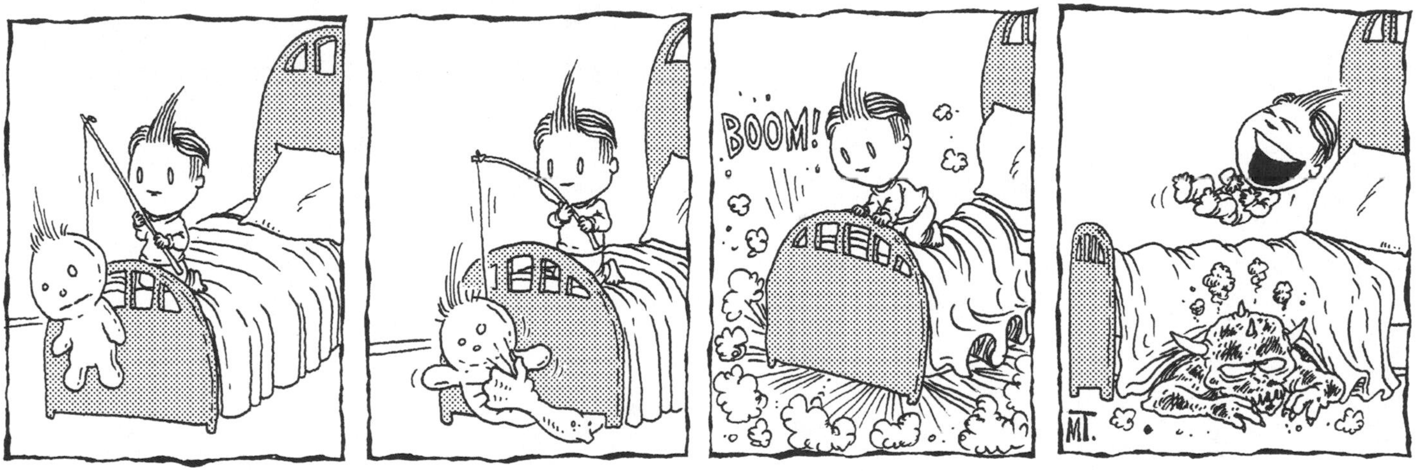
BOOM!
MT.

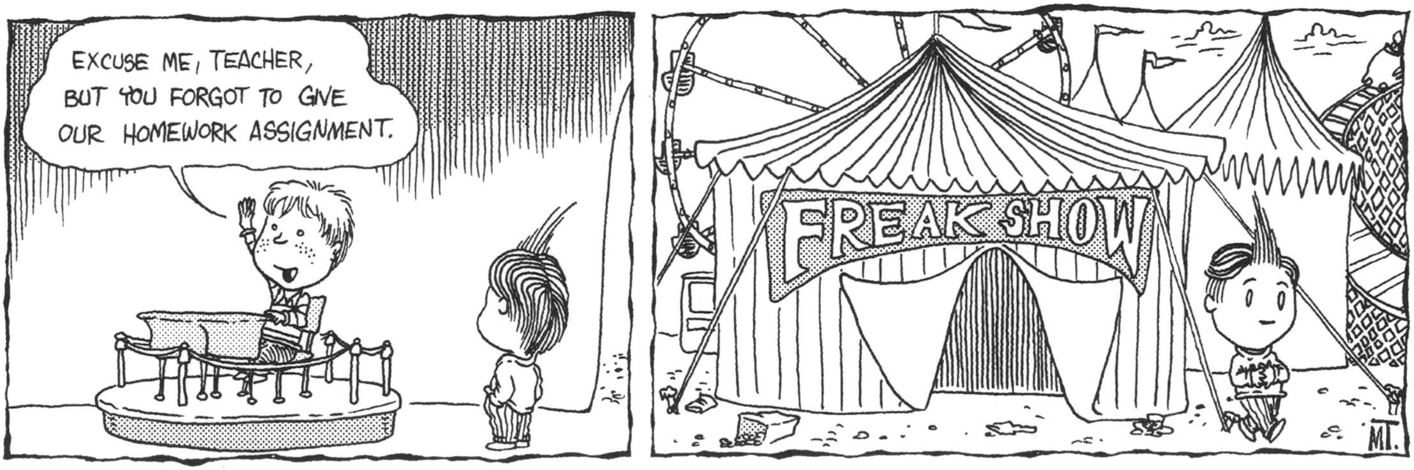
EXCUSE ME, TEACHER, BUT YOU FORGOT TO GIVE OUR HOMEWORK ASSIGNMENT.
FREAK SHOW
MT.

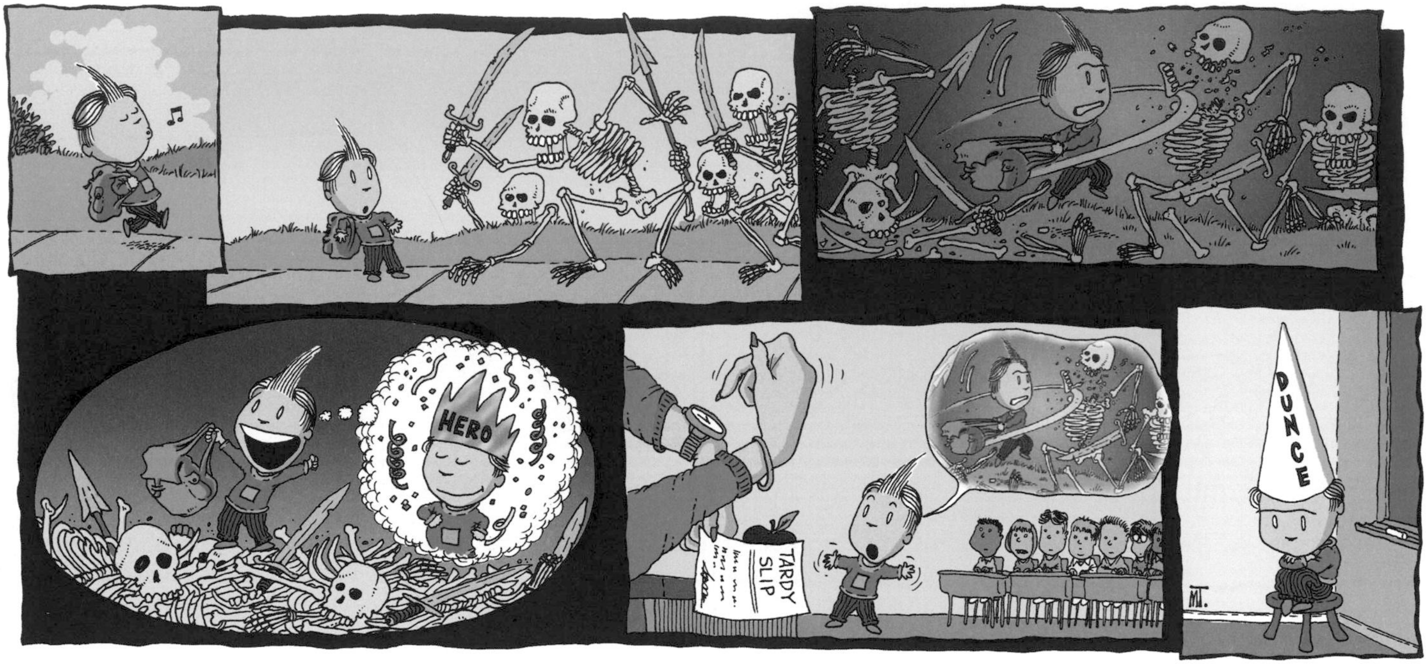
HERO
TARDY SLIP
DUNCE

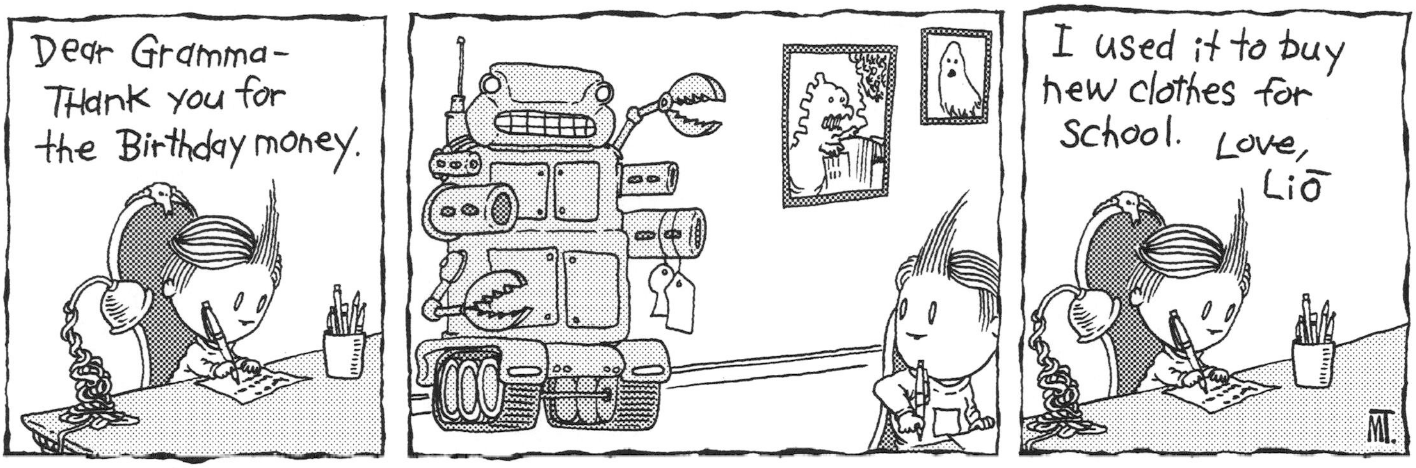
Dear Gramma-
THank you for the Birthday money.
I used it to buy new clothes for School.
Love,
Liō

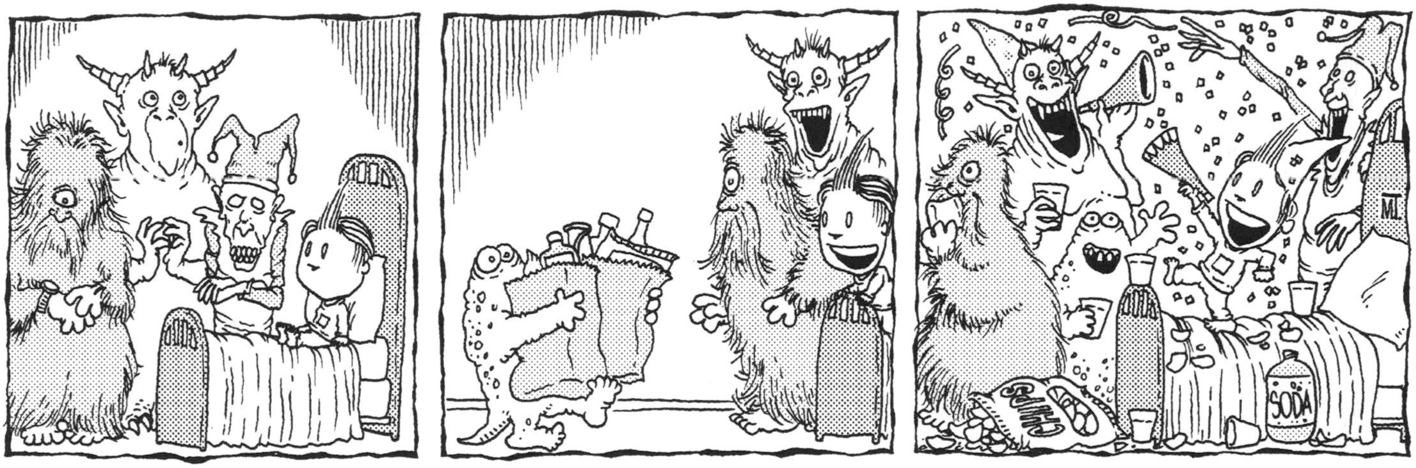
SODA

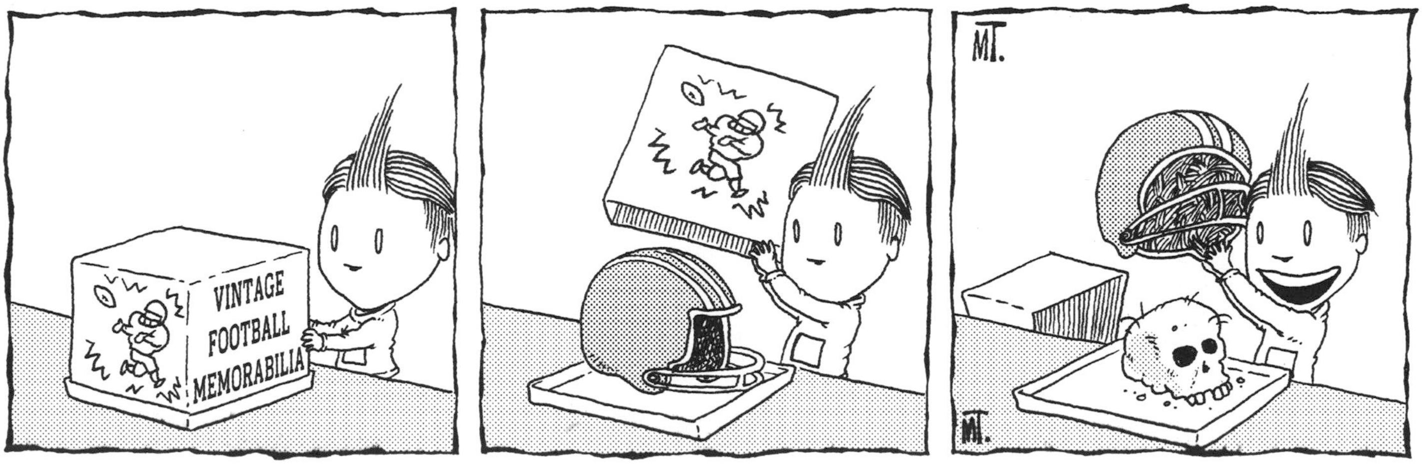
VINTAGE
FOOTBALL
MEMORABILIA

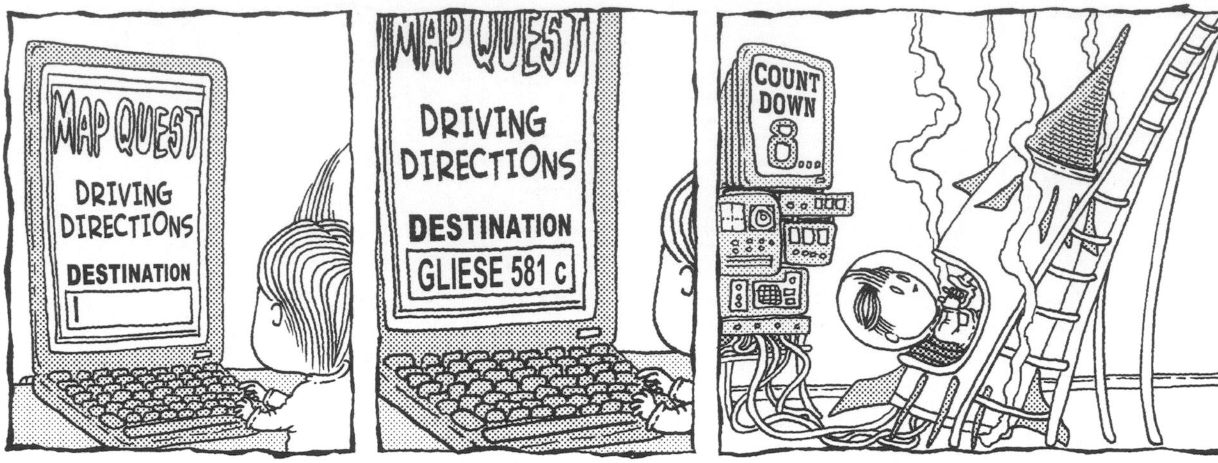
MAP QUEST
DRIVING DIRECTIONS
DESTINATION
MAP QUEST
DRIVING DIRECTIONS
DESTINATION
GLIESE 581 c
COUNT DOWN
8...

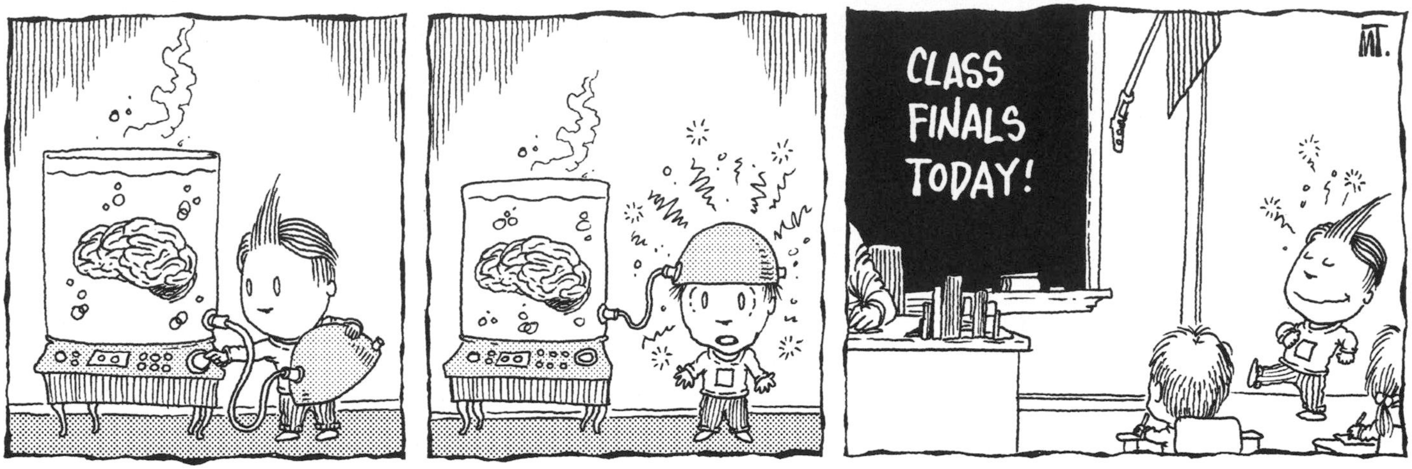
CLASS FINALS TODAY!

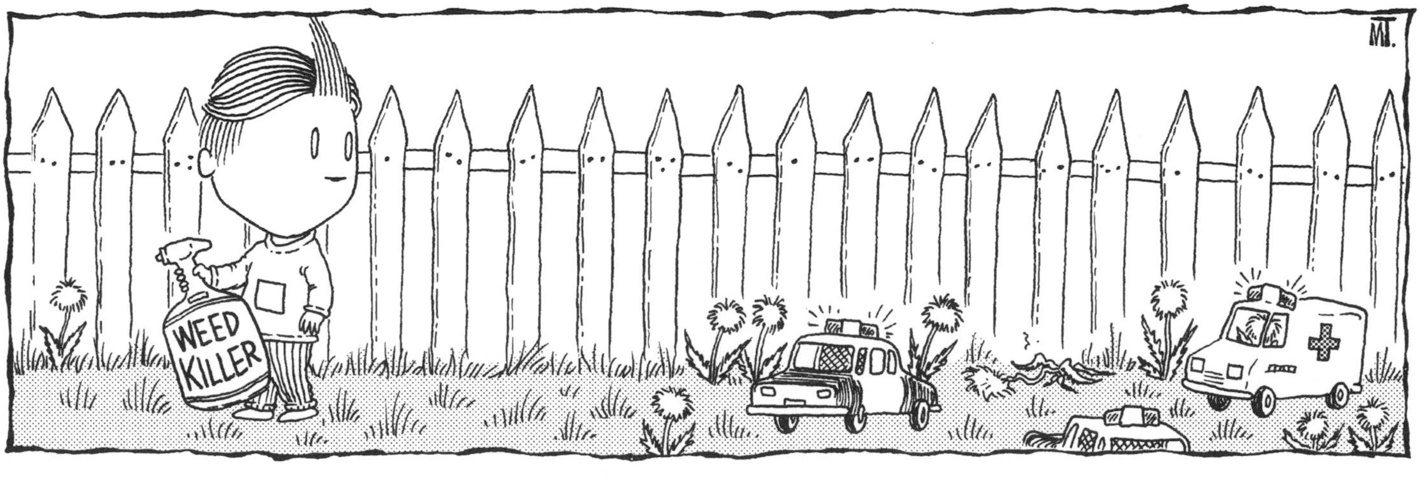
WEED KILLER

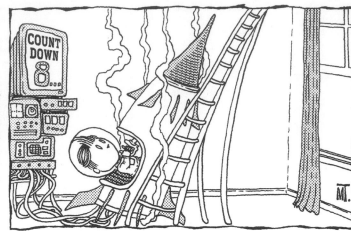

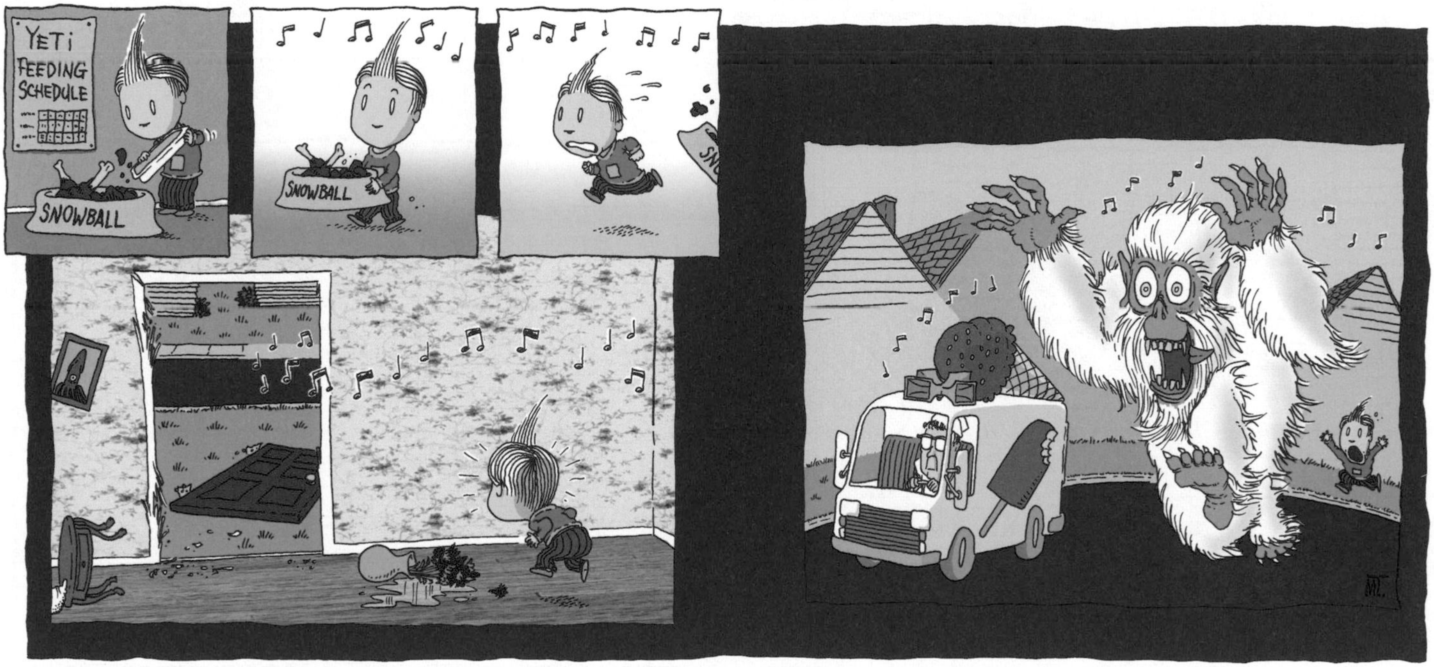
YETi FEEDING SCHEDULE
SNOWBALL
SNOWBALL

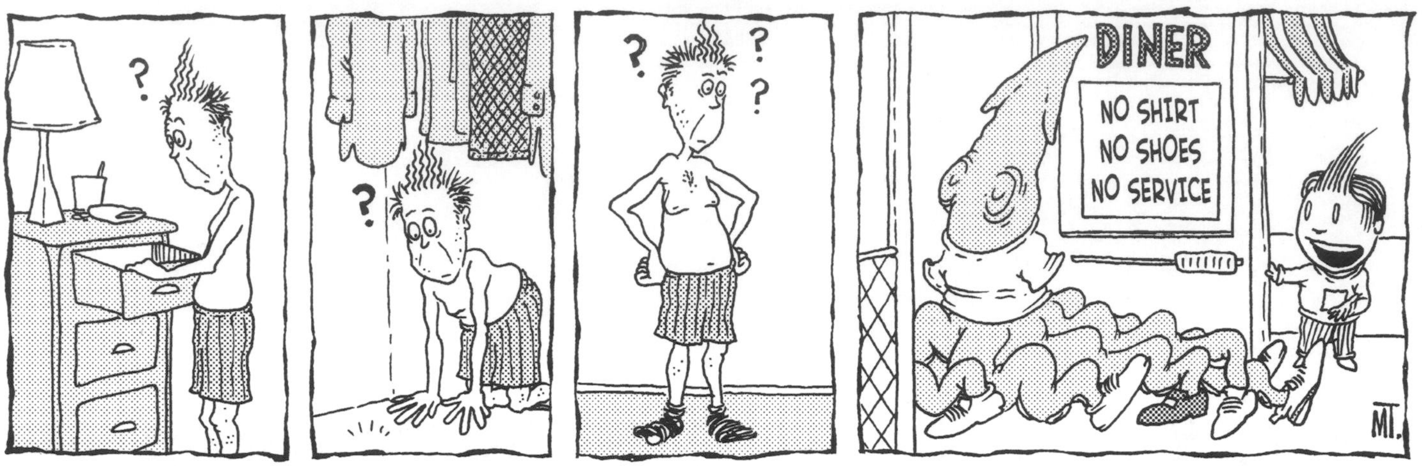
DINER
NO SHIRT
NO SHOES
NO SERVICE
MT.

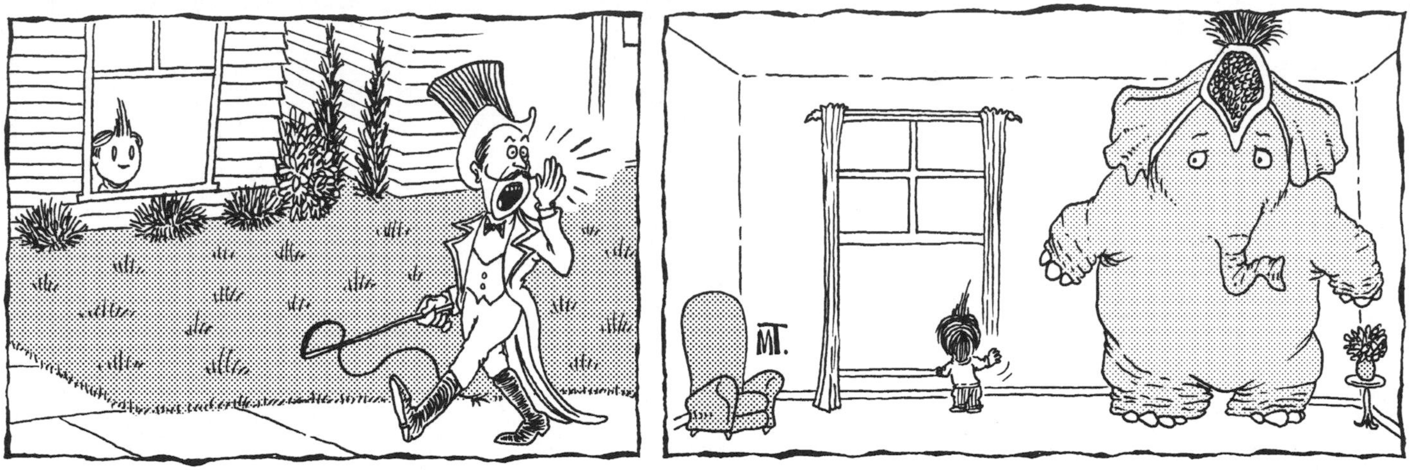
MT.

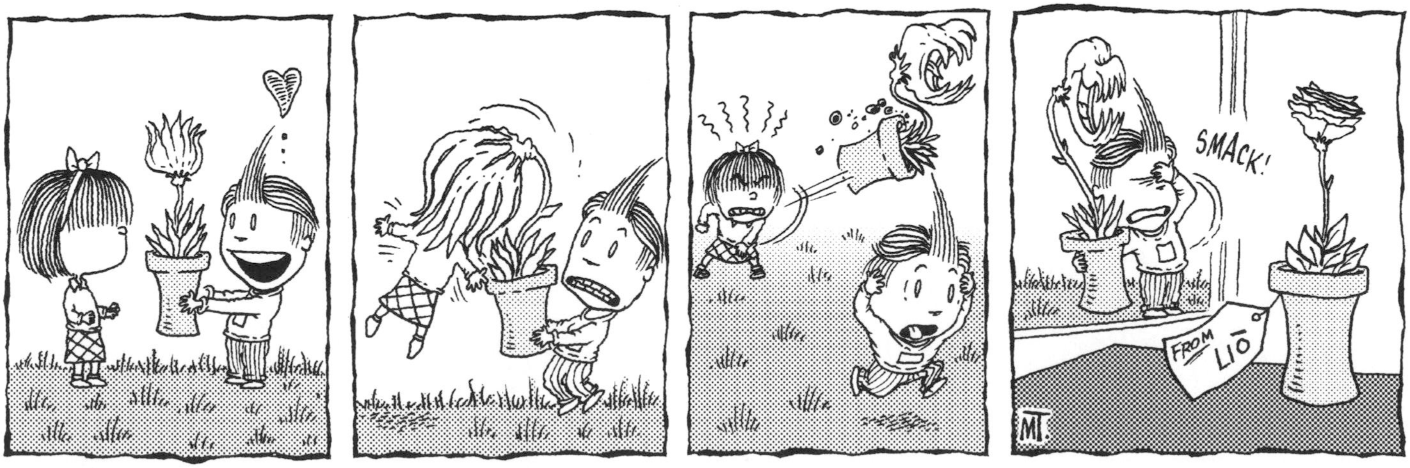
SMACK!
FROM LIO
MT.

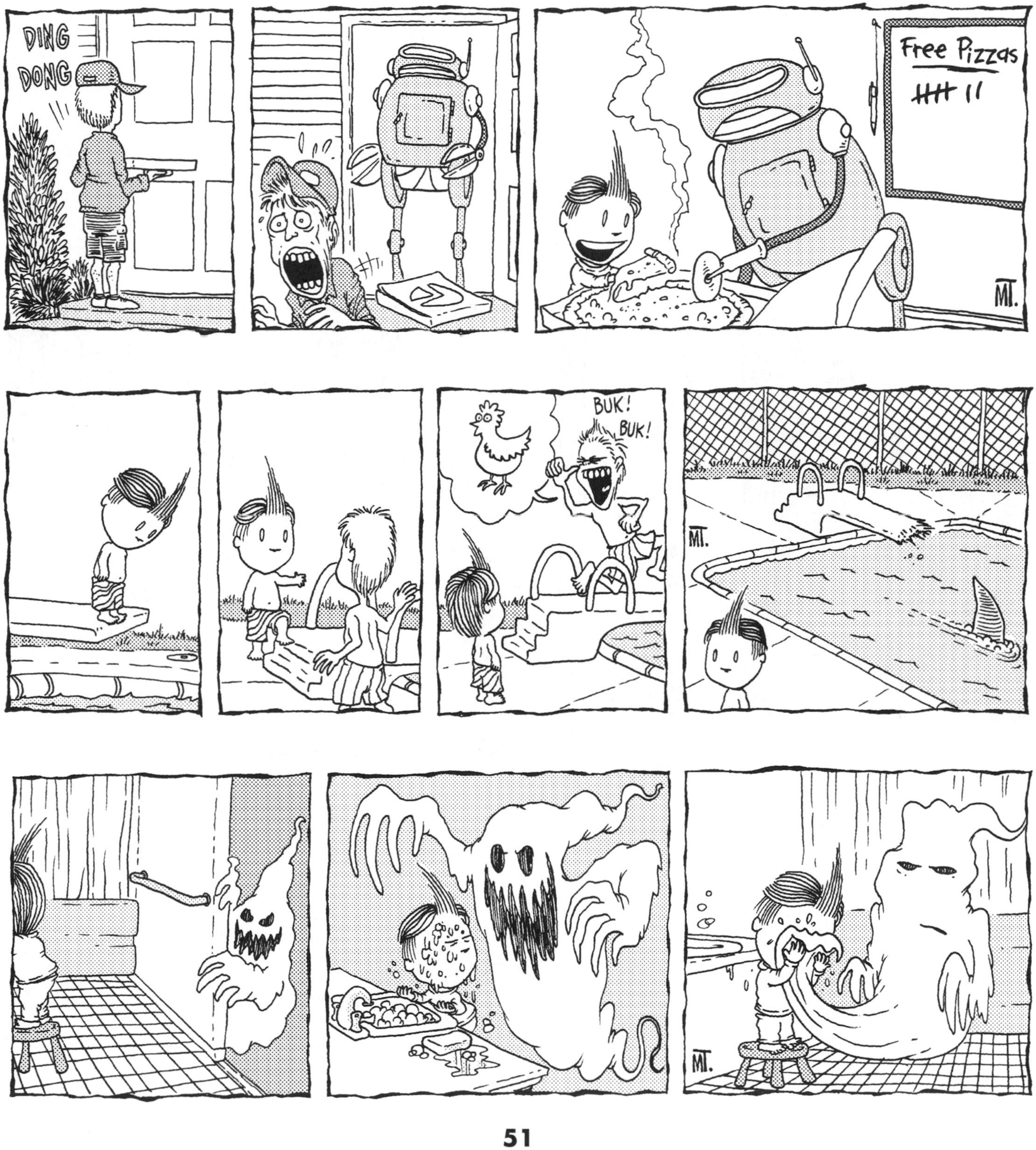
DING
DONG
Free Pizzas
BUK!
BUK!

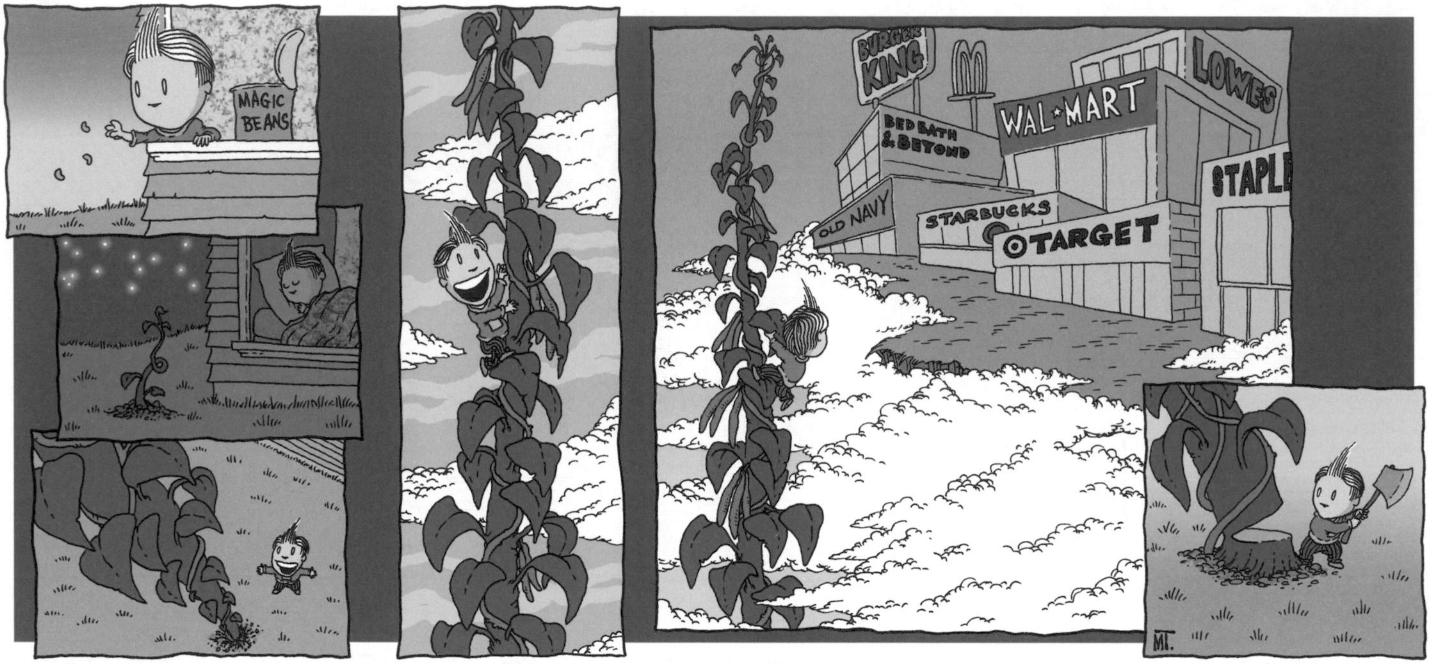
MAGIC BEANS
BURGER KING
BED BATH & BEYOND
WAL★MART
LOWES
STAPLE
OLD NAVY
STARBUCKS
TARGET
MT.

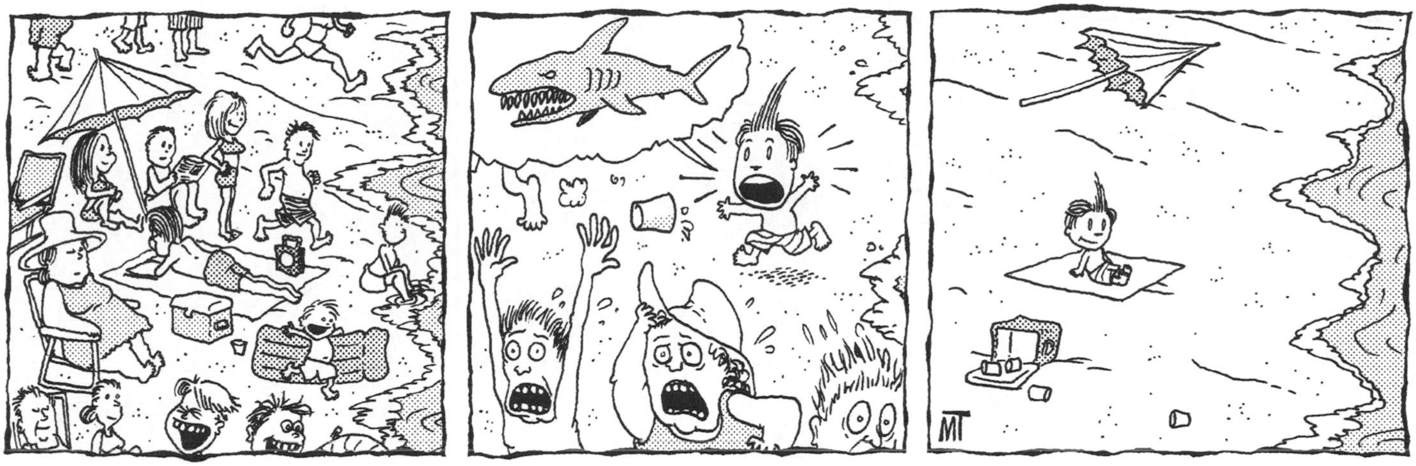
MT

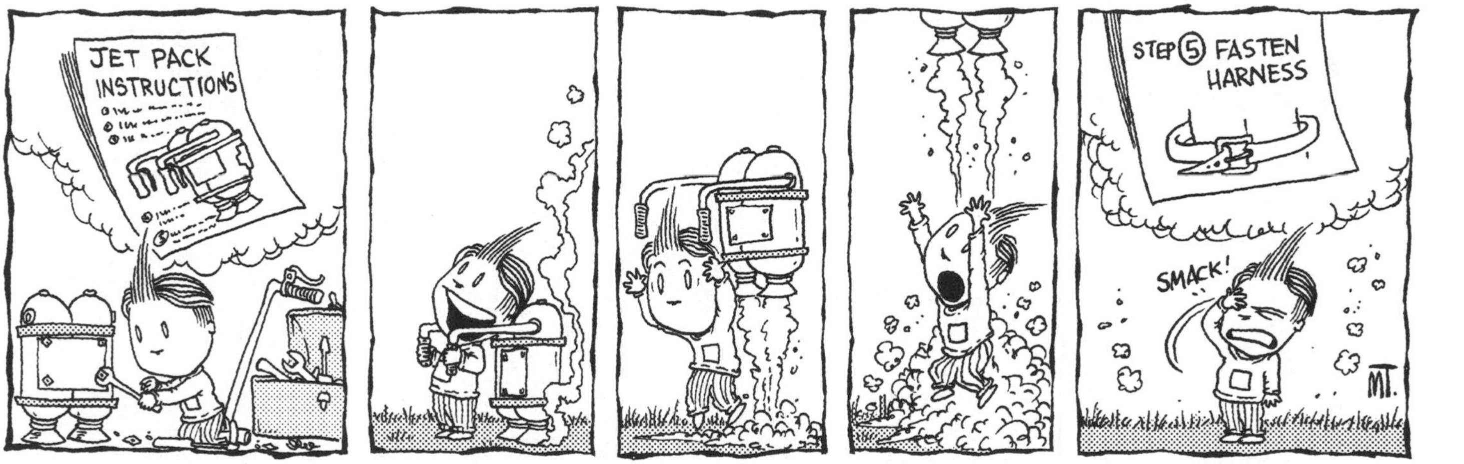
JET PACK
INSTRUCTIONS
STEP 5 FASTEN
HARNESS
SMACK!
MT.

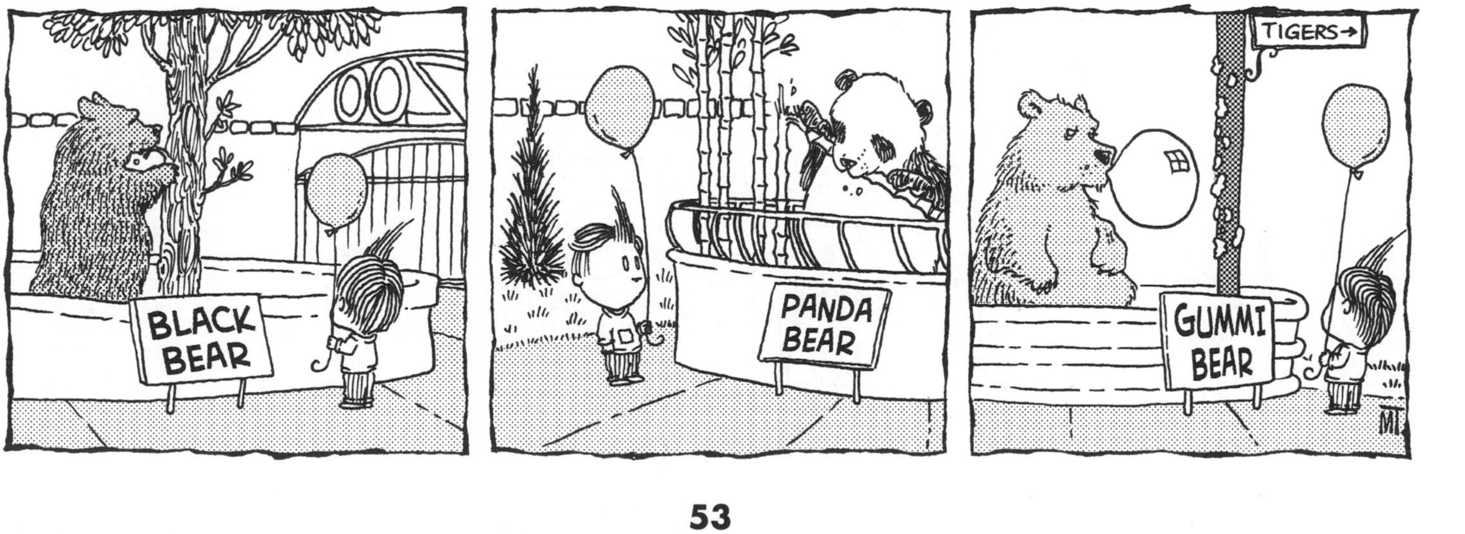
BLACK
BEAR
PANDA
BEAR
TIGERS →
GUMMI
BEAR
MT

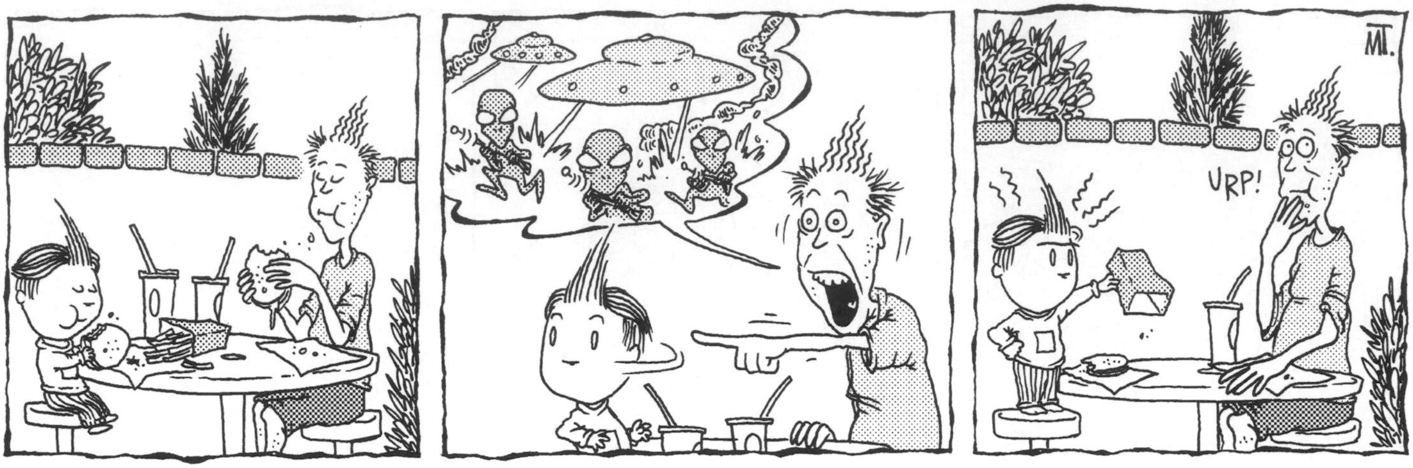

URP!
MT.

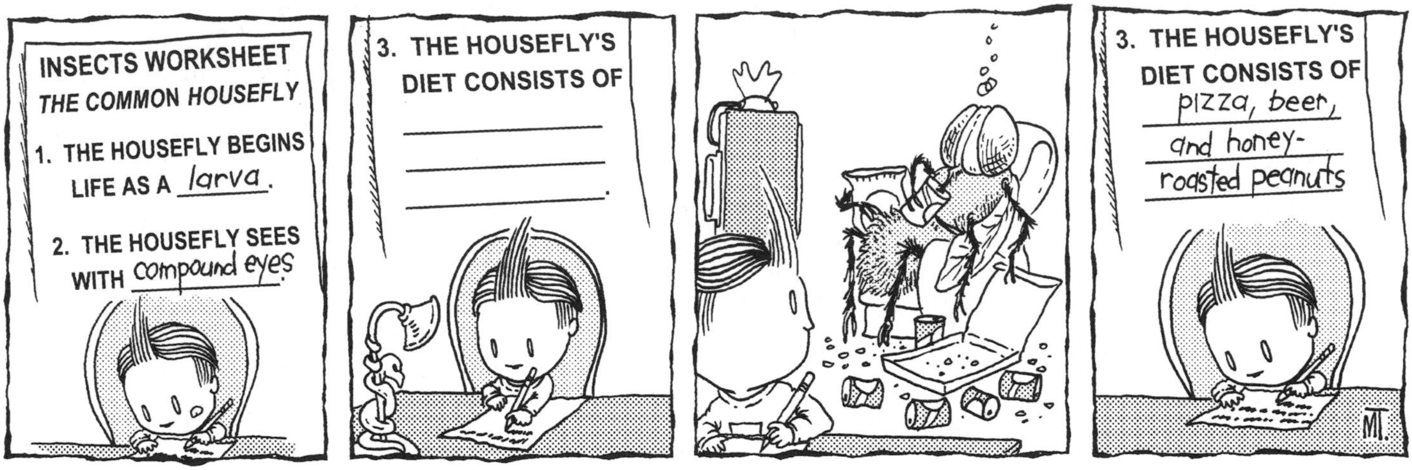

INSECTS WORKSHEET
THE COMMON HOUSEFLY
1. THE HOUSEFLY BEGINS LIFE AS A larva.
2. THE HOUSEFLY SEES WITH compound eyes.
3. THE HOUSEFLY'S DIET CONSISTS OF
3. THE HOUSEFLY'S DIET CONSISTS OF pizza, beer, and honey-roasted peanuts
MT.

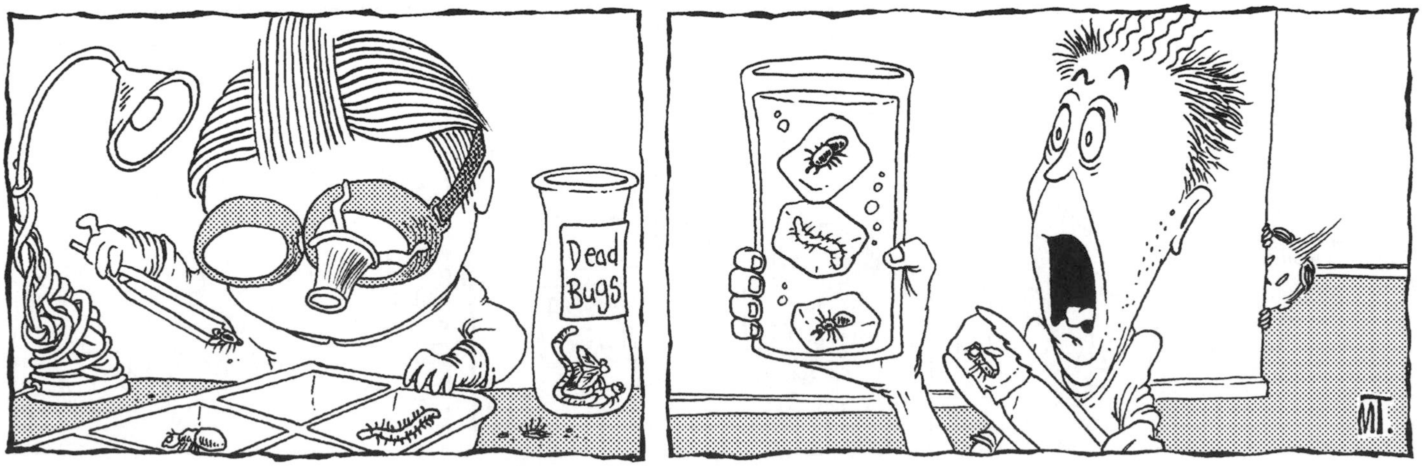

Dead Bugs
MT.

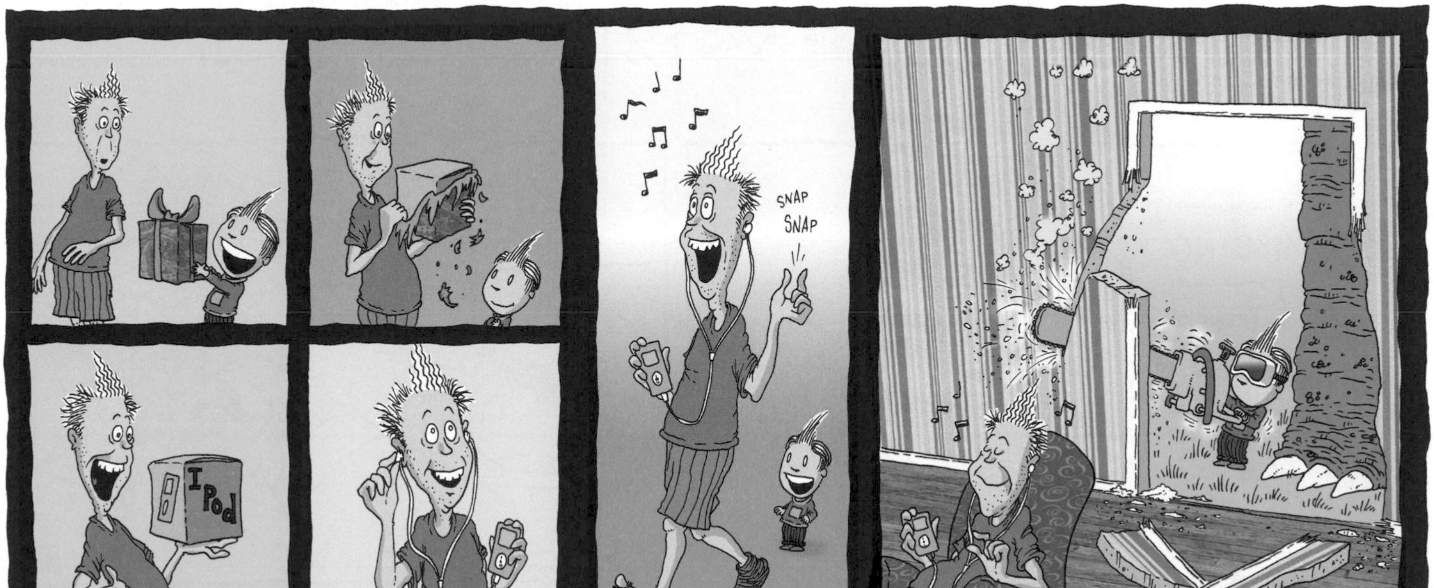
IPod
SNAP
SNAP
MT.

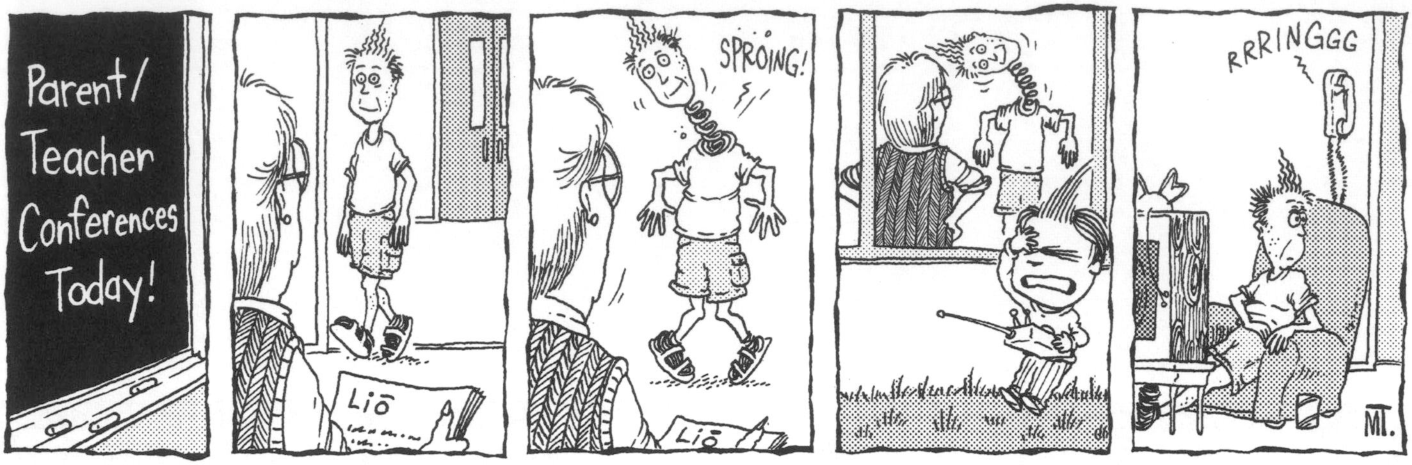
Parent/ Teacher Conferences Today!
LIŌ
SPROING!
LIŌ
RRRINGGG
MT.

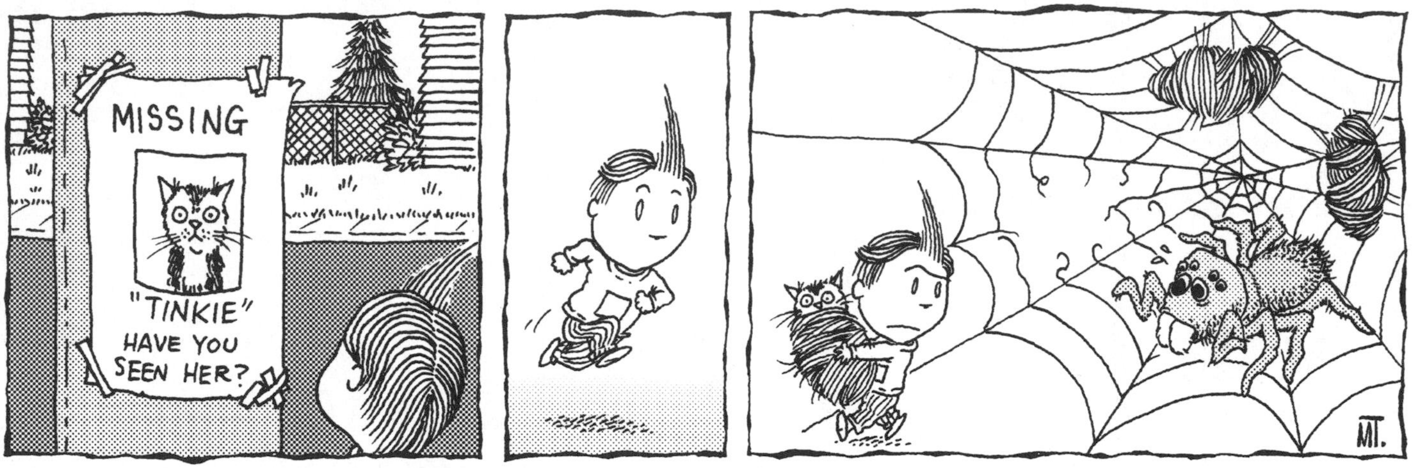
MISSING
"TINKIE"
HAVE YOU SEEN HER?
MT.

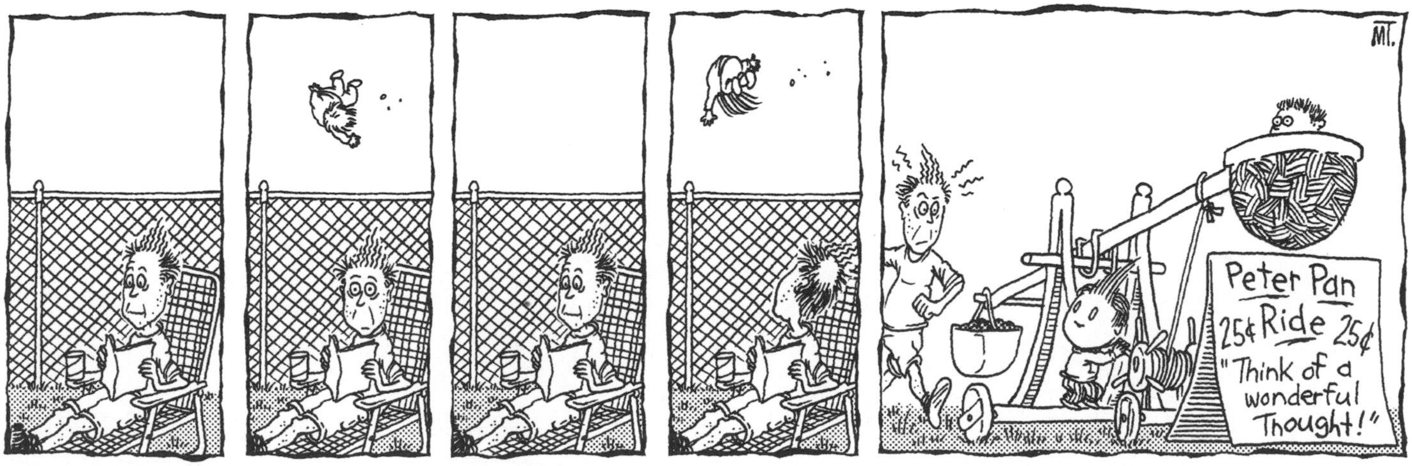
MT.
Peter Pan
25¢ Ride 25¢
"Think of a wonderful Thought!"

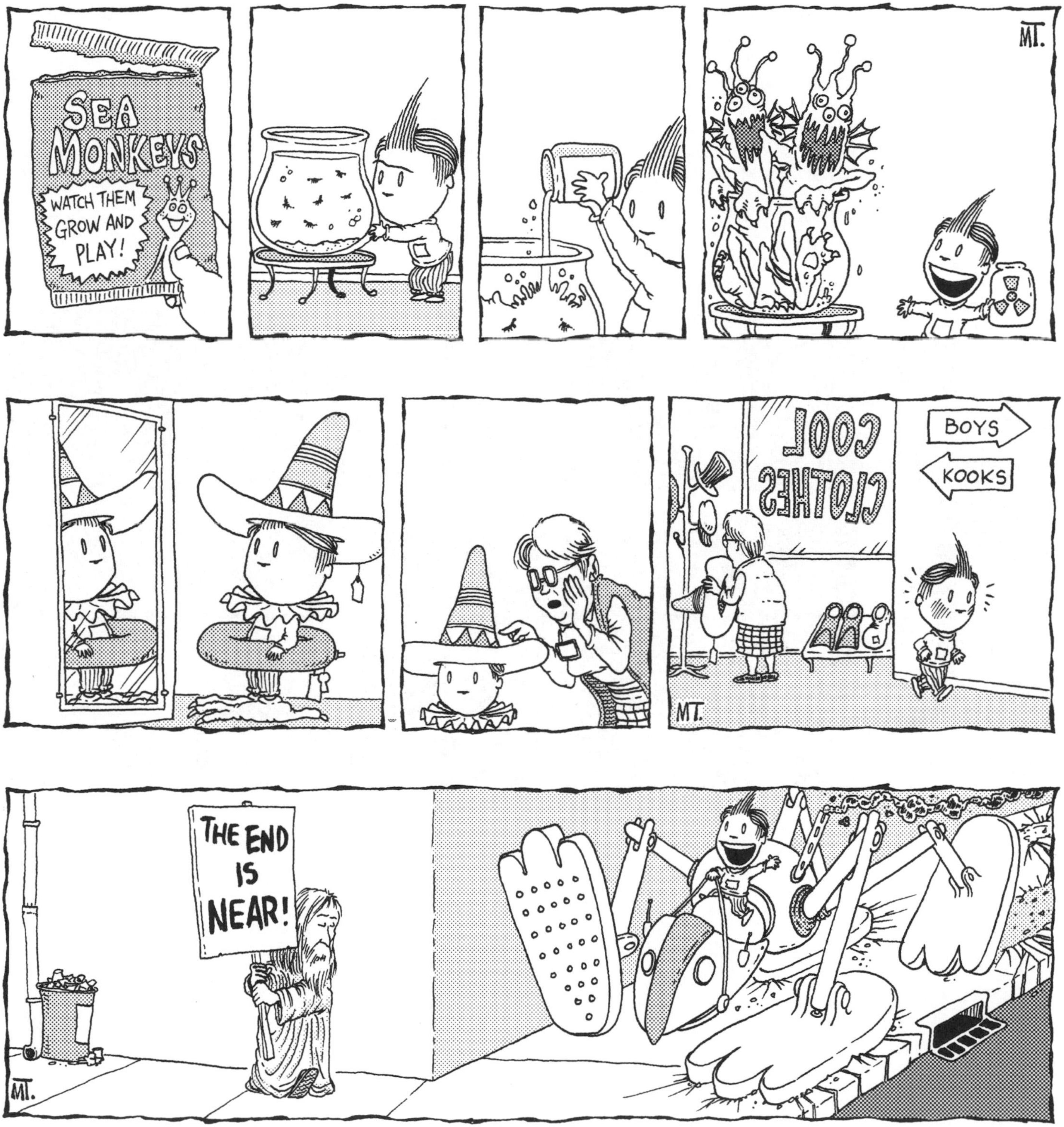
SEA MONKEYS
WATCH THEM GROW AND PLAY!
MT.
COOL CLOTHES
BOYS
KOOKS
MT.
THE END IS NEAR!
MT.

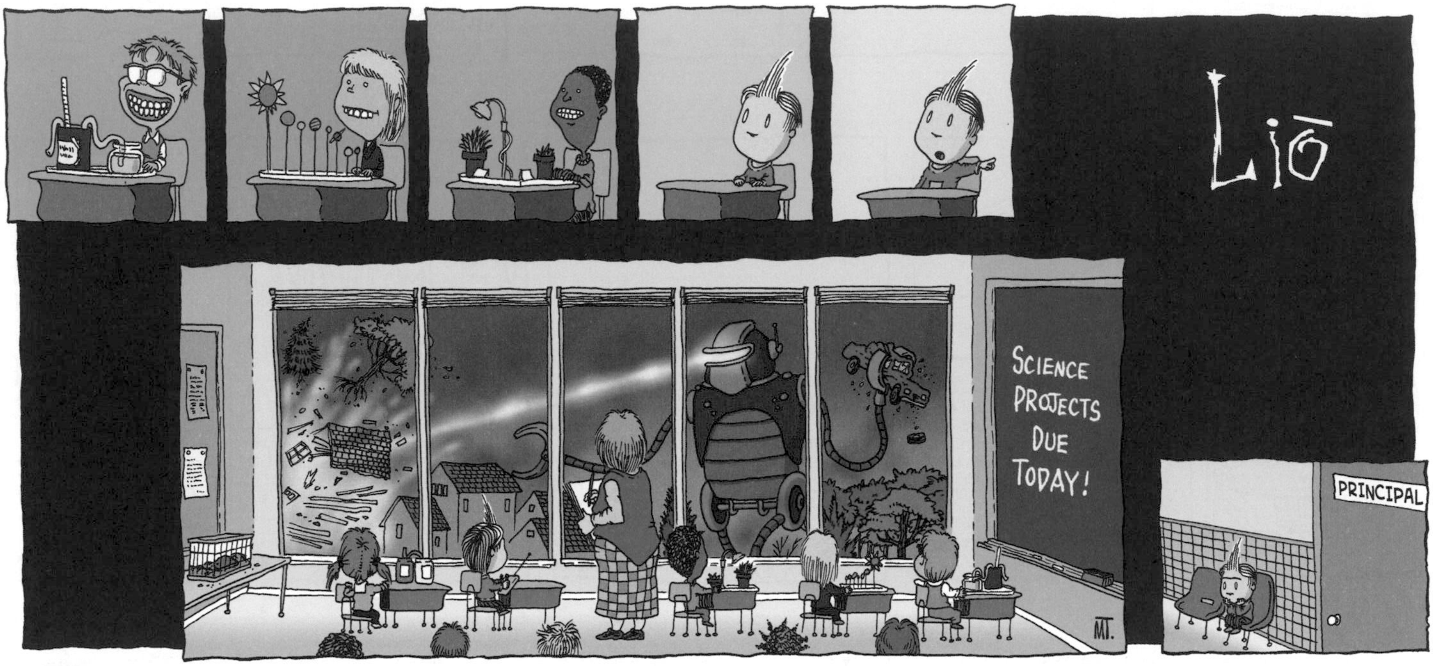
Liō
SCIENCE PROJECTS DUE TODAY!
PRINCIPAL
MT.

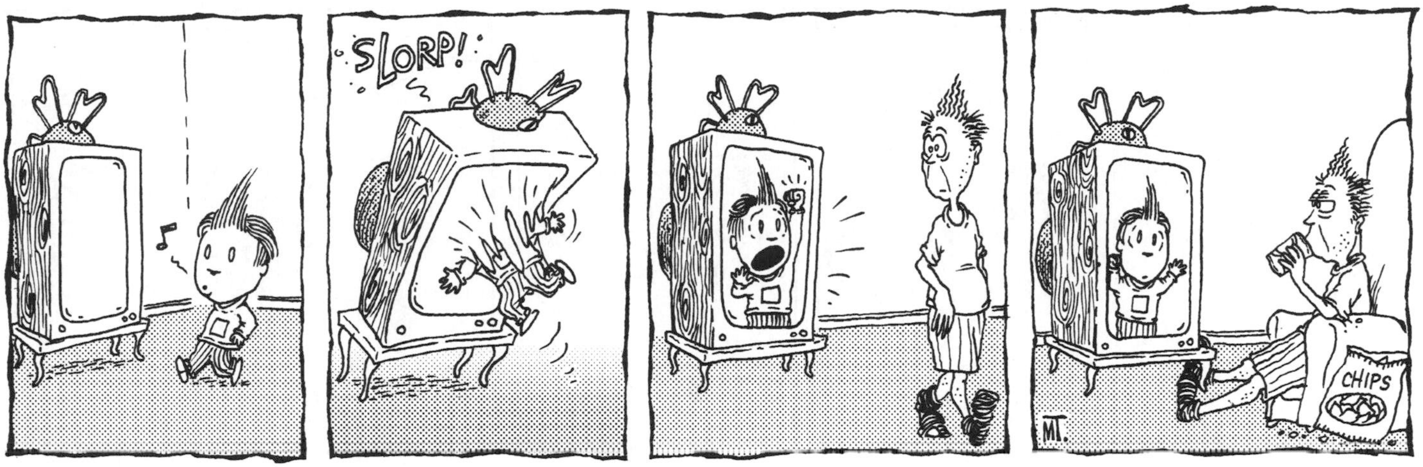
SLORP!
CHIPS

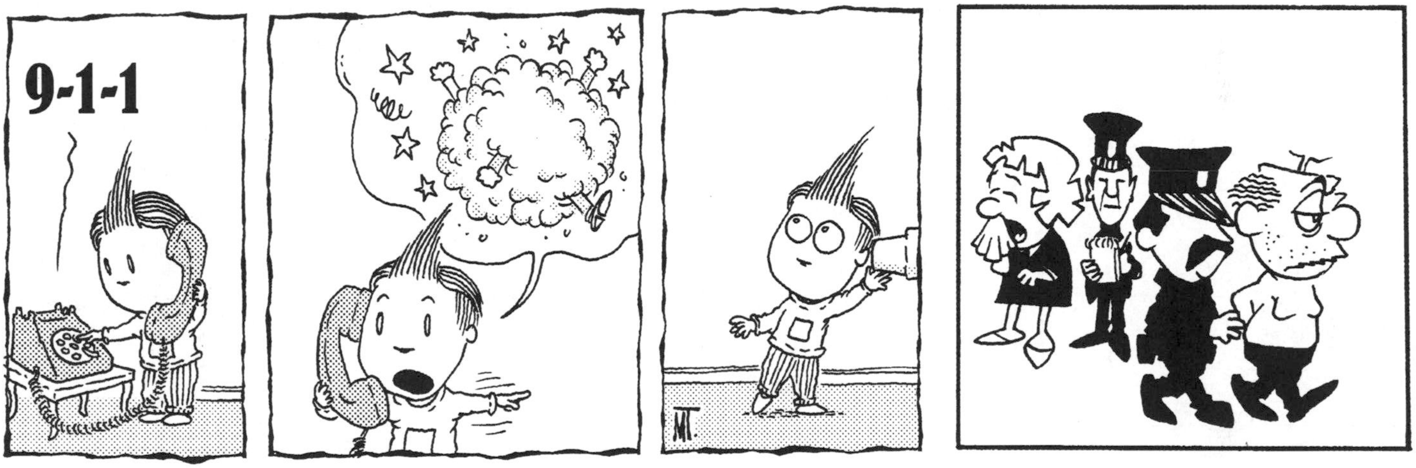
9-1-1

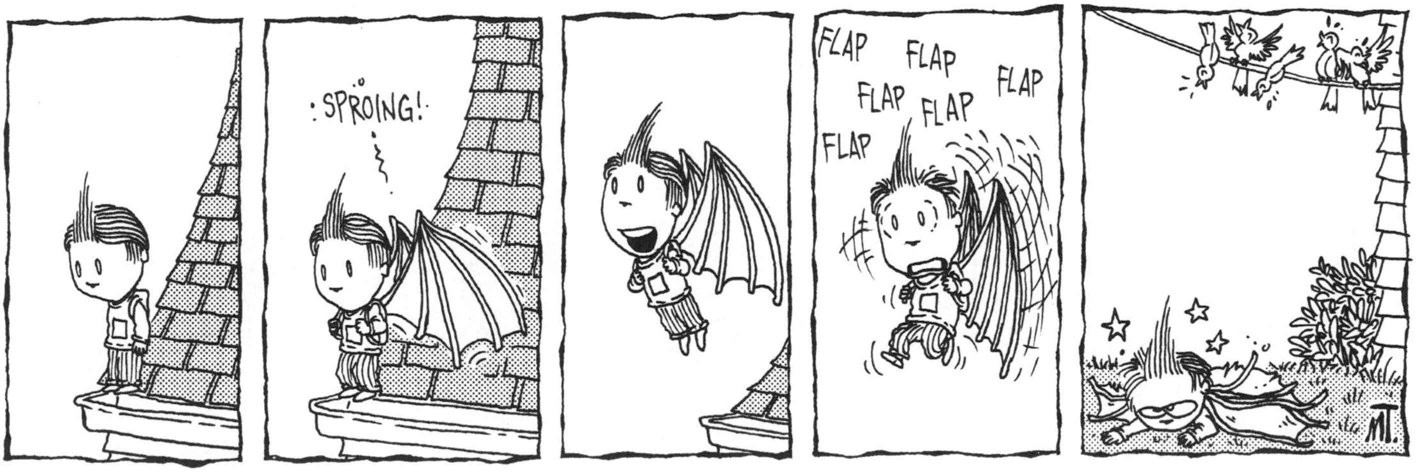
SPROING!
FLAP FLAP FLAP FLAP FLAP FLAP

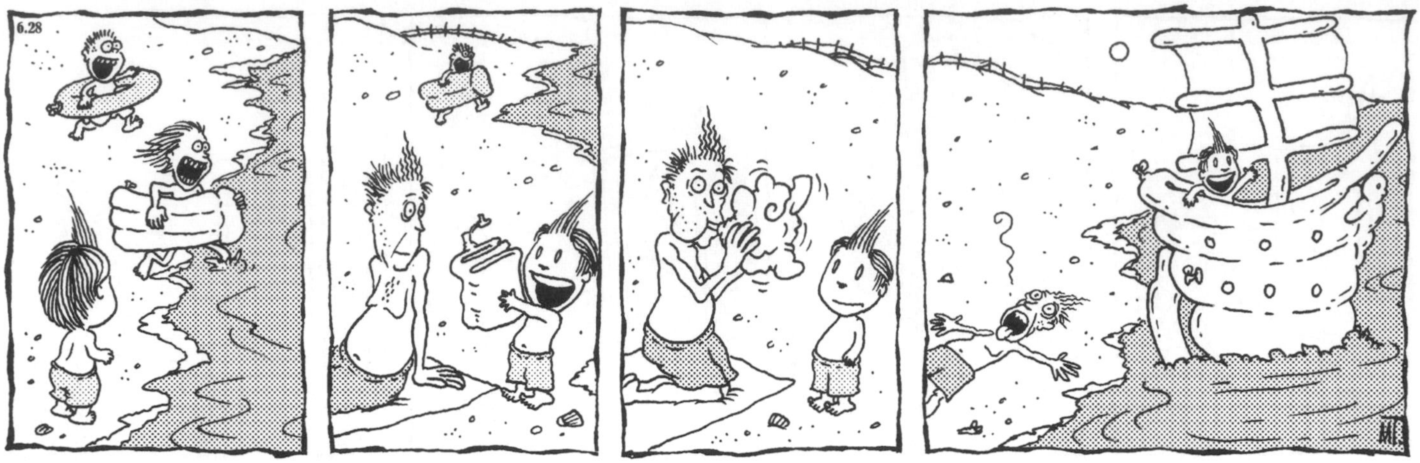
6.28
MT.

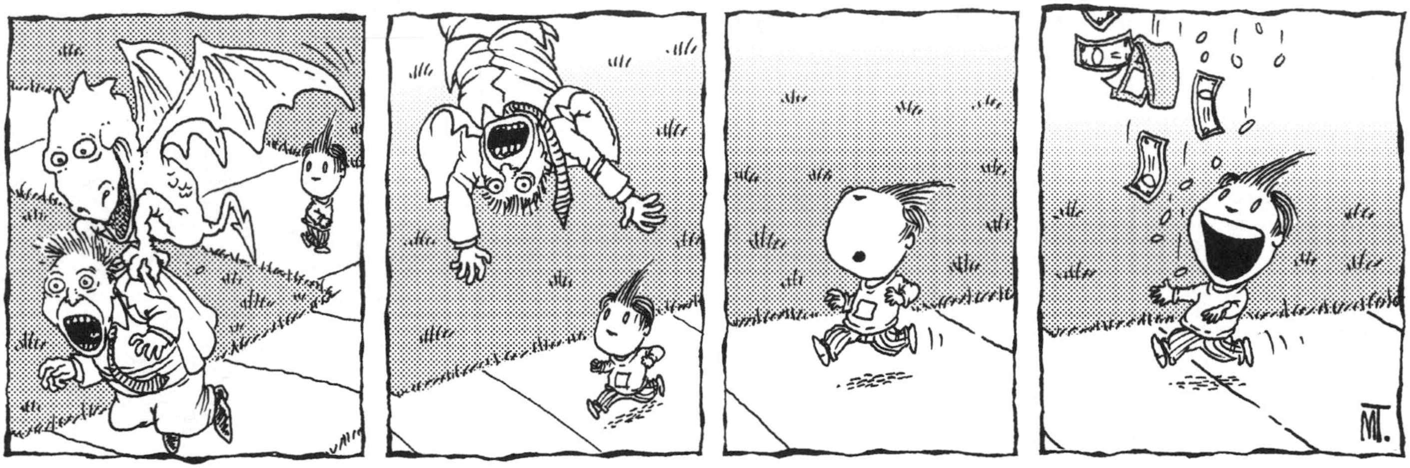
MT.

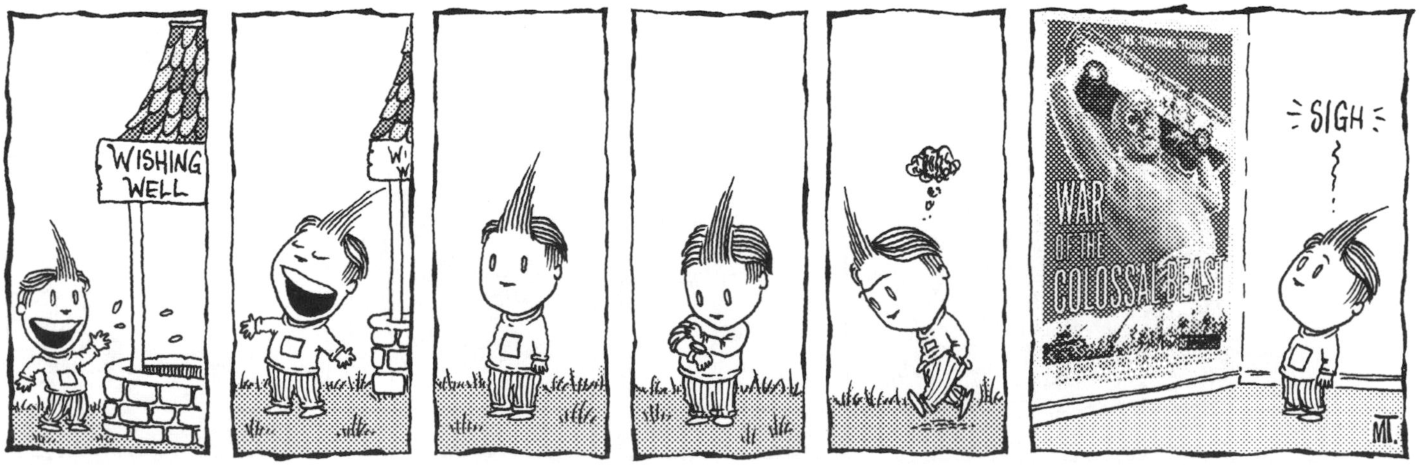
WISHING
WELL
WAR
OF THE
COLOSSAL BEAST
SIGH
MT.

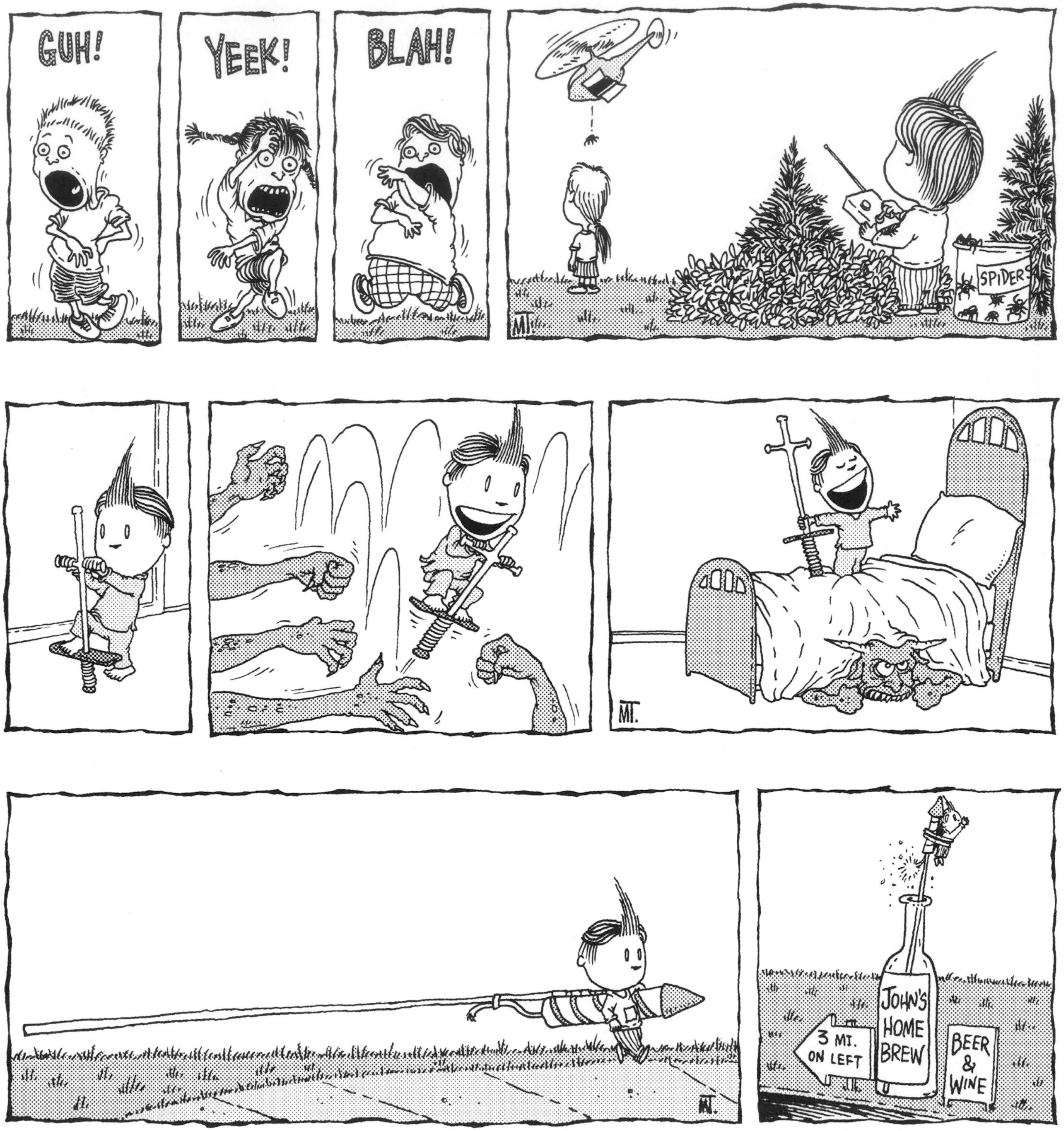
GUH!
YEEK!
BLAH!
SPIDERS
MT.
MT.
MT.
3 MI. ON LEFT
JOHN'S HOME BREW
BEER & WINE

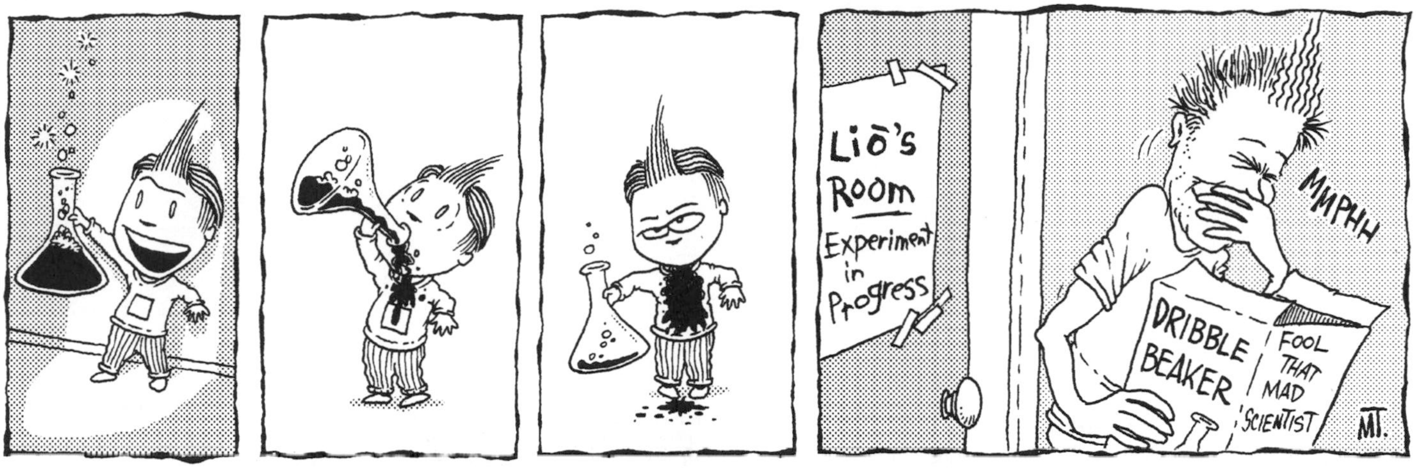
Liō's Room
Experiment in Progress
MMPHH
DRIBBLE BEAKER
FOOL THAT MAD SCIENTIST

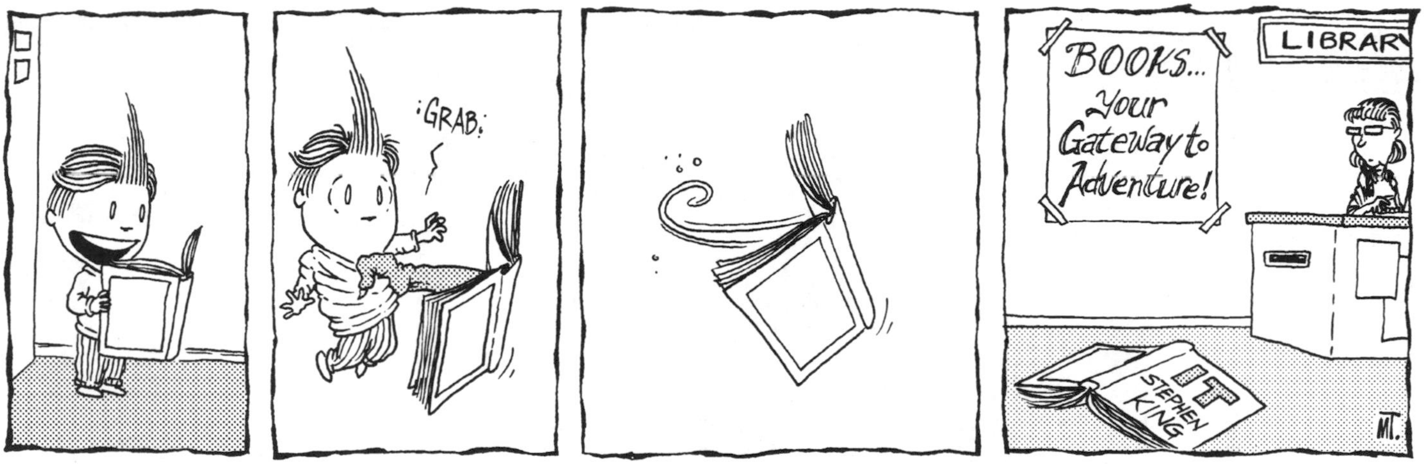
¡GRAB¡
BOOKS... Your Gateway to Adventure!
LIBRARY
IT
STEPHEN KING

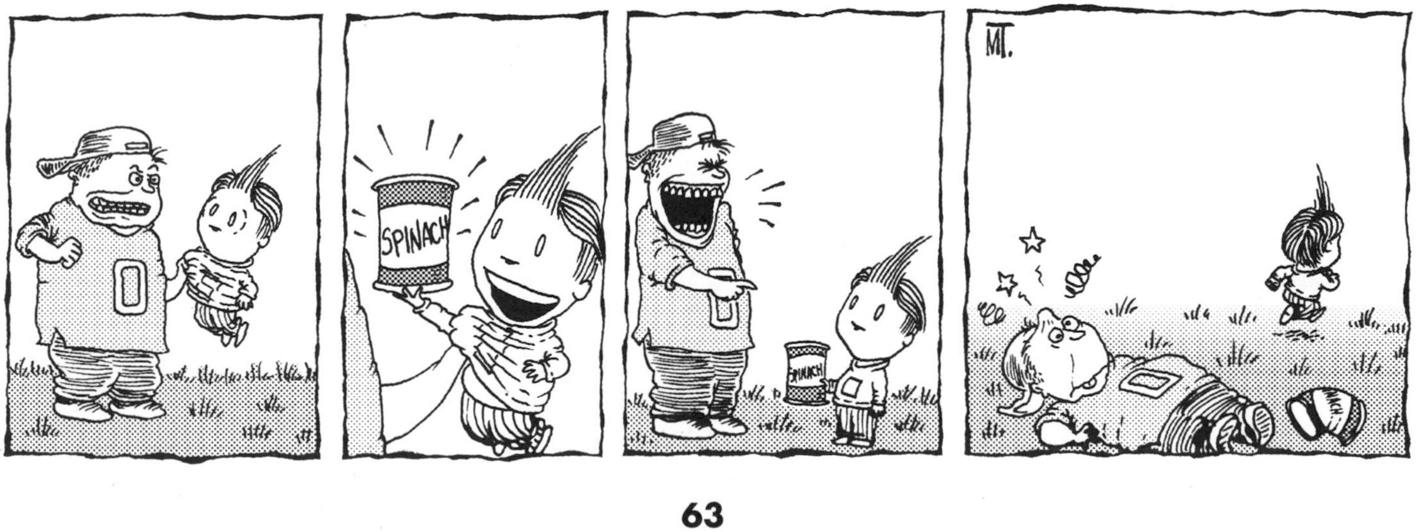
SPINACH

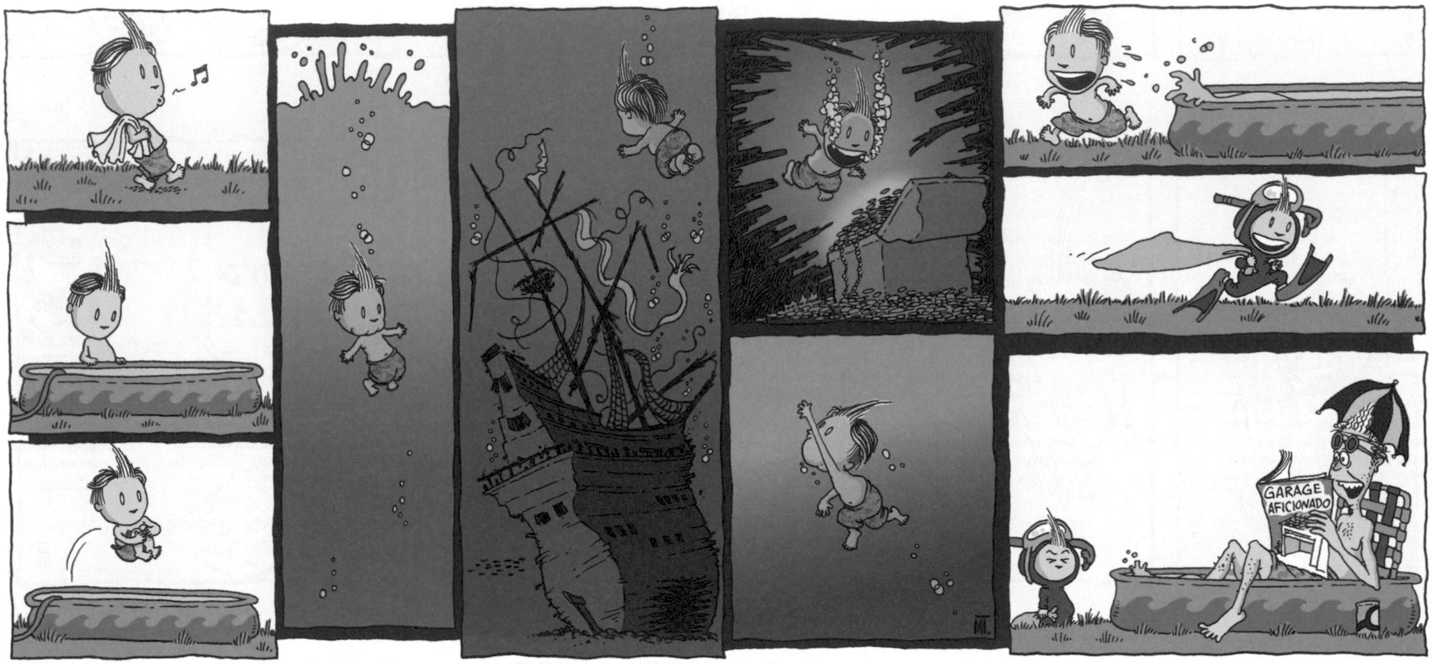
GARAGE AFICIONADO

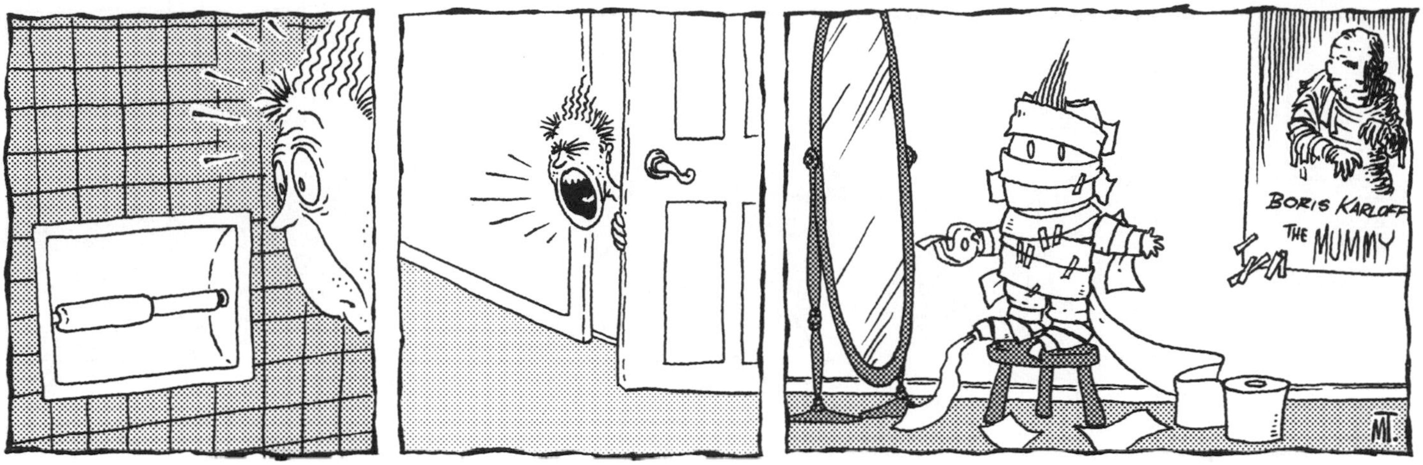
BORIS KARLOFF
THE MUMMY

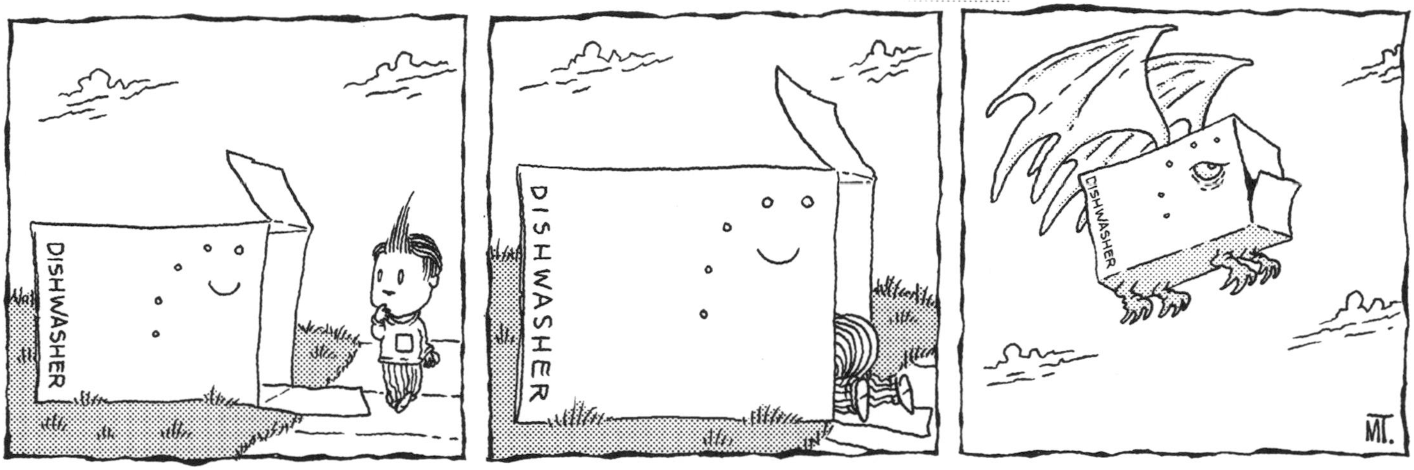
DISHWASHER
DISHWASHER
DISHWASHER

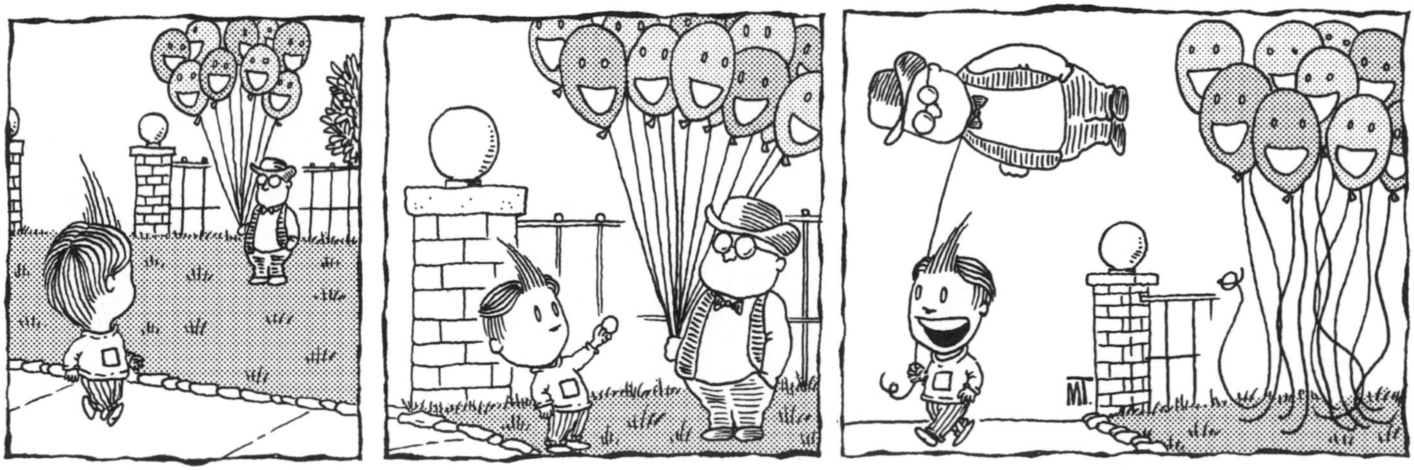

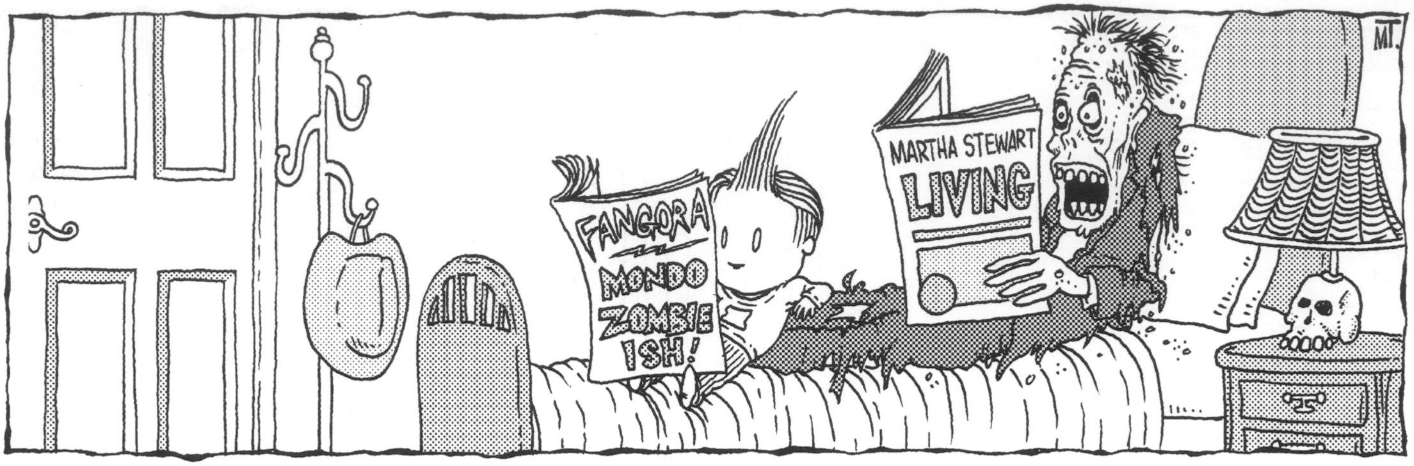
FANGORA
MONDO ZOMBIE ISH!
MARTHA STEWART
LIVING

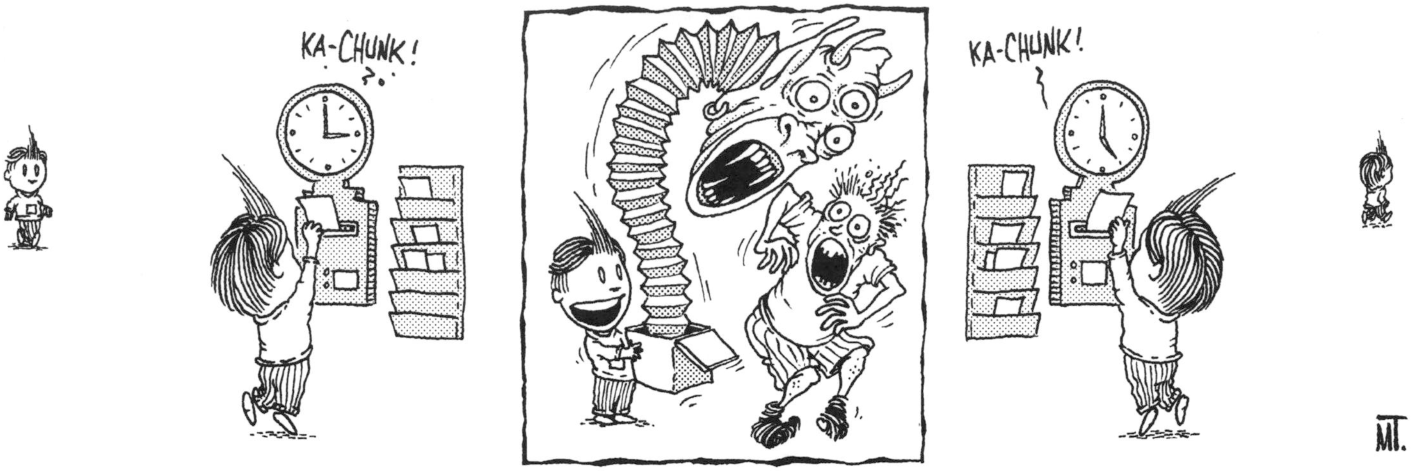
KA-CHUNK!
KA-CHUNK!

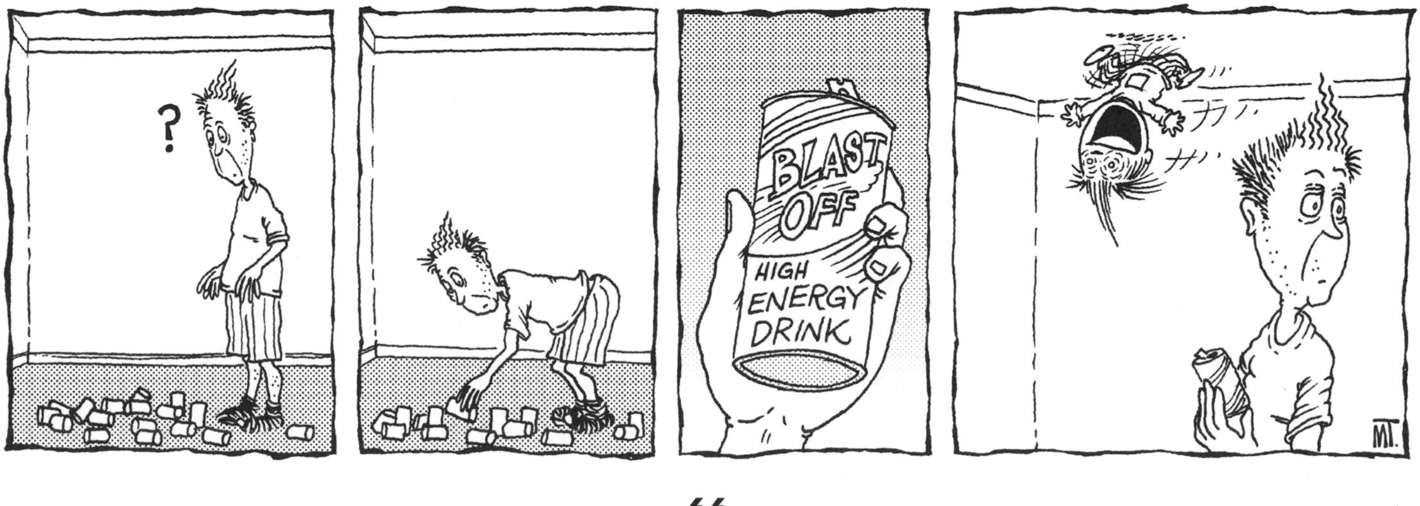
?
BLAST OFF
HIGH ENERGY DRINK

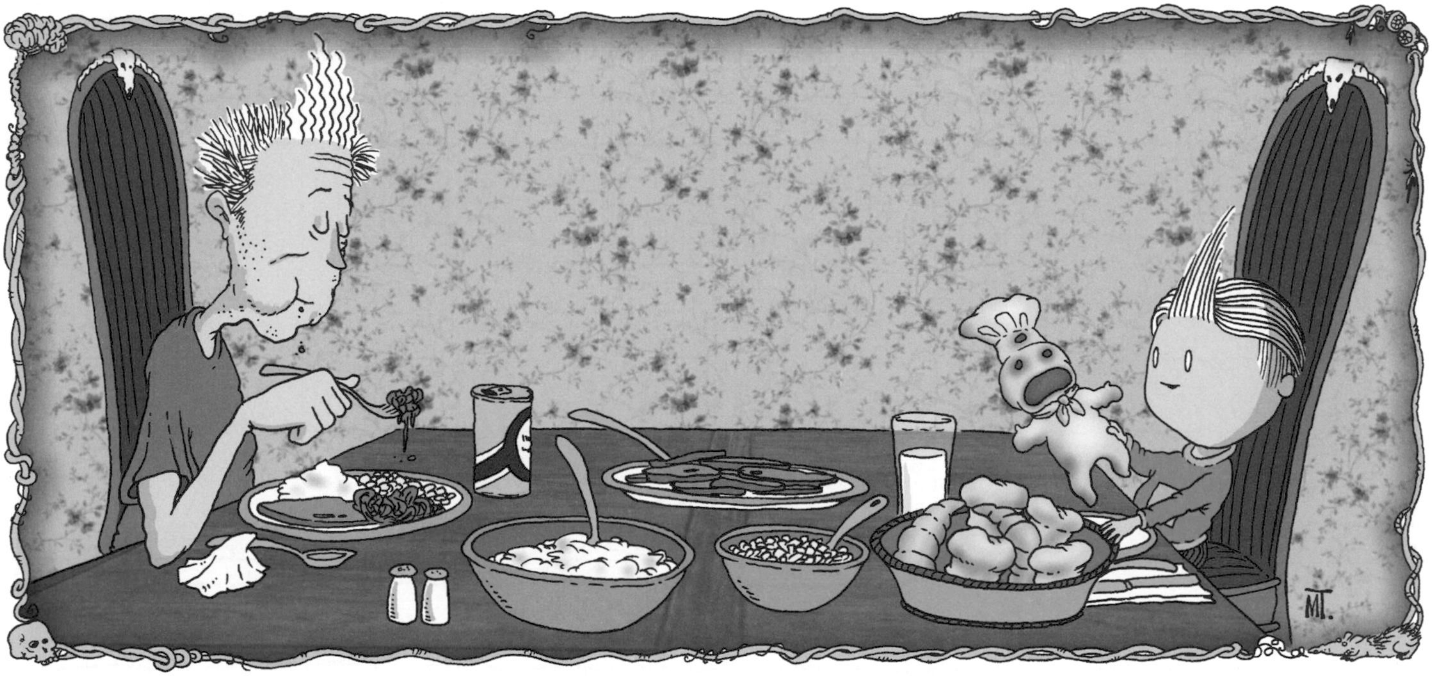
MT.

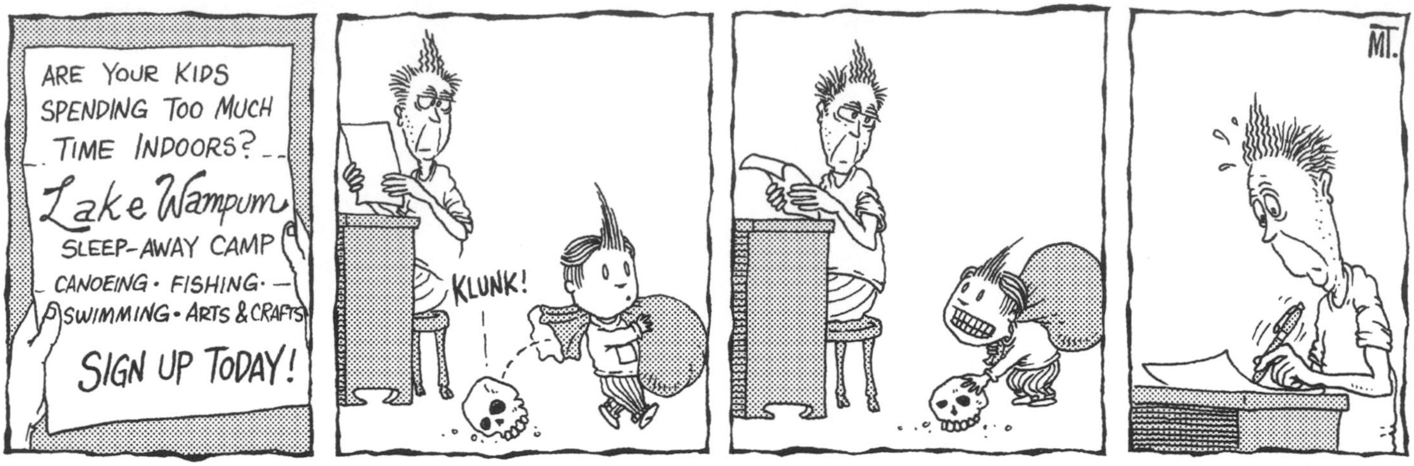
ARE YOUR KIDS SPENDING TOO MUCH TIME INDOORS?
Lake Wampum
SLEEP-AWAY CAMP
CANOEING · FISHING · SWIMMING · ARTS & CRAFTS
SIGN UP TODAY!
KLUNK!
MT.

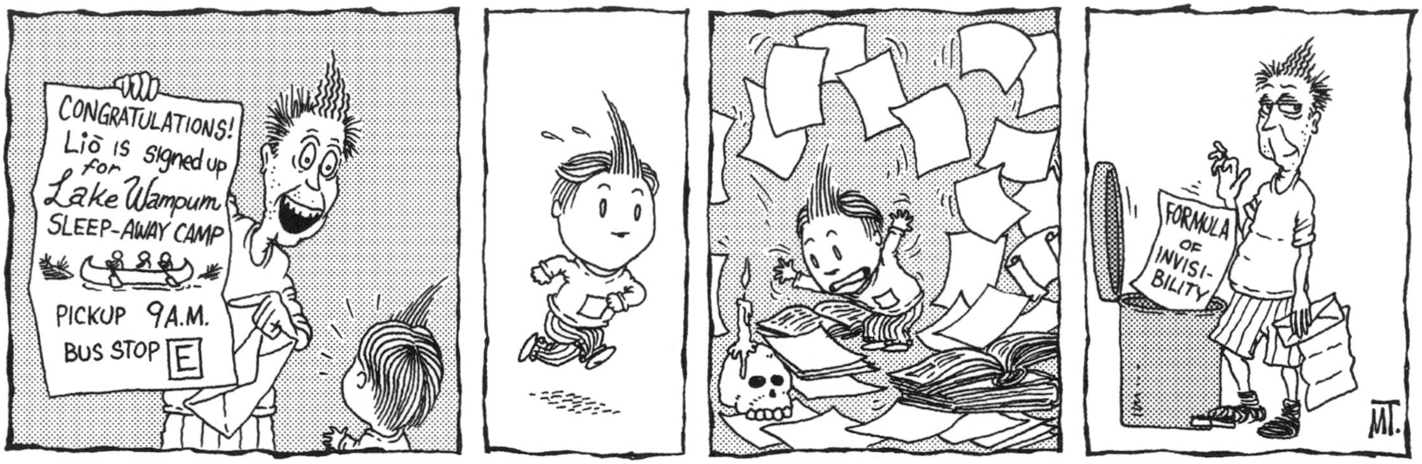
CONGRATULATIONS!
Liō is signed up for
Lake Wampum
SLEEP-AWAY CAMP
PICKUP 9 A.M.
BUS STOP E
FORMULA OF INVISI-BILITY
MT.

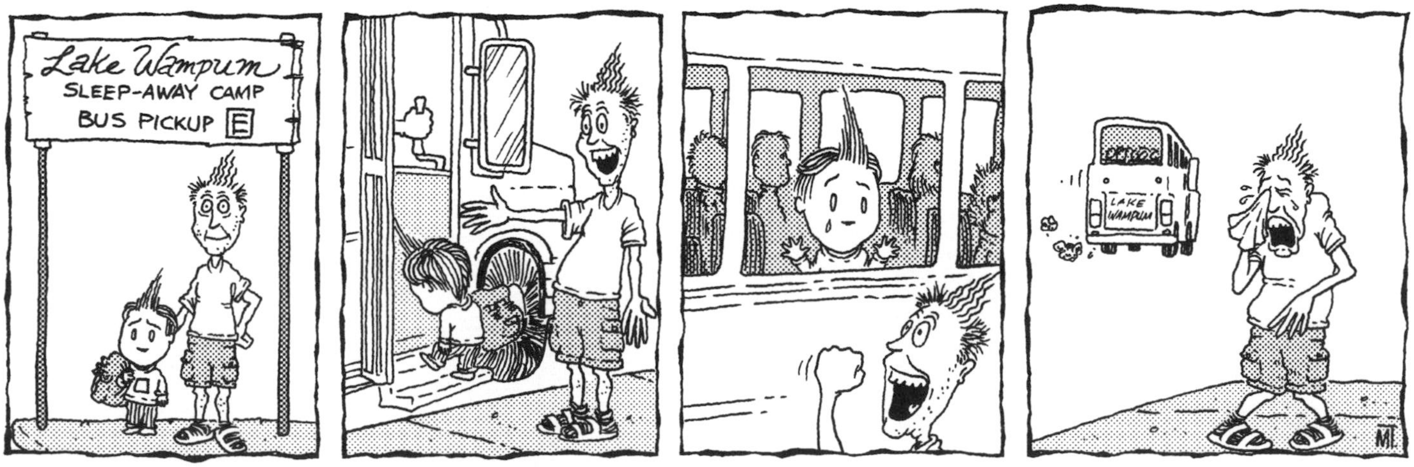
Lake Wampum
SLEEP-AWAY CAMP
BUS PICKUP E
LAKE WAMPUM
MT.

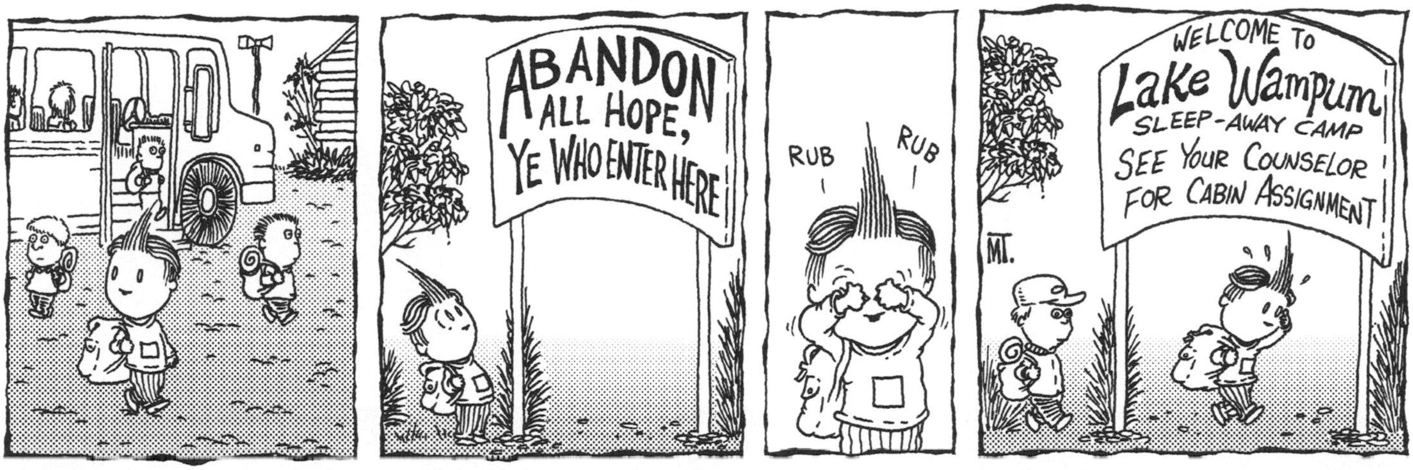
ABANDON ALL HOPE, YE WHO ENTER HERE
RUB RUB
WELCOME TO Lake Wampum SLEEP-AWAY CAMP
SEE YOUR COUNSELOR FOR CABIN ASSIGNMENT
MT.

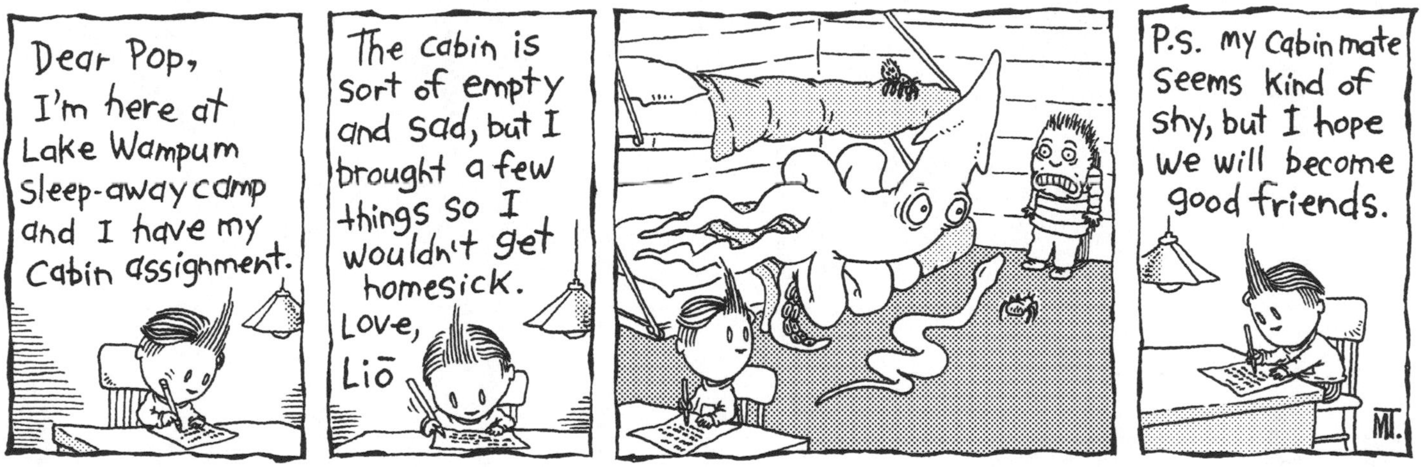
Dear Pop,
I'm here at Lake Wampum Sleep-away camp and I have my cabin assignment.
The cabin is sort of empty and sad, but I brought a few things so I wouldn't get homesick.
Love,
Lio
P.S. my cabinmate seems kind of shy, but I hope we will become good friends.
MT.

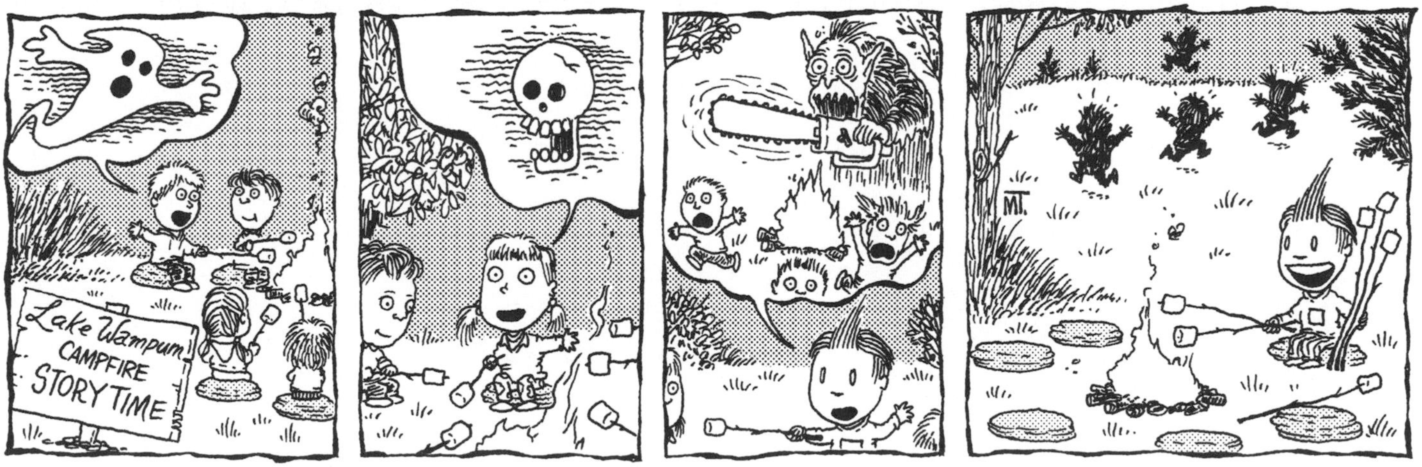
Lake Wampum CAMPFIRE STORY TIME
MT.

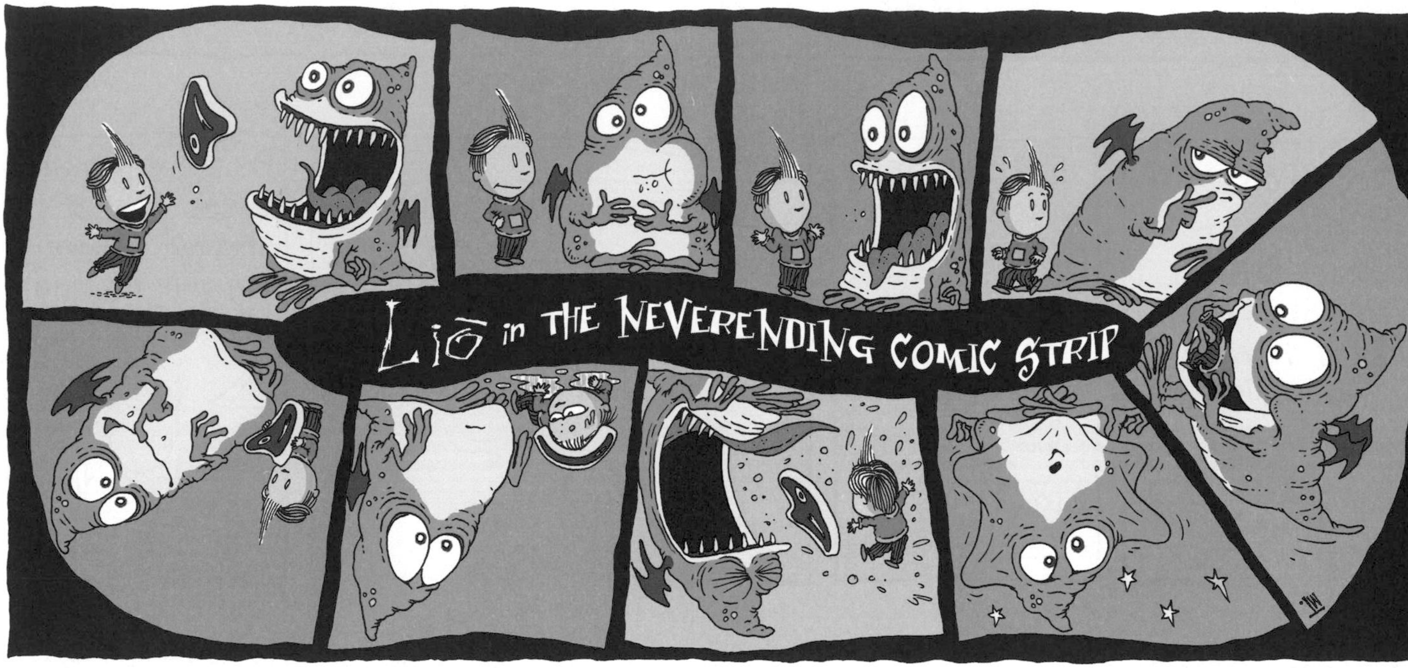
Liō in THE NEVERENDING COMIC STRIP

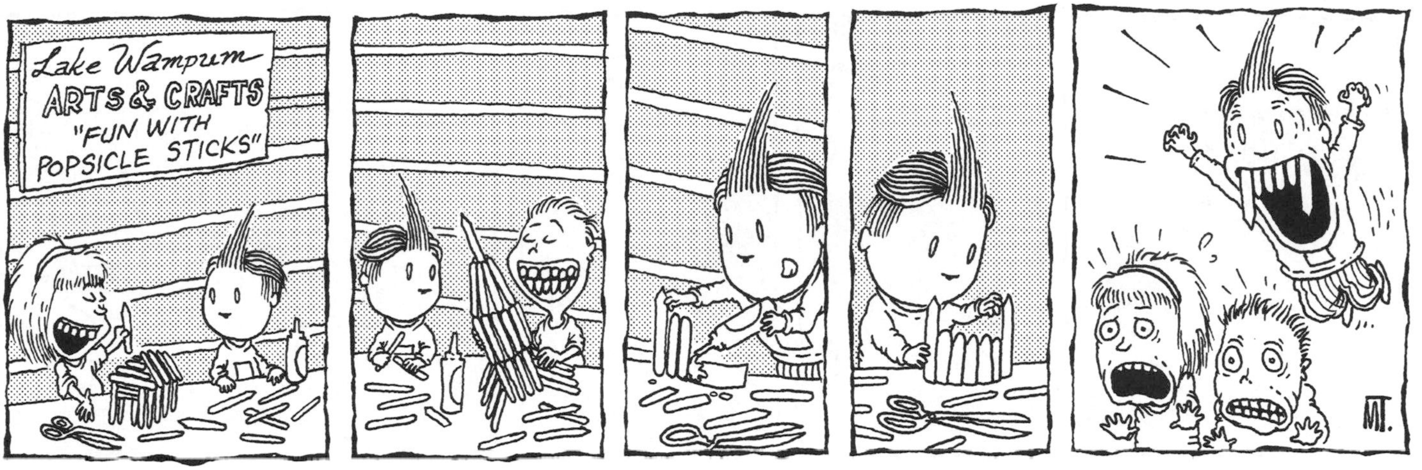
Lake Wampum
ARTS & CRAFTS
"FUN WITH
POPSICLE STICKS"

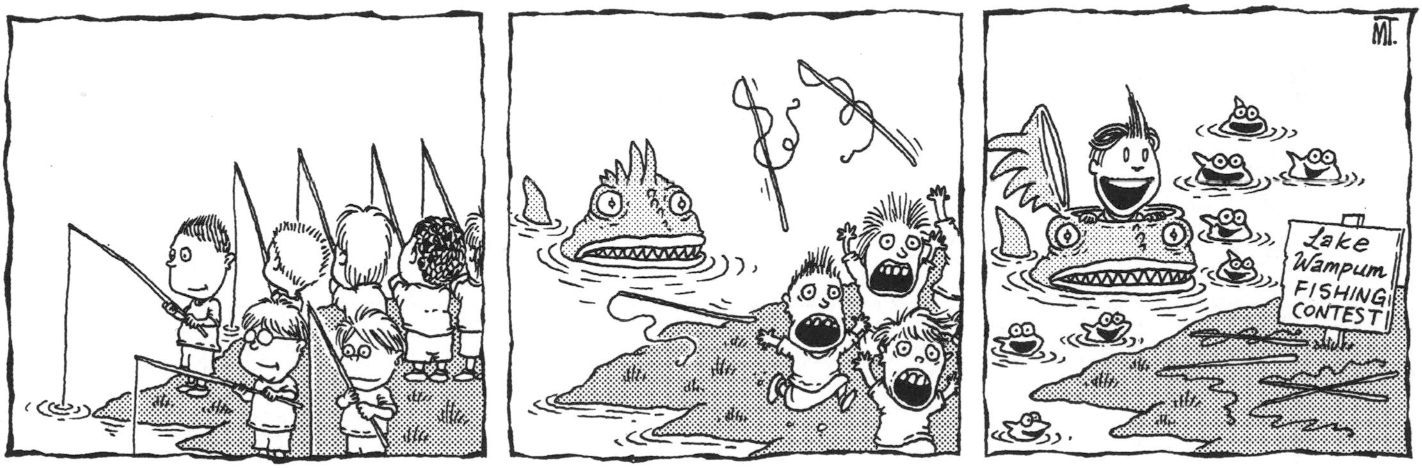
Lake Wampum
FISHING
CONTEST

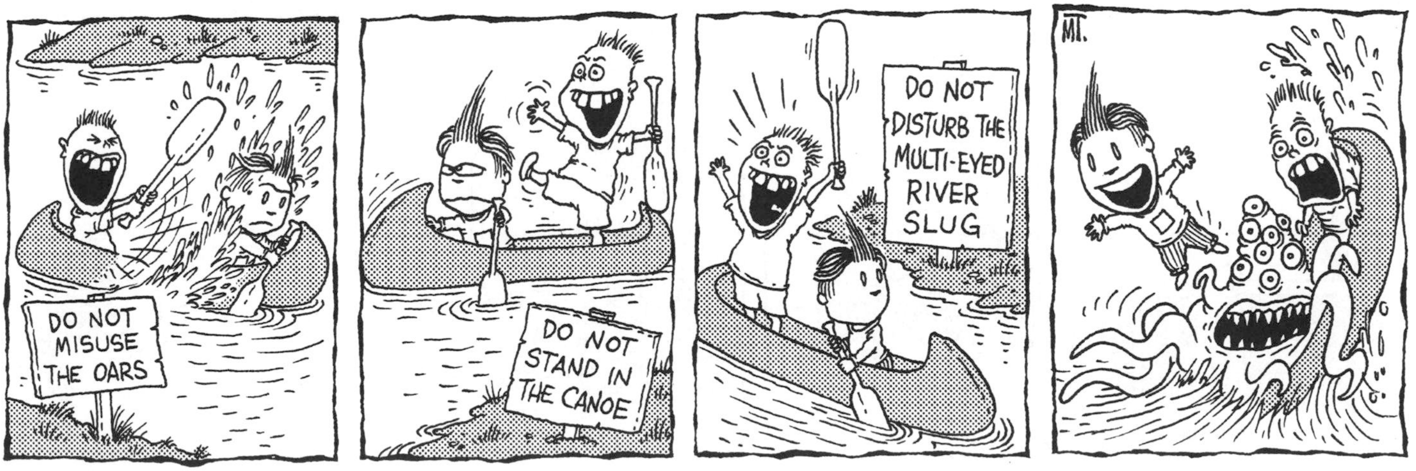
DO NOT
MISUSE
THE OARS
DO NOT
STAND IN
THE CANOE
DO NOT
DISTURB THE
MULTI-EYED
RIVER
SLUG

Lake Wampum
CANOE RETURN
STILL OUT:
LIŌ AND BIFF 05
Lake Wampum CAMP COUNSELOR
05 Lake Wampum
CAMP KITCHEN
POTATOES
Lake Wampum
SLEEP-AWAY CAMP
CAMPER PICKUP
BUS E

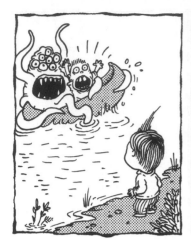

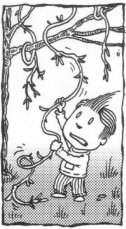

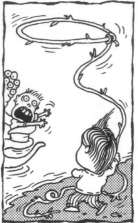

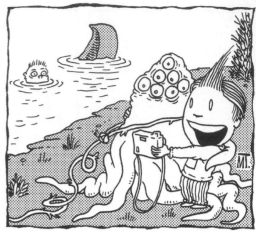

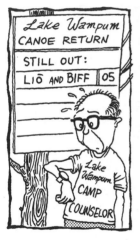

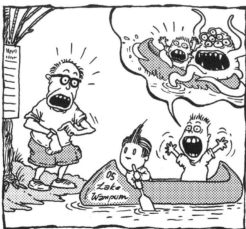

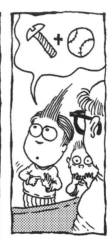

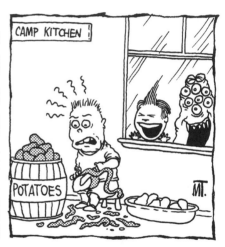

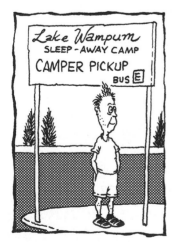

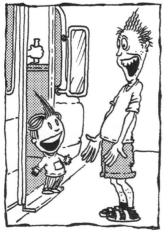

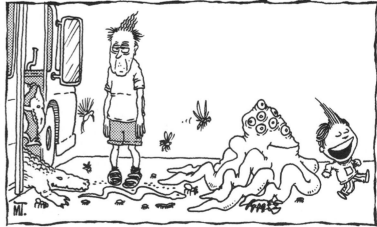

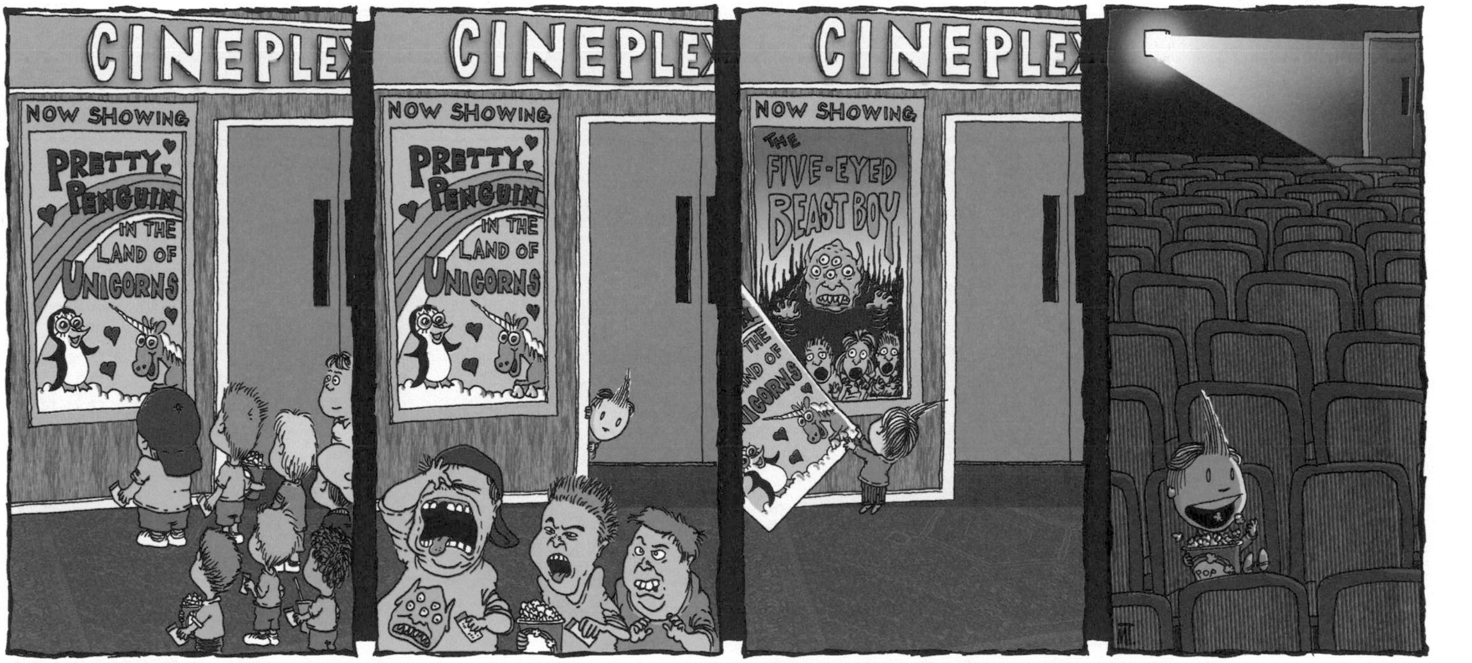
CINEPLEX
NOW SHOWING
PRETTY PENGUIN IN THE LAND OF UNICORNS
CINEPLEX
NOW SHOWING
PRETTY PENGUIN IN THE LAND OF UNICORNS
CINEPLEX
NOW SHOWING
THE FIVE-EYED BEAST BOY
POP

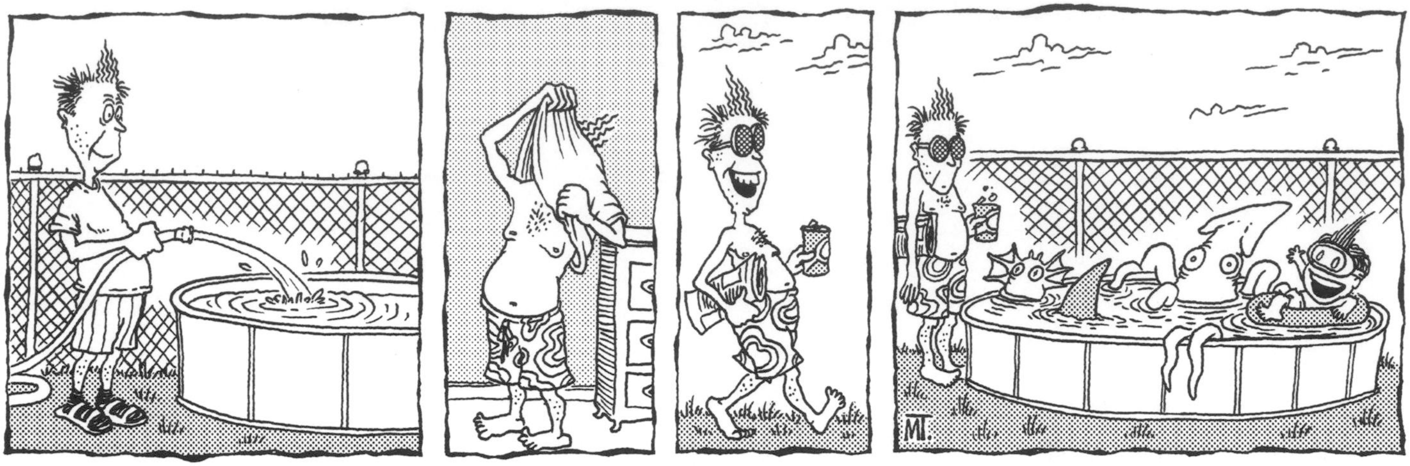
MT.

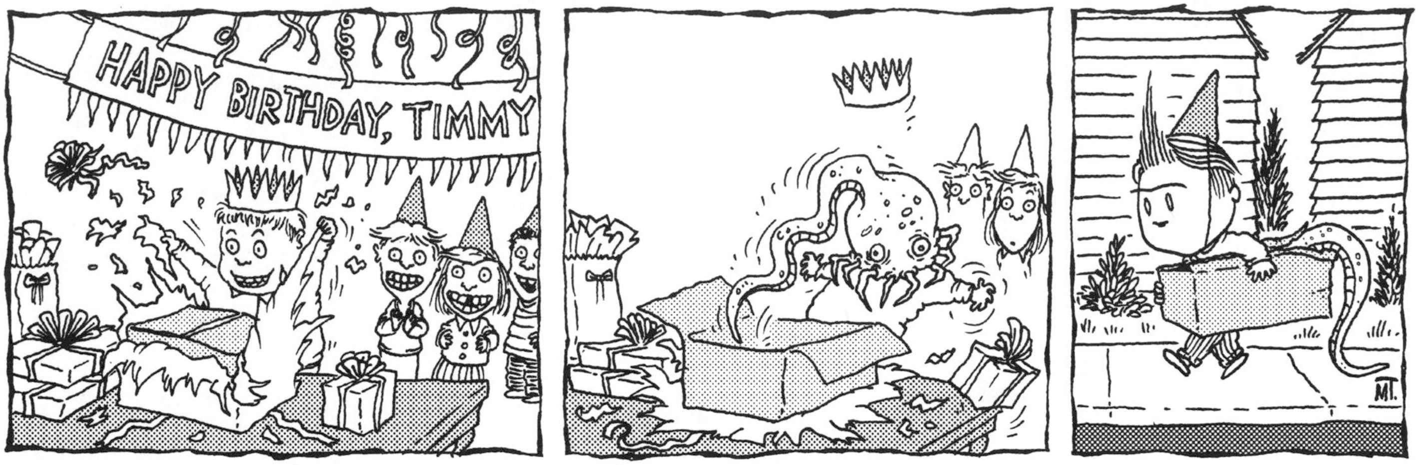
HAPPY BIRTHDAY, TIMMY
MT.

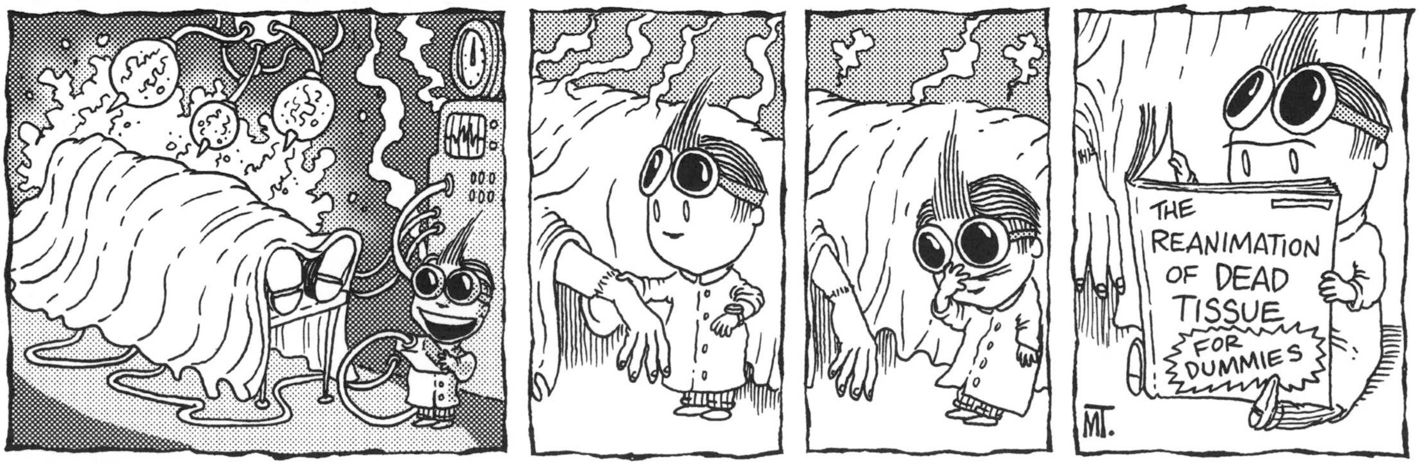
THE REANIMATION OF DEAD TISSUE
FOR DUMMIES
MT.

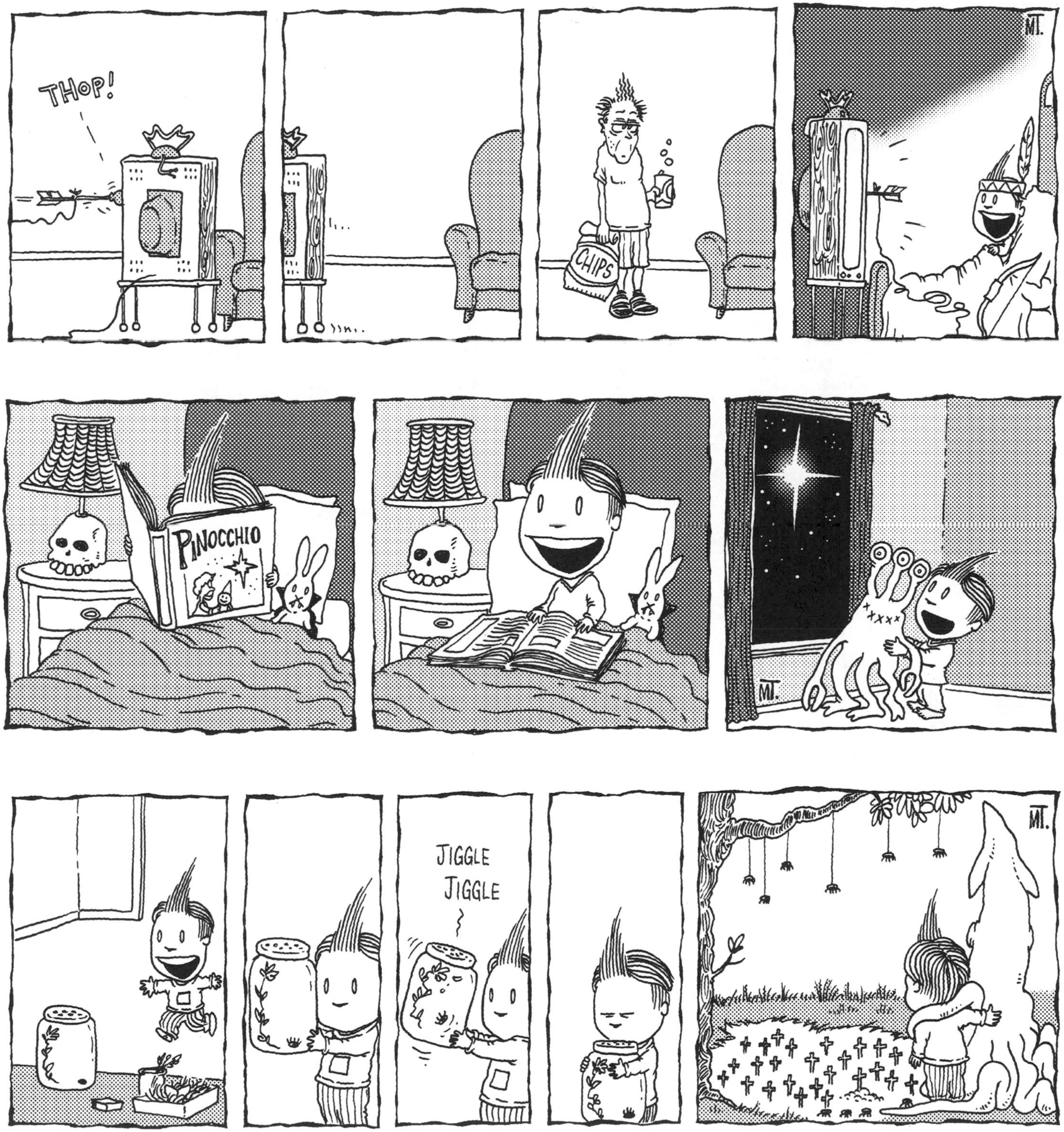
THOP!
CHIPS
MT.
PINOCCHIO
MT.
JIGGLE
JIGGLE
MT.

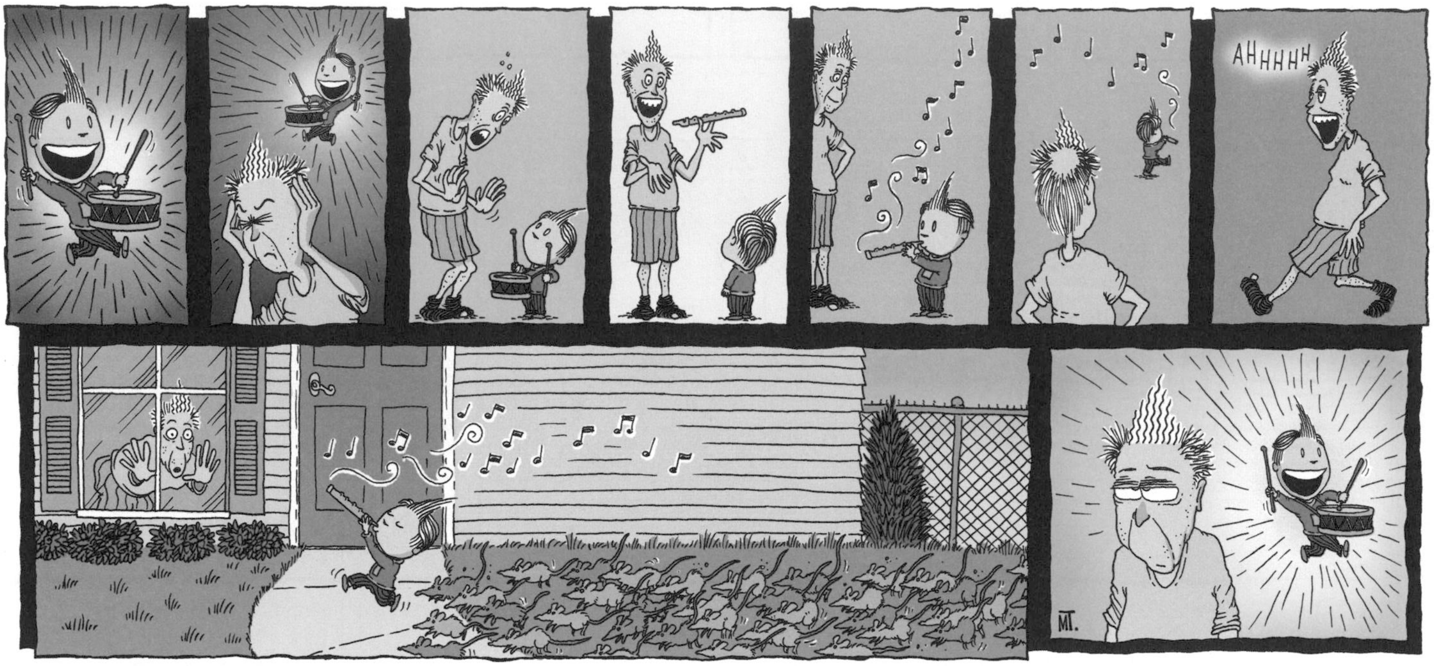
AHHHHH
MT.

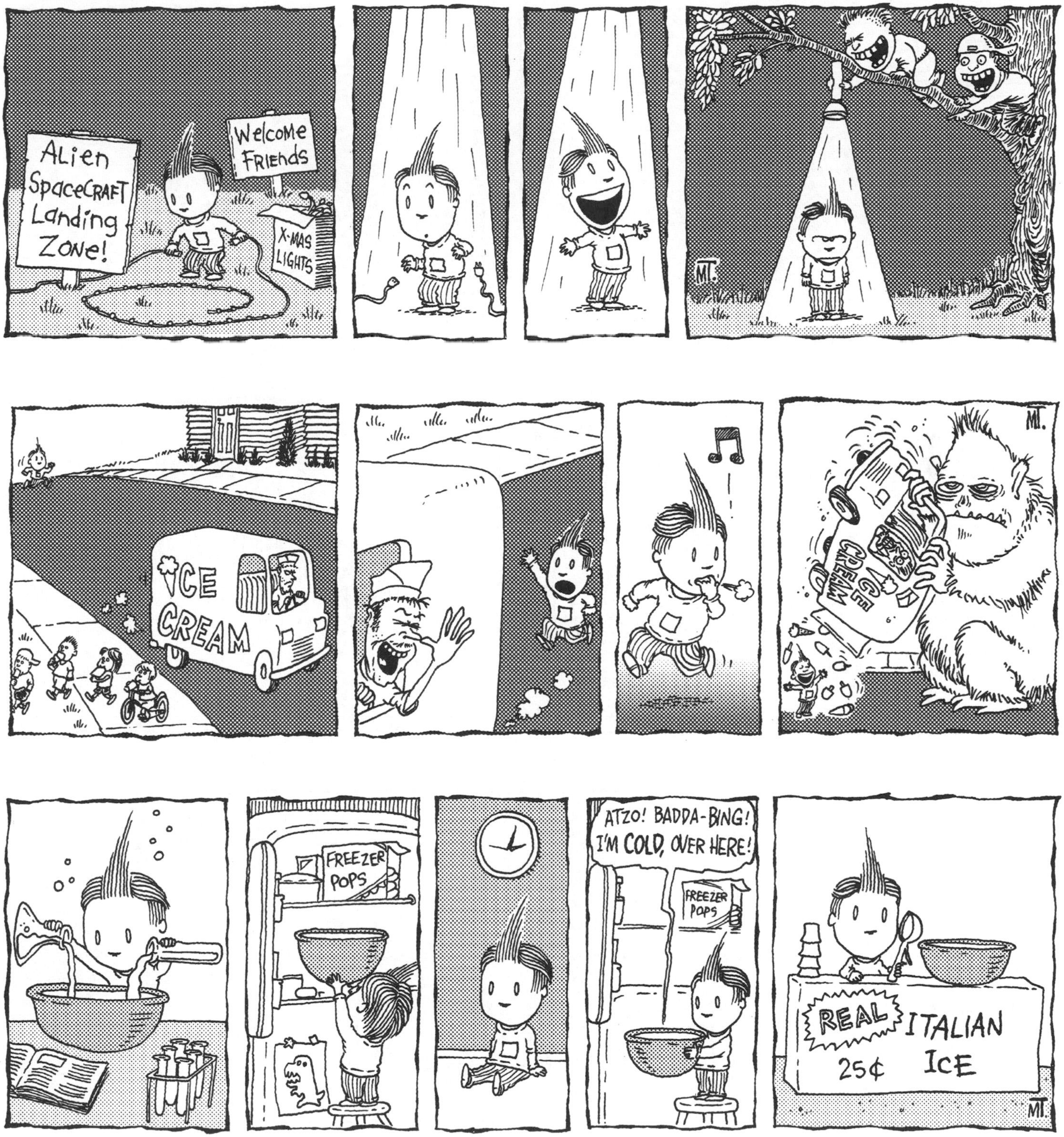
Alien SpaceCRAFT Landing Zone!
Welcome Friends
X-MAS LIGHTS
ICE CREAM
ICE CREAM
FREEZER POPS
ATZO! BADDA-BING! I'M COLD, OVER HERE!
FREEZER POPS
REAL ITALIAN ICE
25¢

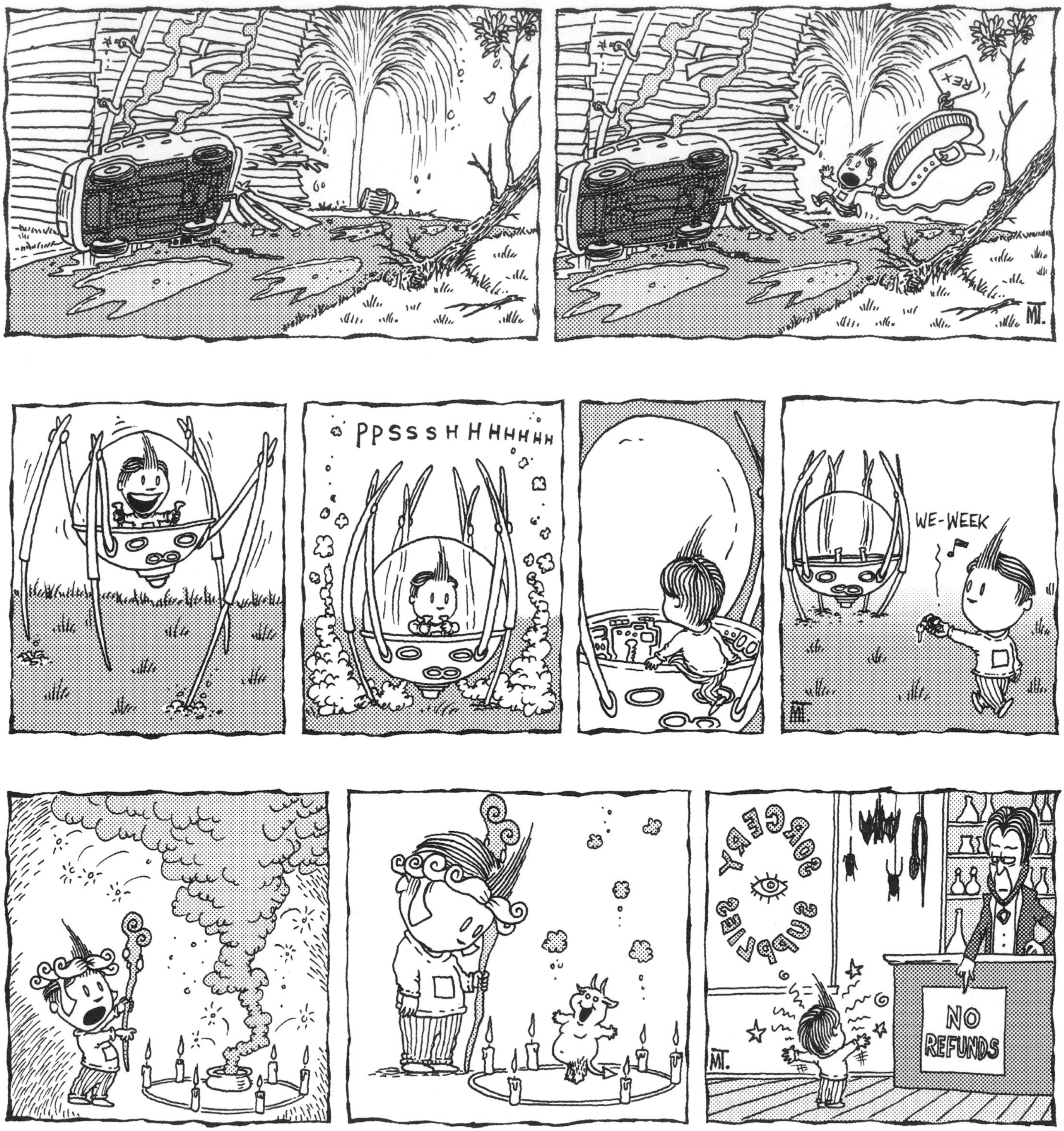
REX
MT.
PPSSSHHHHHHH
WE-WEEK
MT.
SORCERY SUPPLIES
NO REFUNDS
MT.

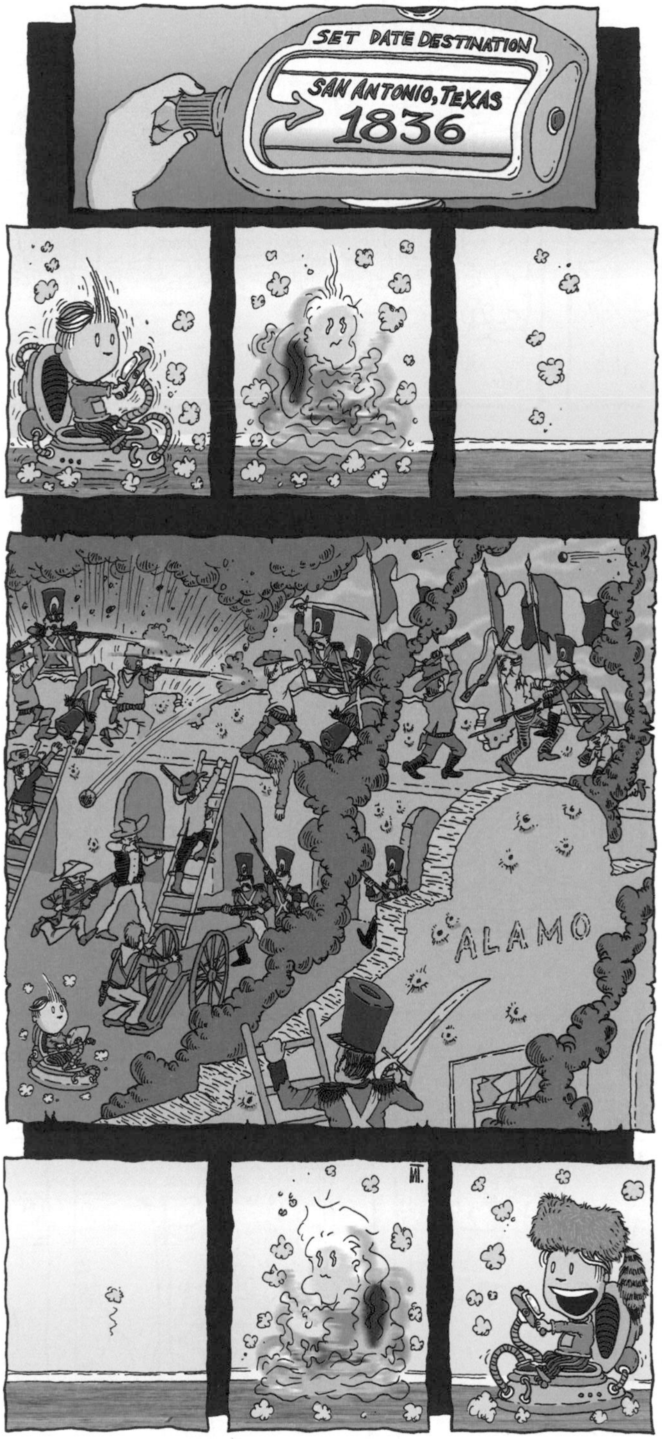
SET DATE DESTINATION
SAN ANTONIO, TEXAS
1836
ALAMO

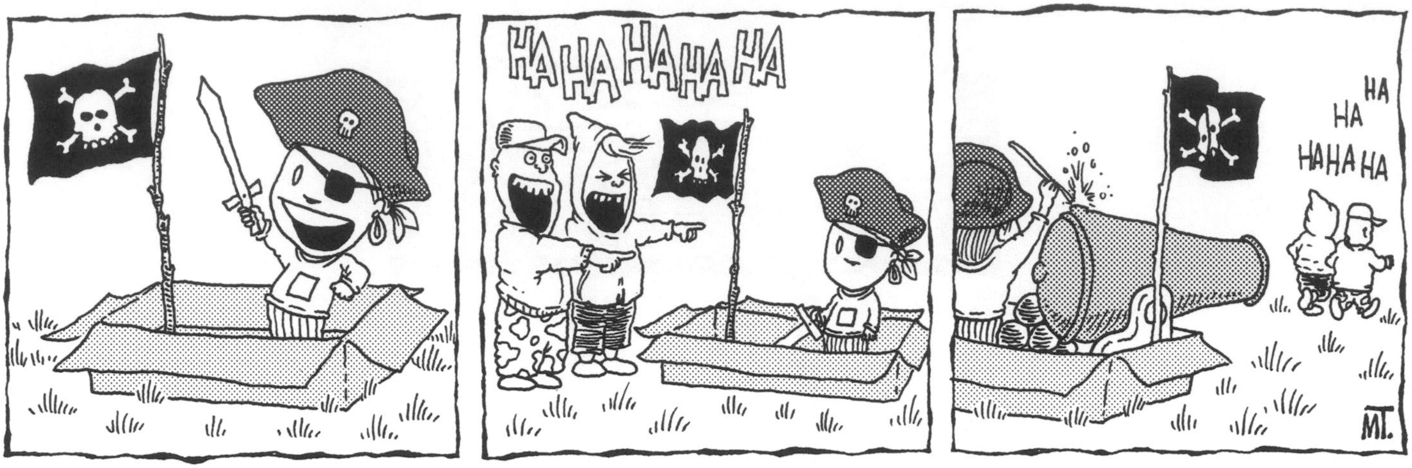
HA HA HA HA HA HA
HA
HA
HA HA HA
MT.

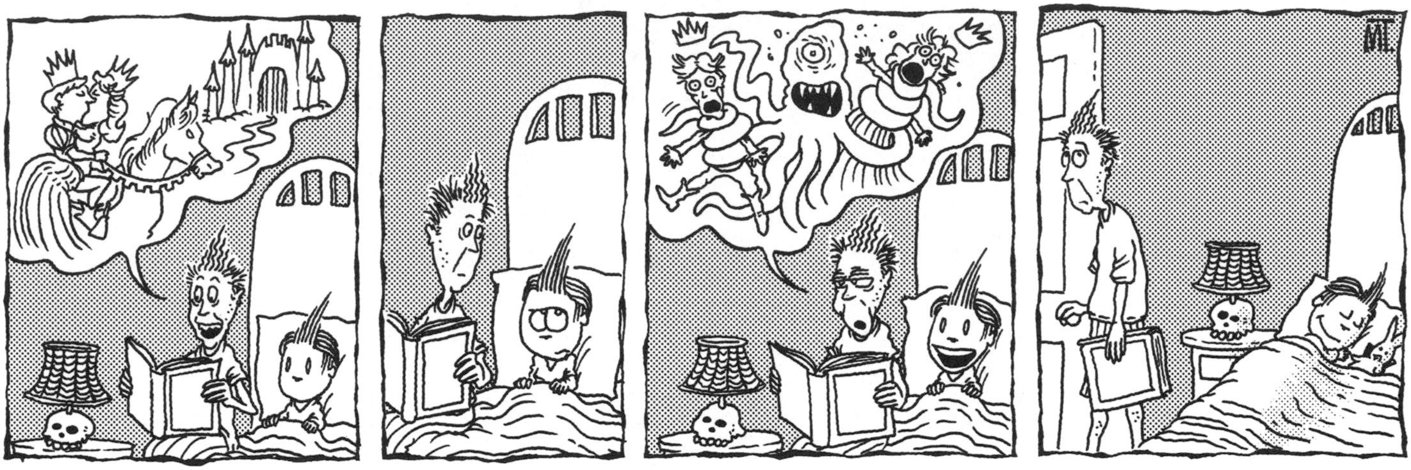
MT.

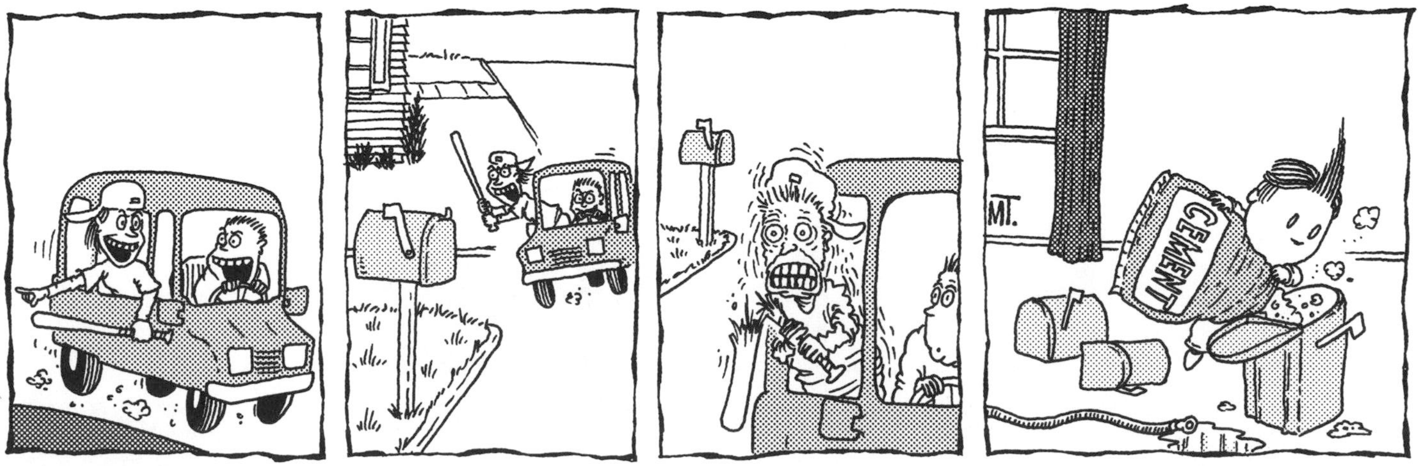
MT.
CEMENT

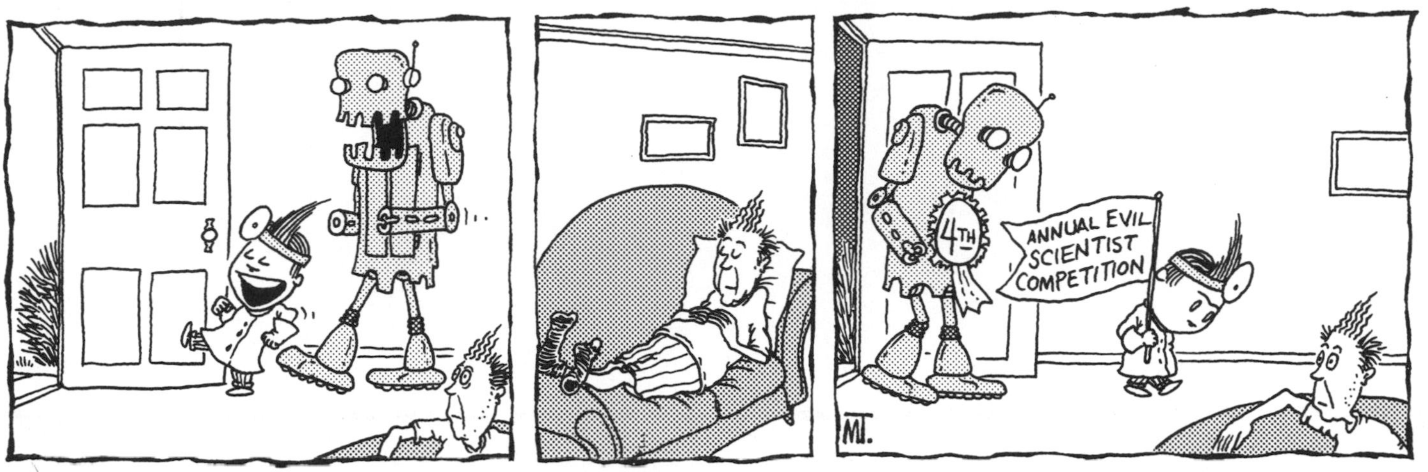
4TH
ANNUAL EVIL SCIENTIST COMPETITION

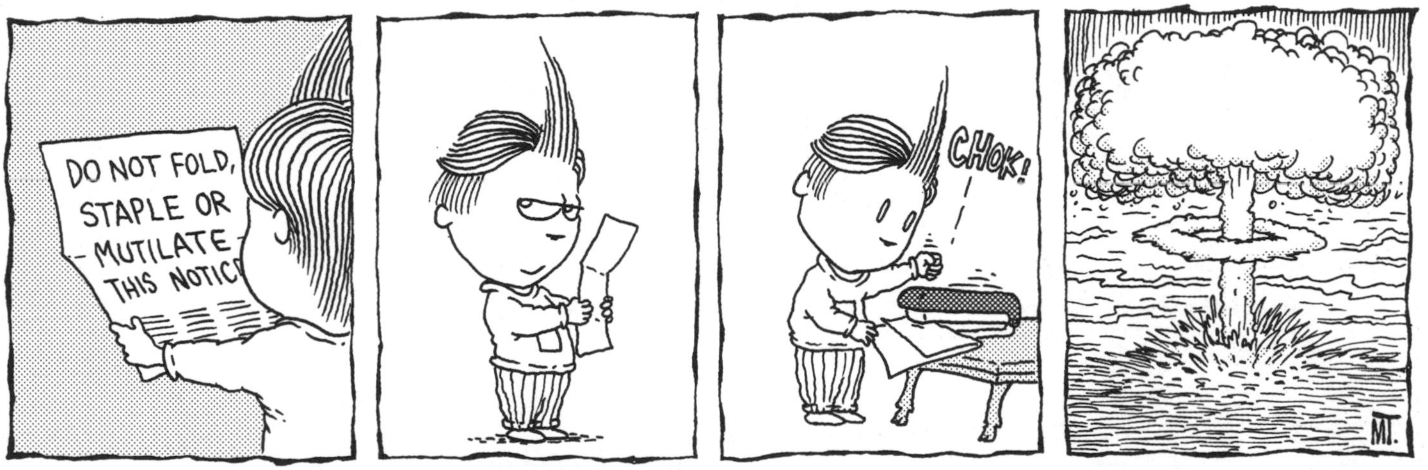
DO NOT FOLD, STAPLE OR MUTILATE THIS NOTIC
CHOK!

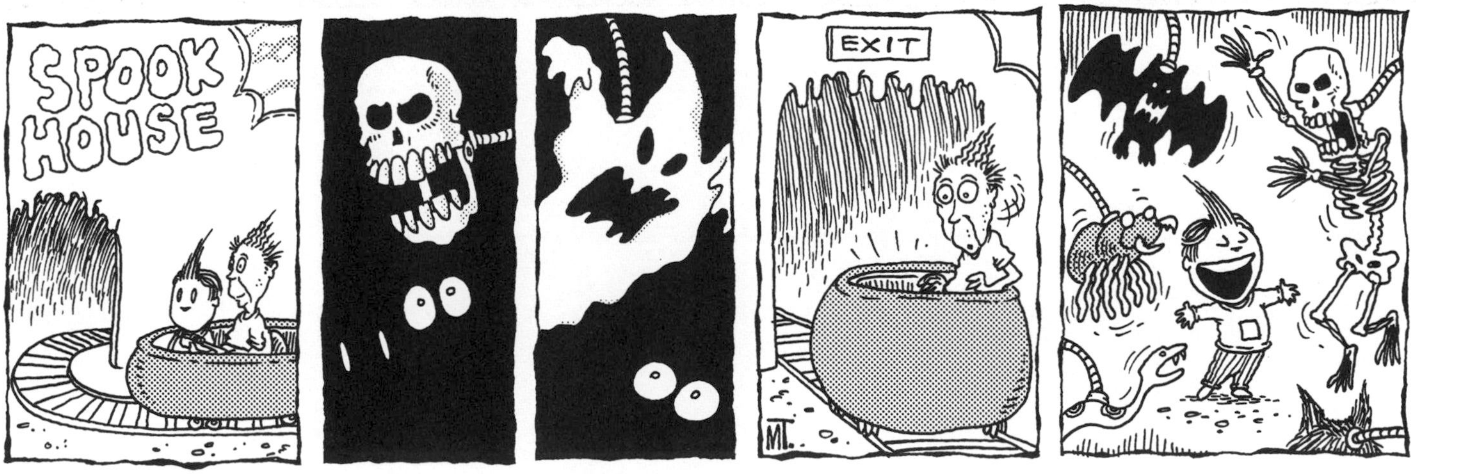
SPOOK HOUSE
EXIT

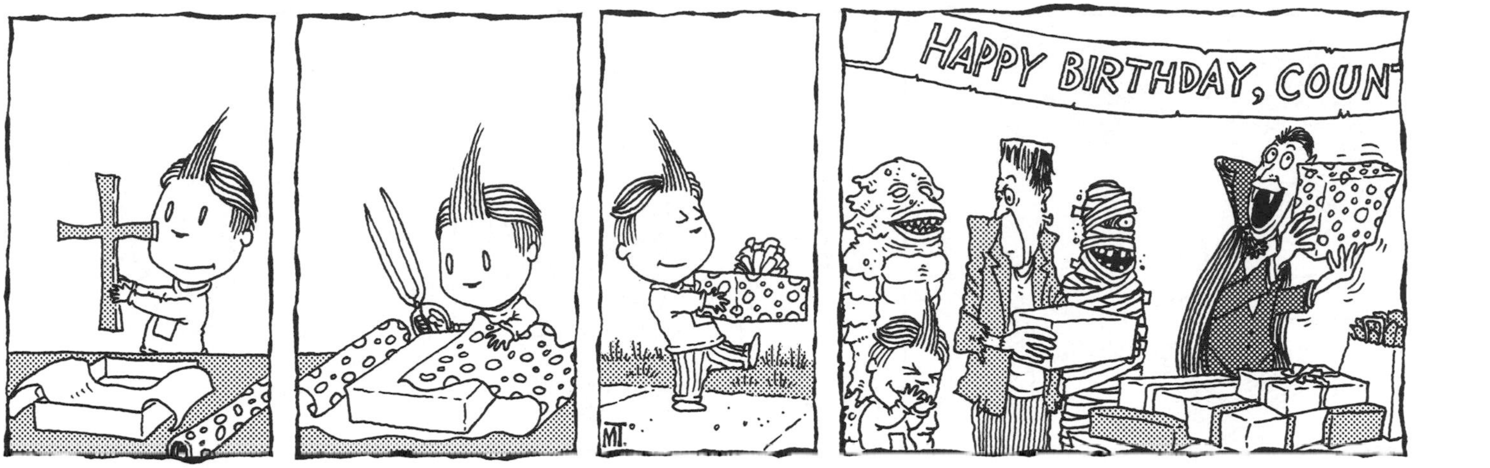
HAPPY BIRTHDAY, COUN

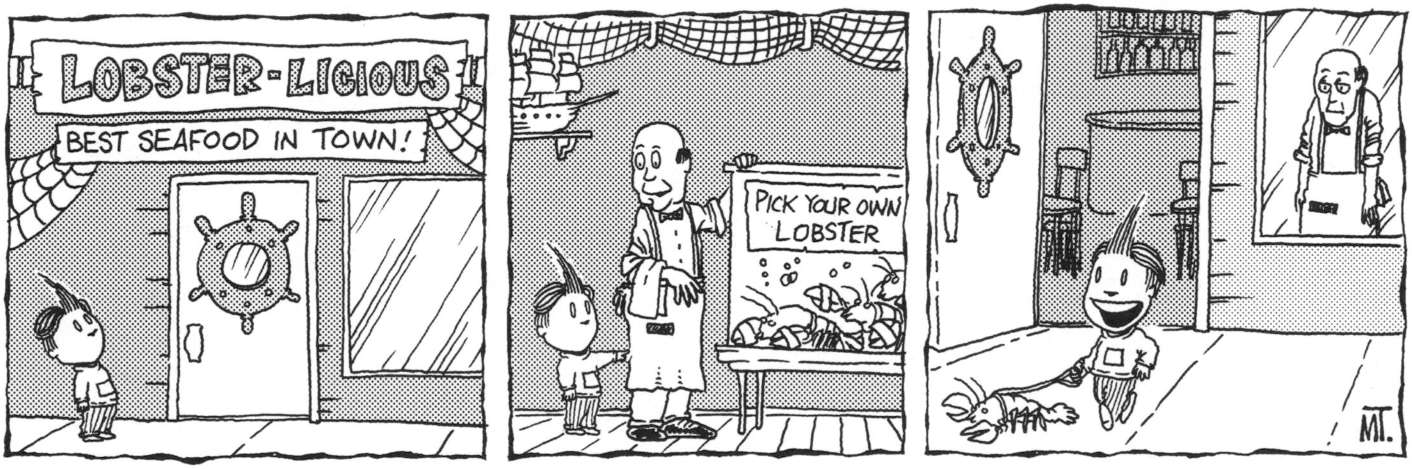
LOBSTER-LICIOUS
BEST SEAFOOD IN TOWN!
PICK YOUR OWN LOBSTER

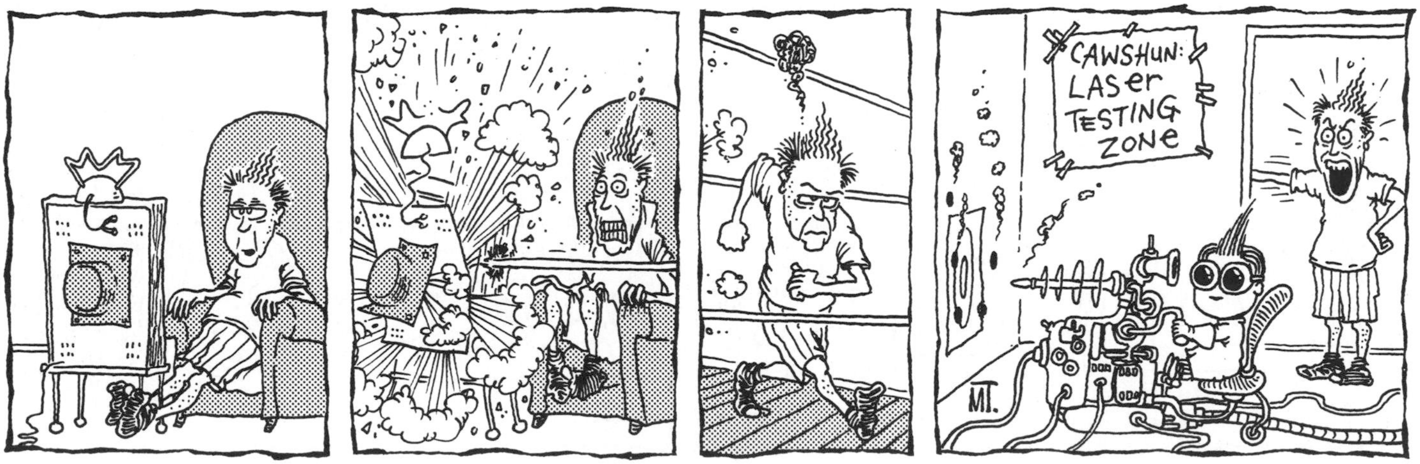
CAWSHUN: LASer TESTING ZONe

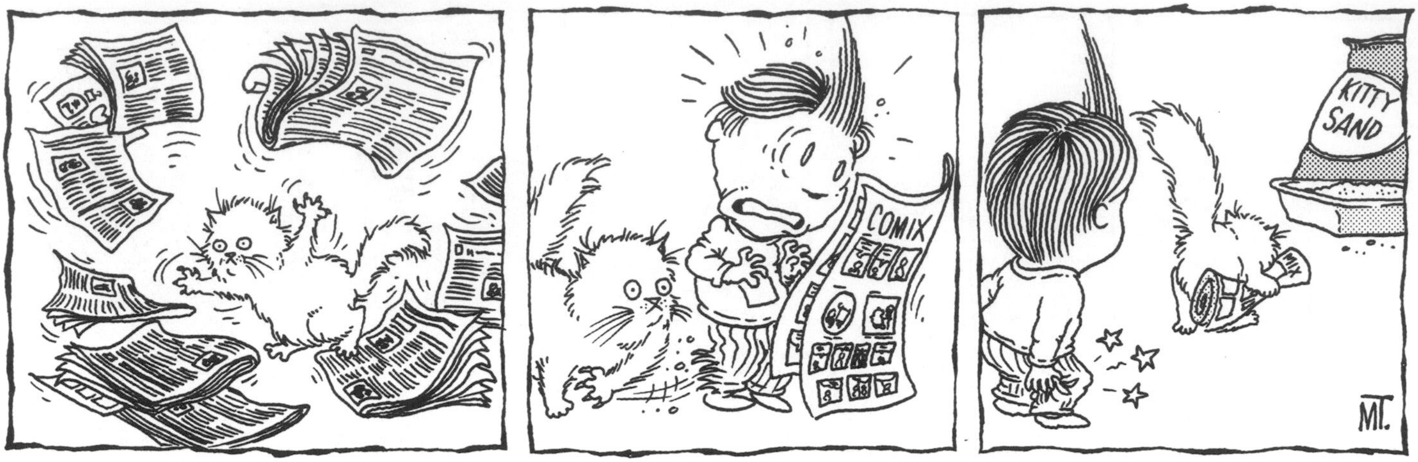
COMIX
KITTY SAND
MT.

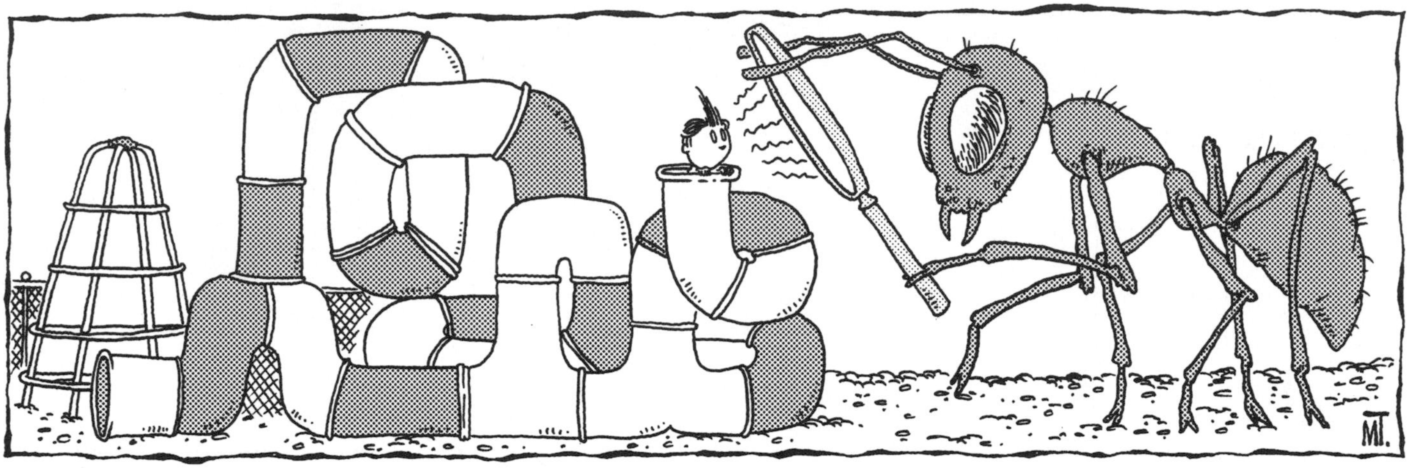
MT.

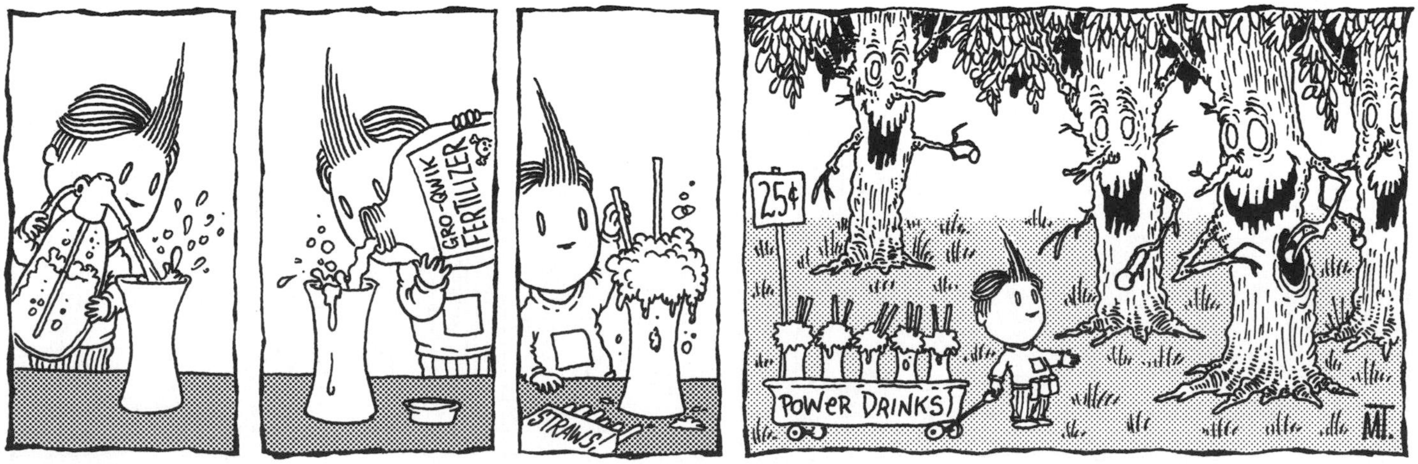
GRO-QWIK FERTILIZER
STRAWS!
25¢
POWER DRINKS
MT.

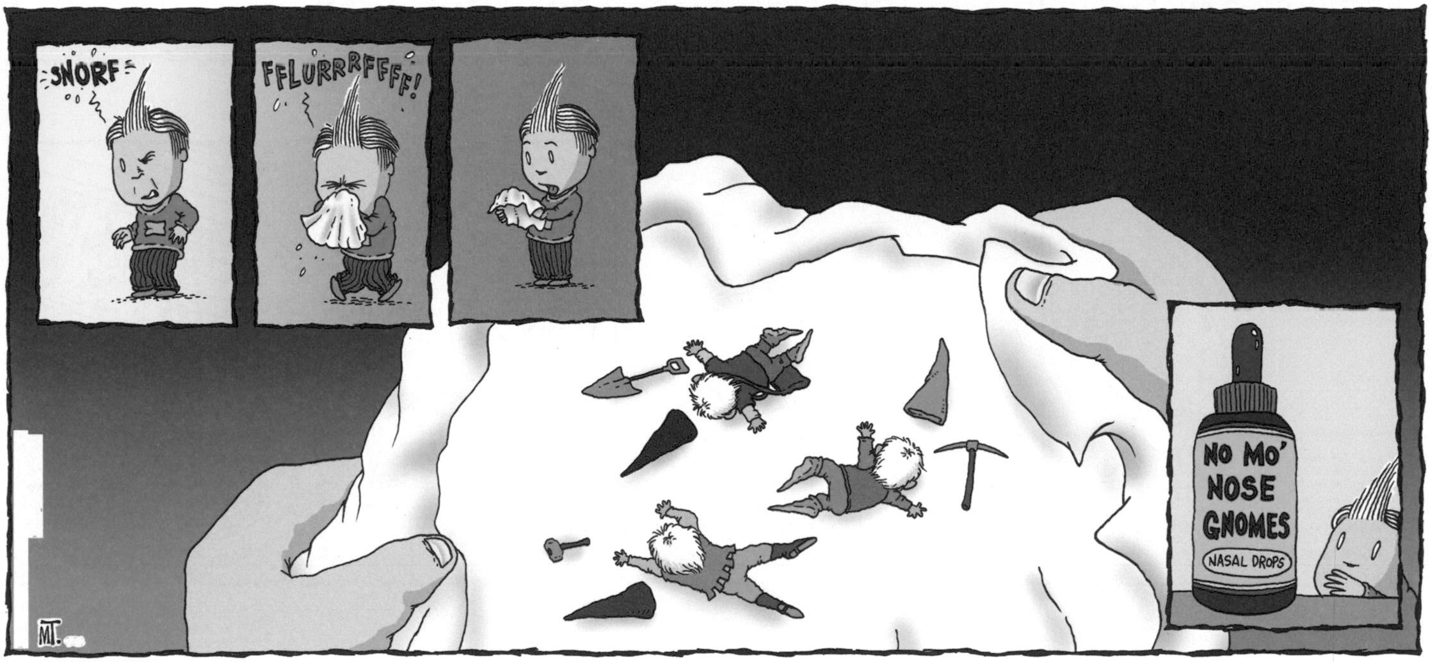
SNORF
FFLURRRFFFF!
NO MO' NOSE GNOMES
NASAL DROPS

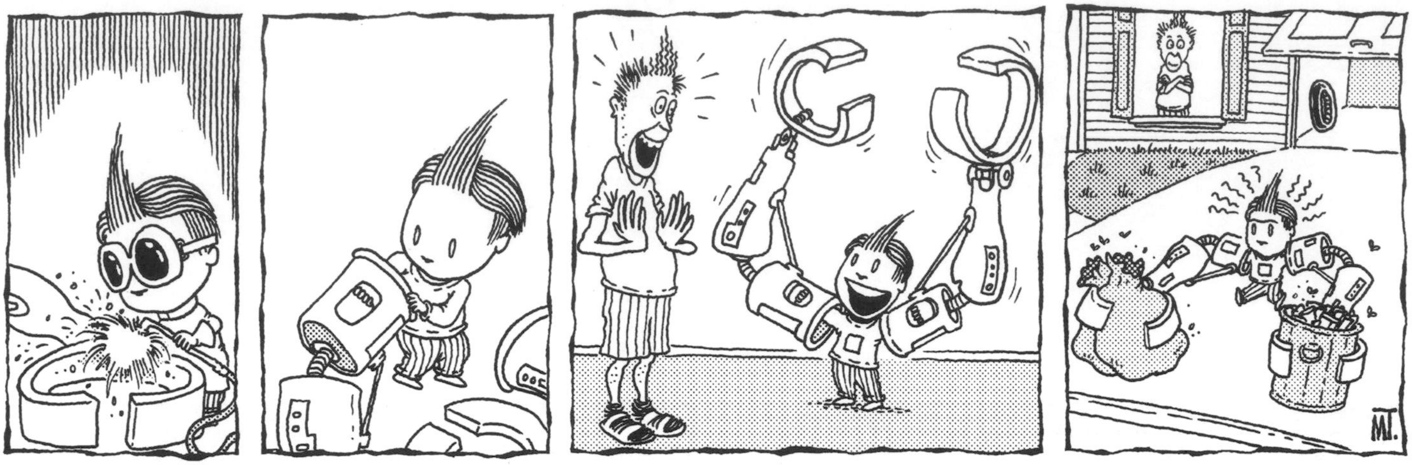

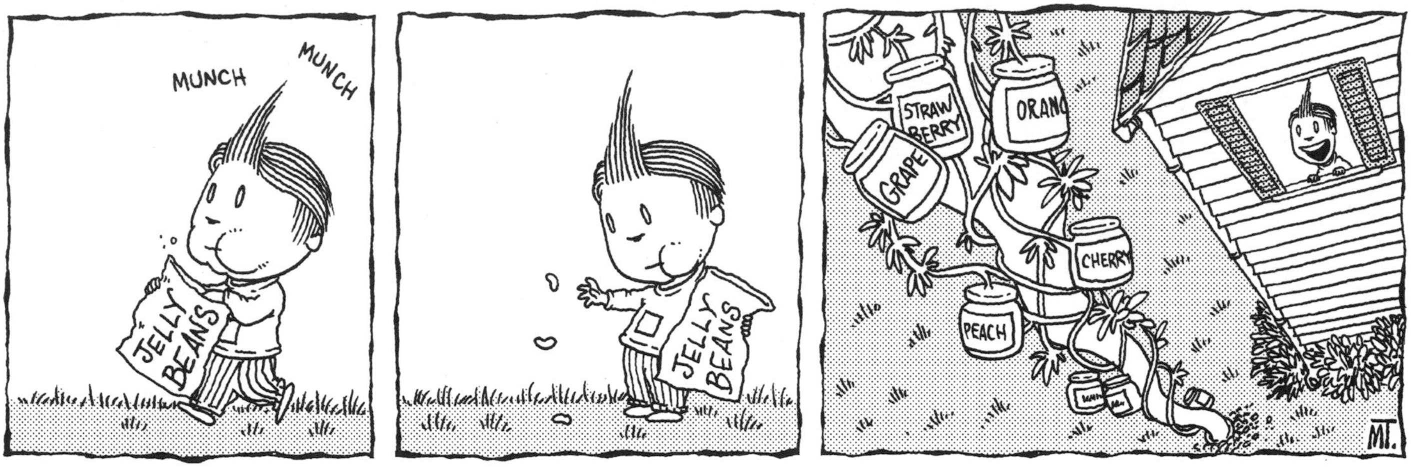
MUNCH
MUNCH
JELLY BEANS
JELLY BEANS
STRAW BERRY
ORANG
GRAPE
CHERRY
PEACH

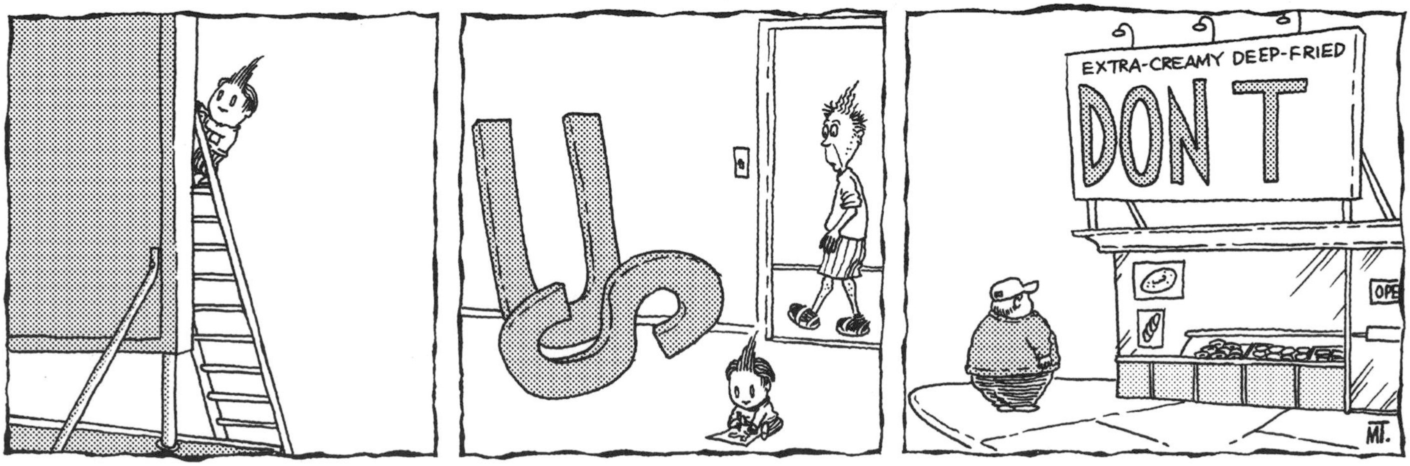
EXTRA-CREAMY DEEP-FRIED
DON T
OPE

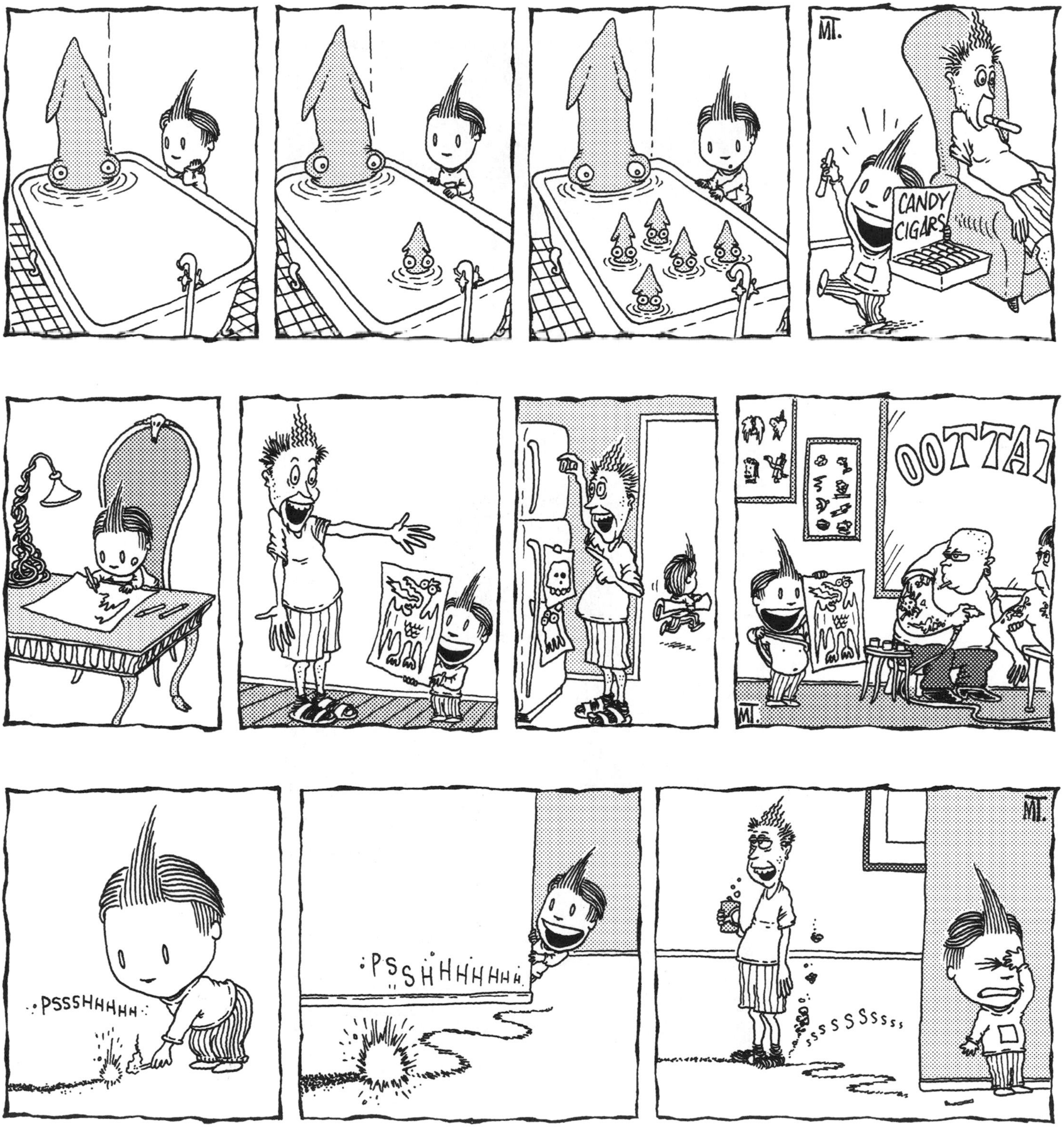
MT.
CANDY CIGARS
MT.
OOTTAT
PSSSHHHHH
PSSHHHHHHH
SSSSSSSSS
MT.

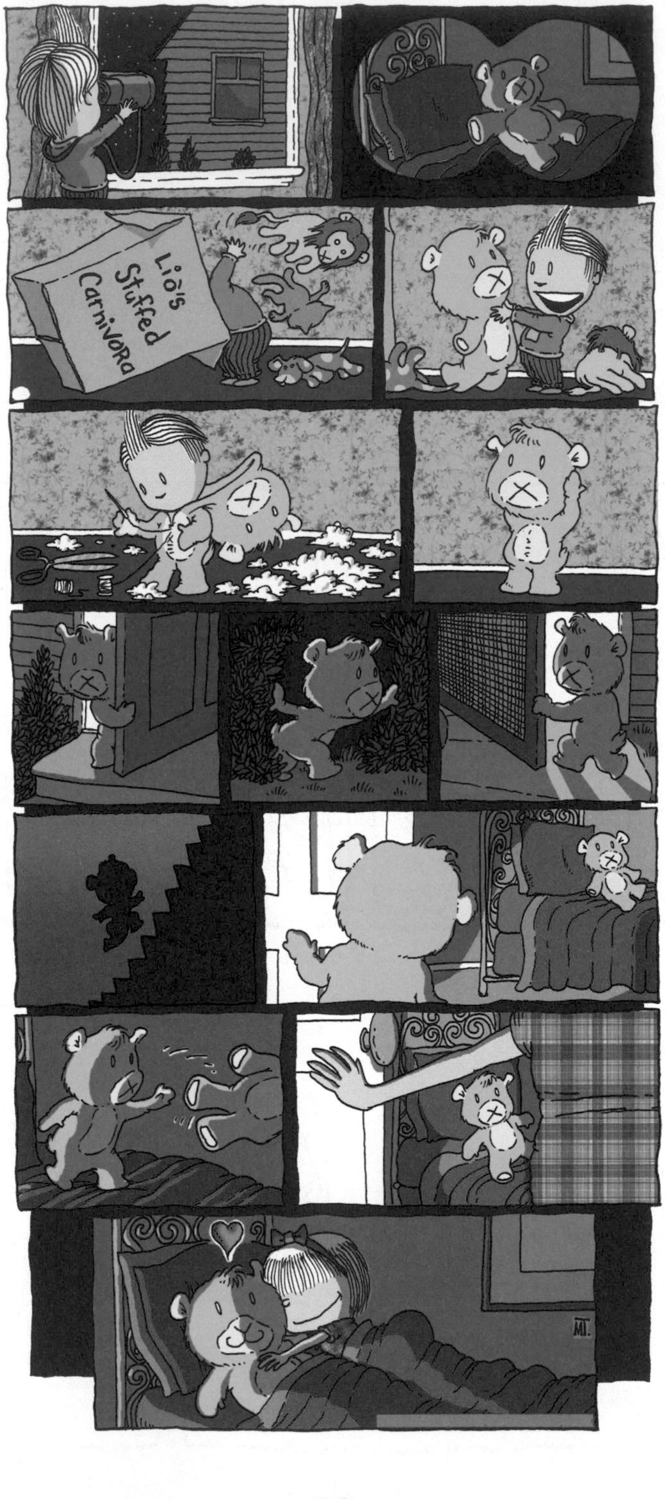
Lio's Stuffed Carnivora
MT.

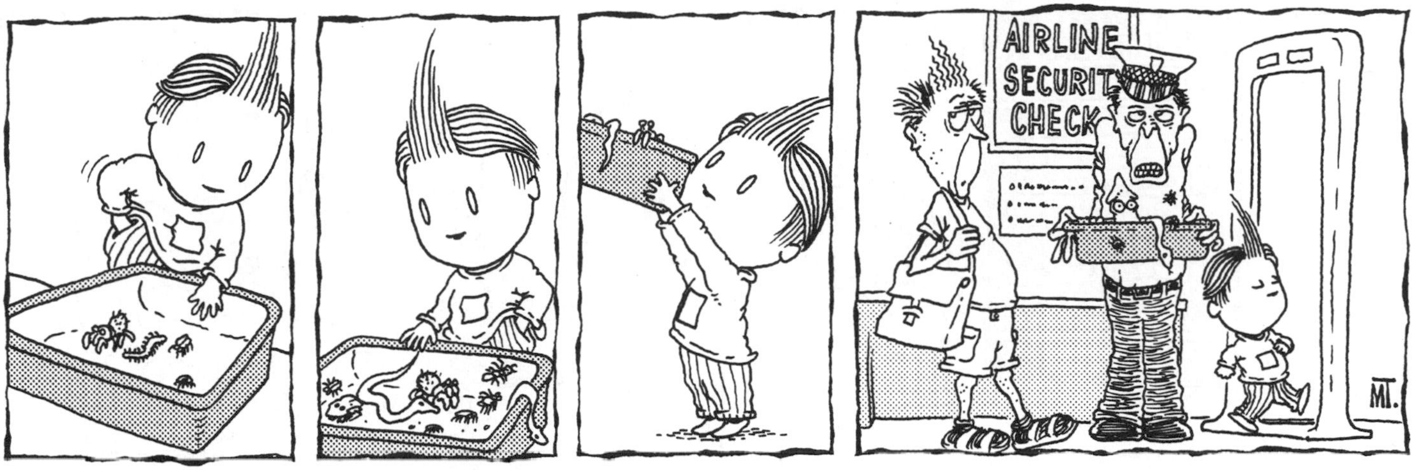
AIRLINE
SECURIT
CHECK
MT.

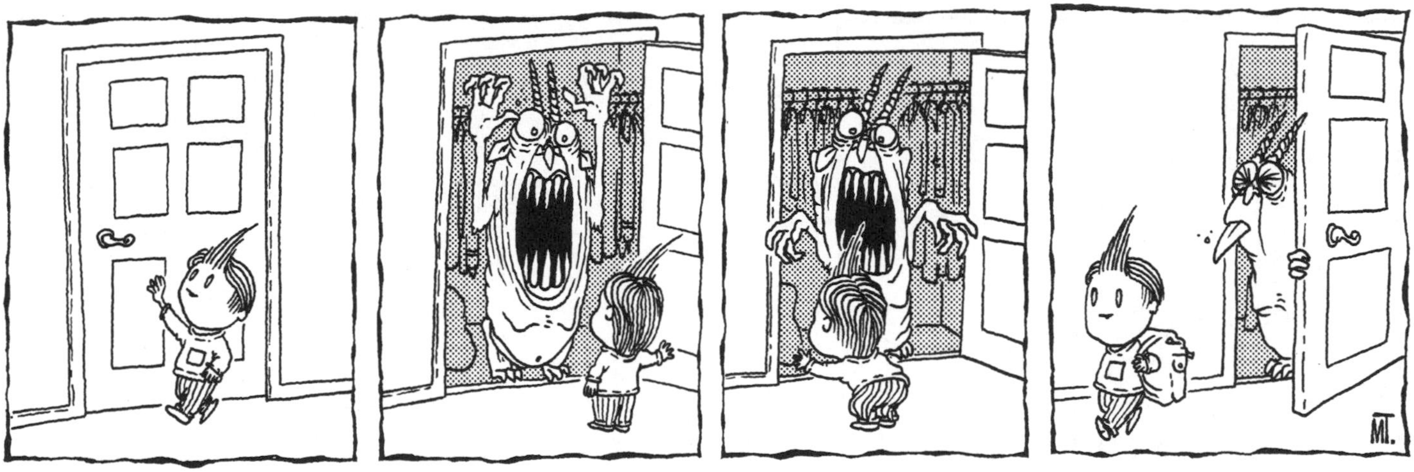
MT.

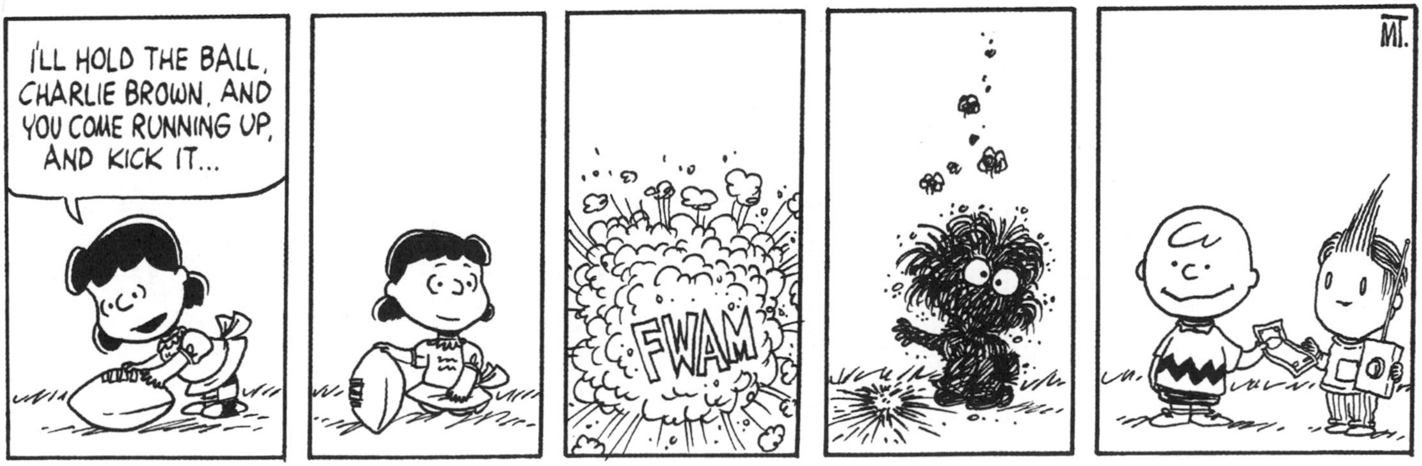
I'LL HOLD THE BALL, CHARLIE BROWN, AND YOU COME RUNNING UP, AND KICK IT...
FWAM
MT.

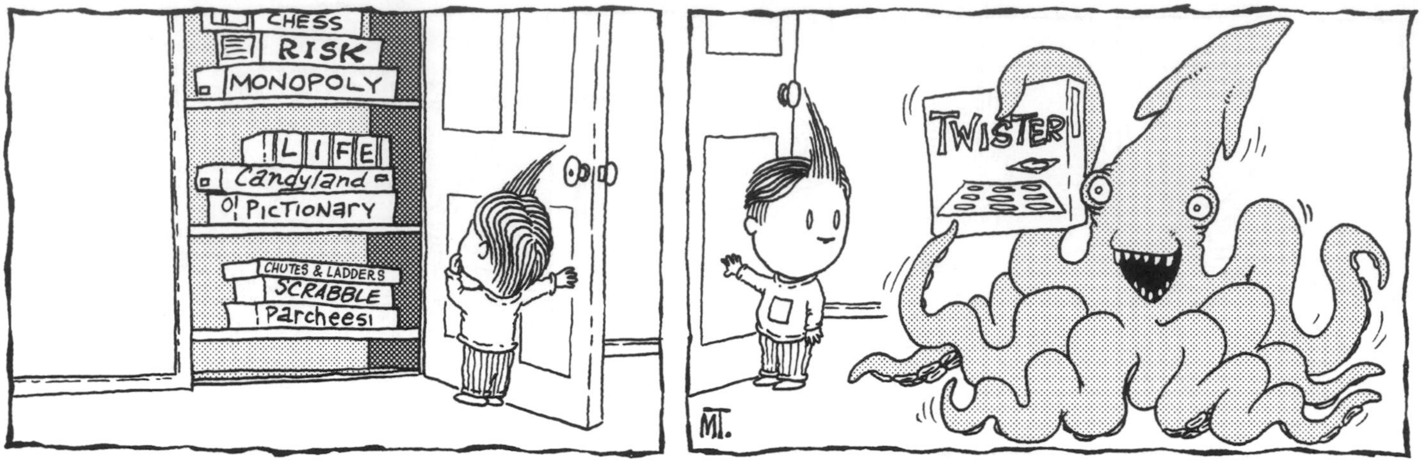
CHESS
RISK
MONOPOLY
LIFE
Candyland
PICTIONARY
CHUTES & LADDERS
SCRABBLE
Parcheesi
TWISTER
MT.

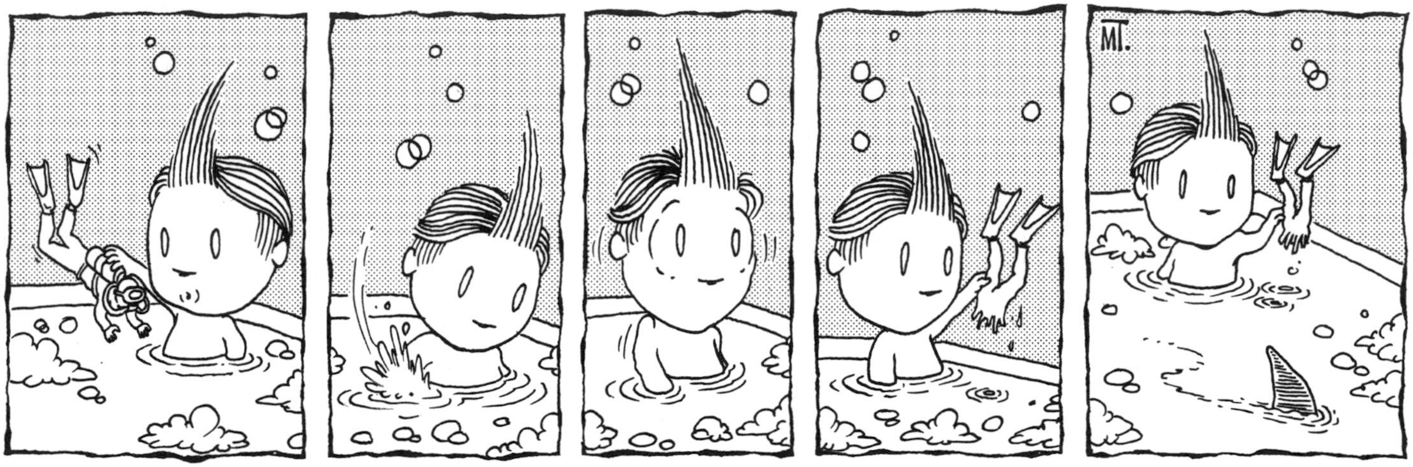
MT.

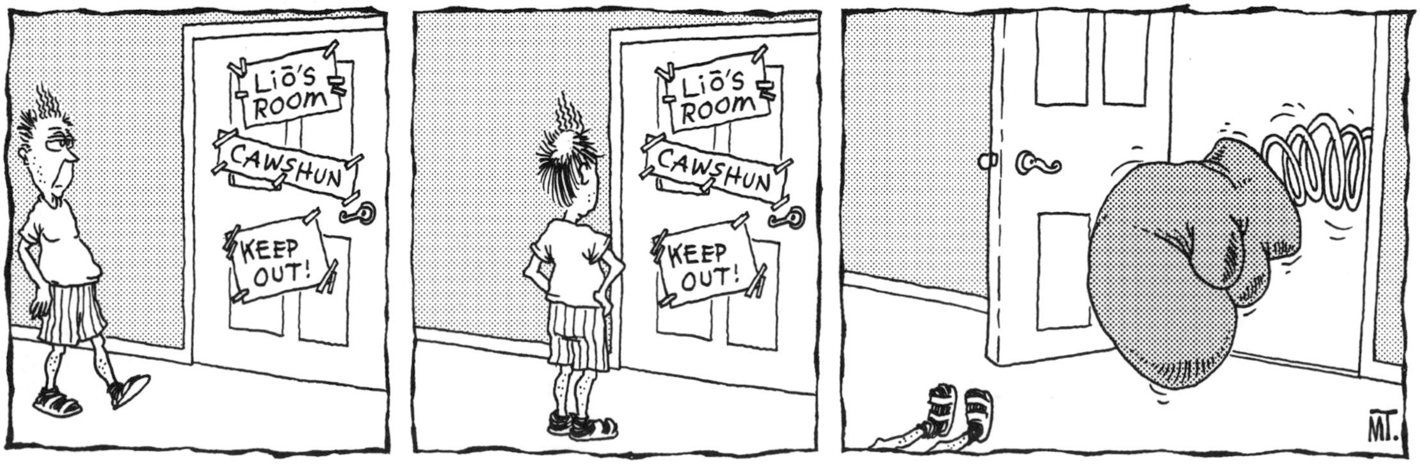
LIŌ'S ROOM
CAWSHUN
KEEP OUT!
LIŌ'S ROOM
CAWSHUN
KEEP OUT!
MT.

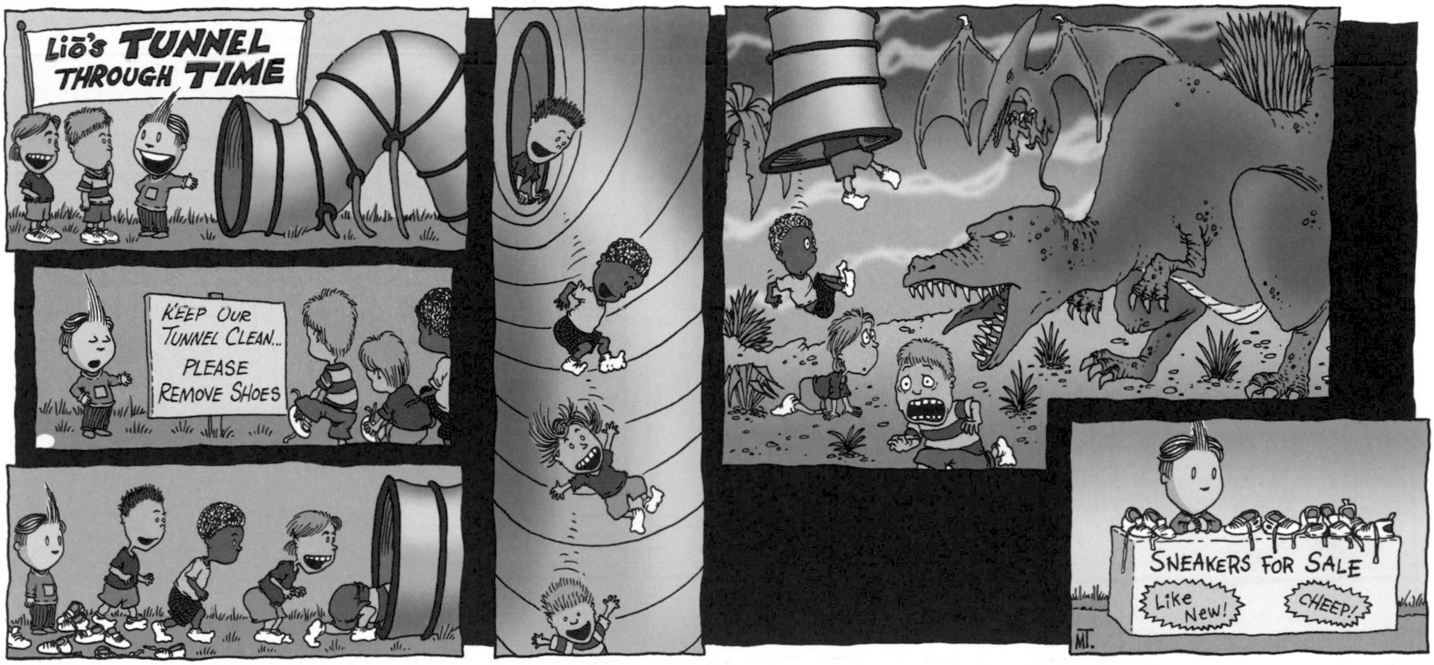

Liō's TUNNEL THROUGH TIME
KEEP OUR TUNNEL CLEAN... PLEASE REMOVE SHOES
SNEAKERS FOR SALE
Like New!
CHEEP!
MT.

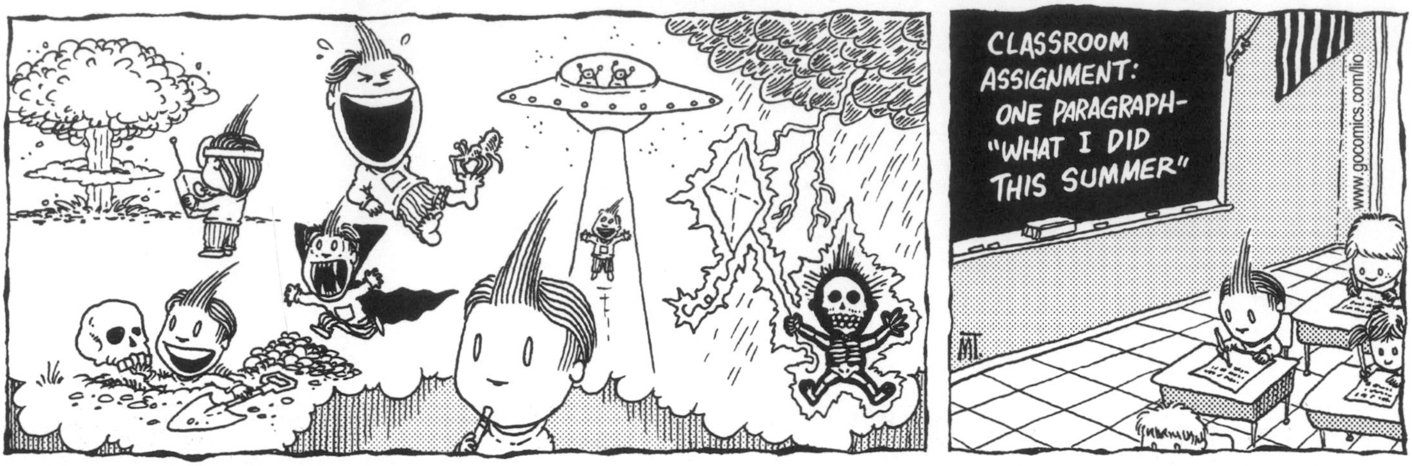
CLASSROOM ASSIGNMENT: ONE PARAGRAPH- "WHAT I DID THIS SUMMER"
www.gocomics.com/lio
MT.

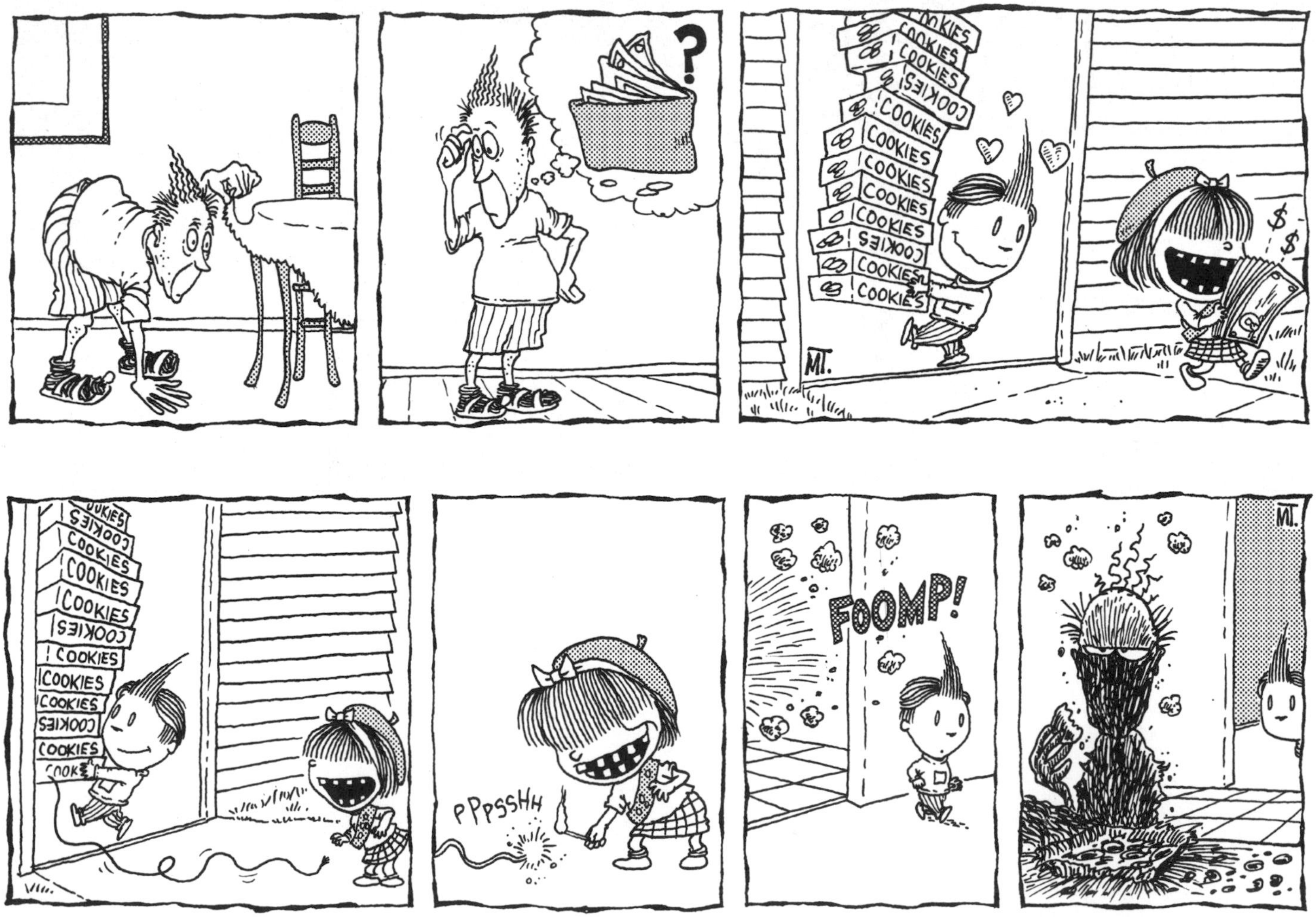
?
COOKIES
MT.
PPPSSHH
FOOMP!
MT.

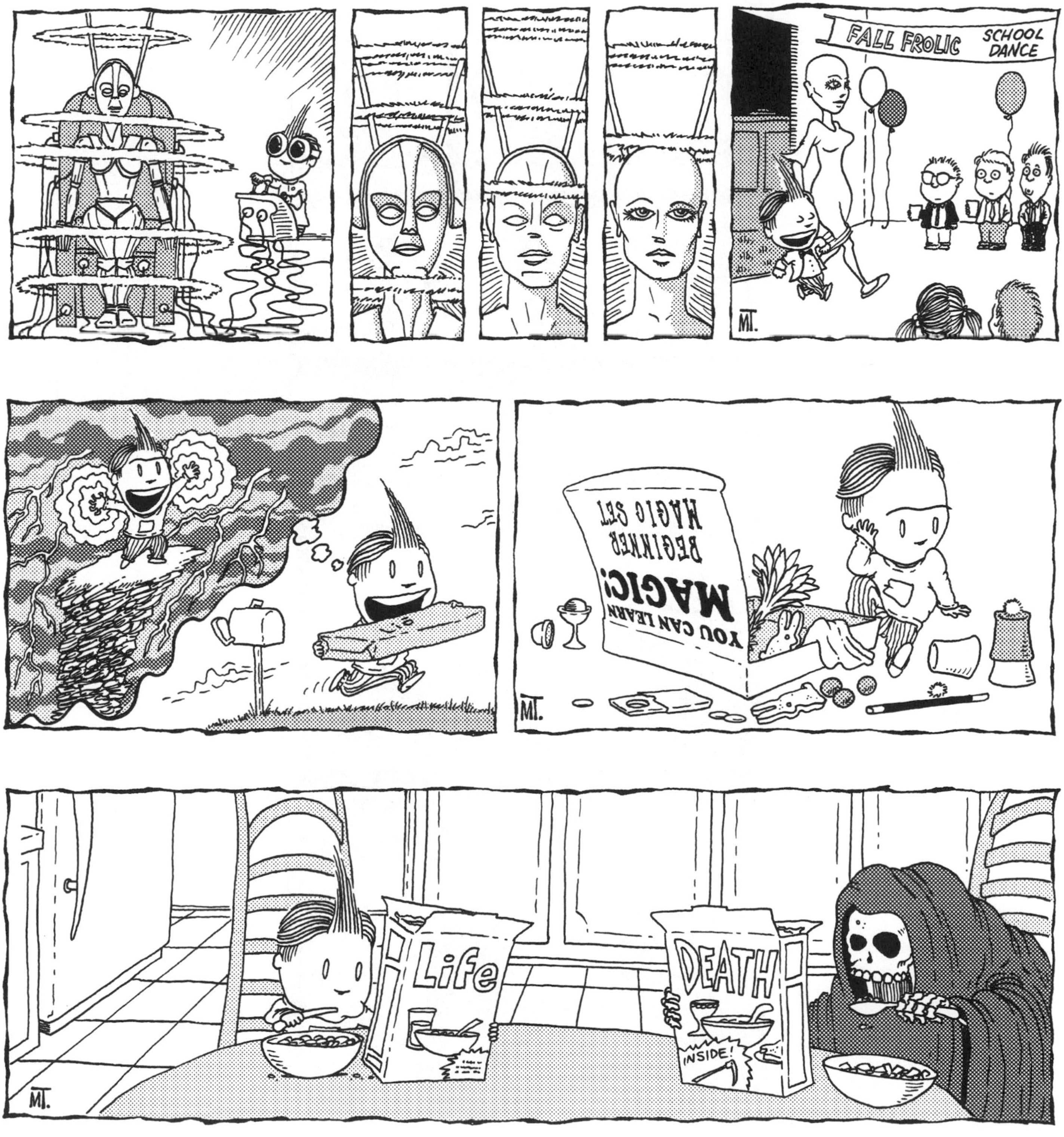
FALL FROLIC
SCHOOL DANCE
MT.
YOU CAN LEARN MAGIC!
BEGINNER MAGIC SET
MT.
Life
DEATH
INSIDE!
MT.

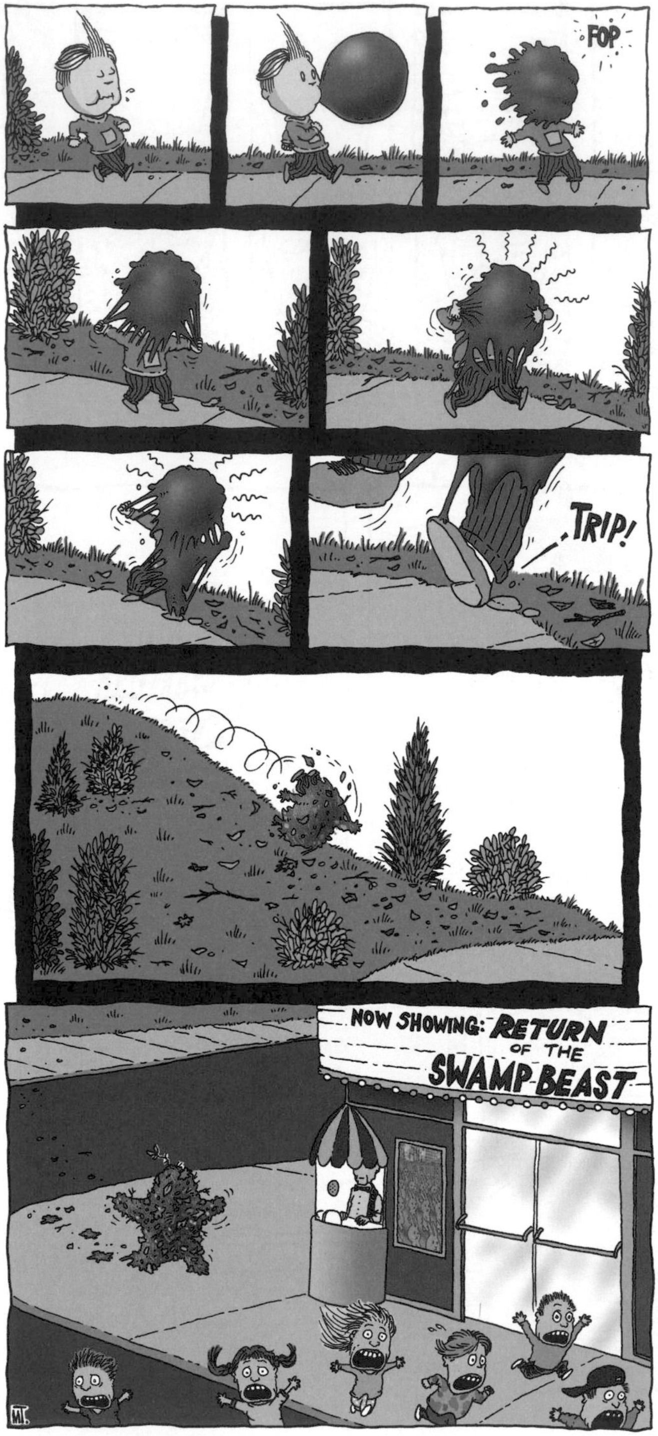
FOP
TRIP!
NOW SHOWING: RETURN OF THE SWAMP-BEAST

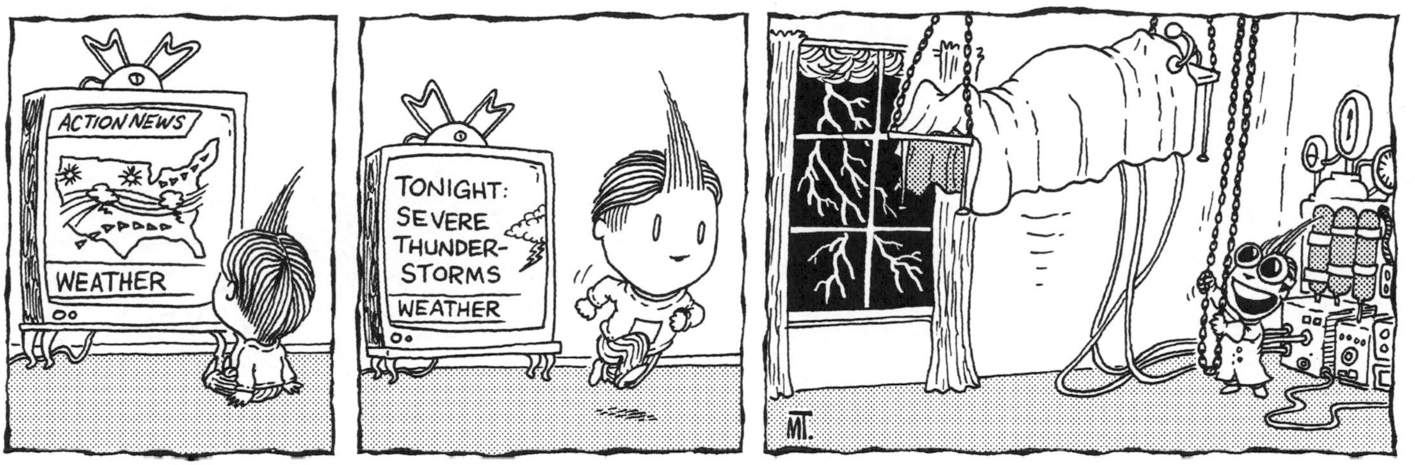
ACTION NEWS
WEATHER
TONIGHT:
SEVERE
THUNDER-
STORMS
WEATHER
MT.

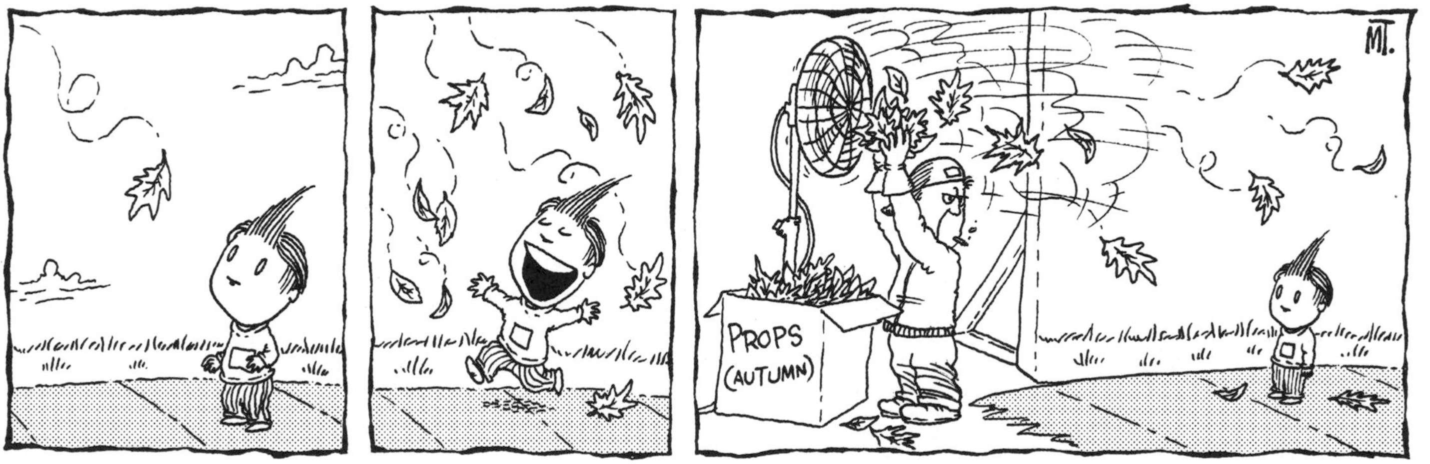
MT.
PROPS
(AUTUMN)

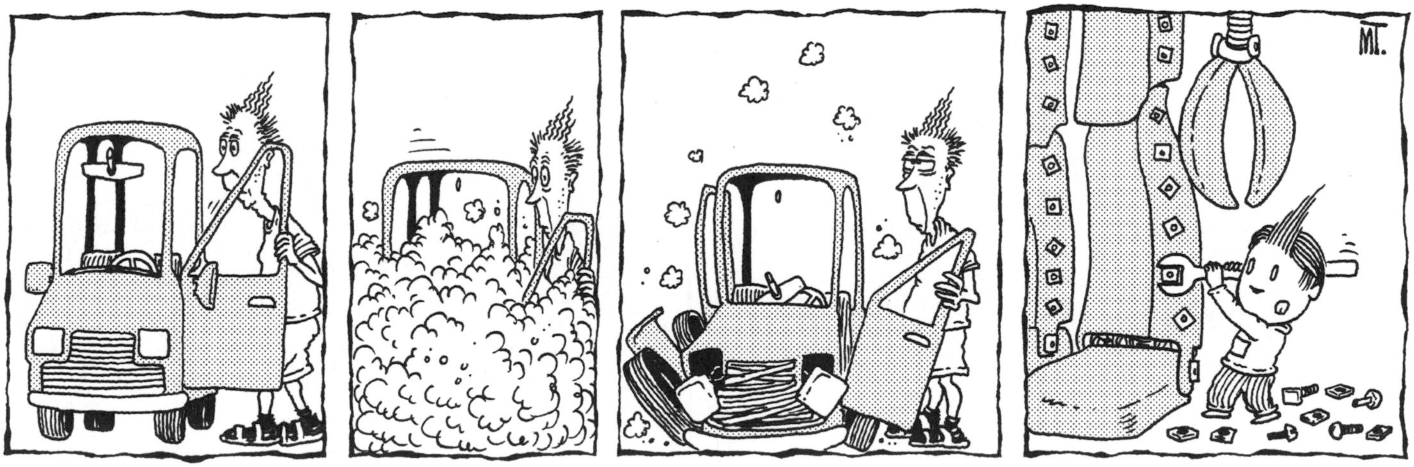
MT.

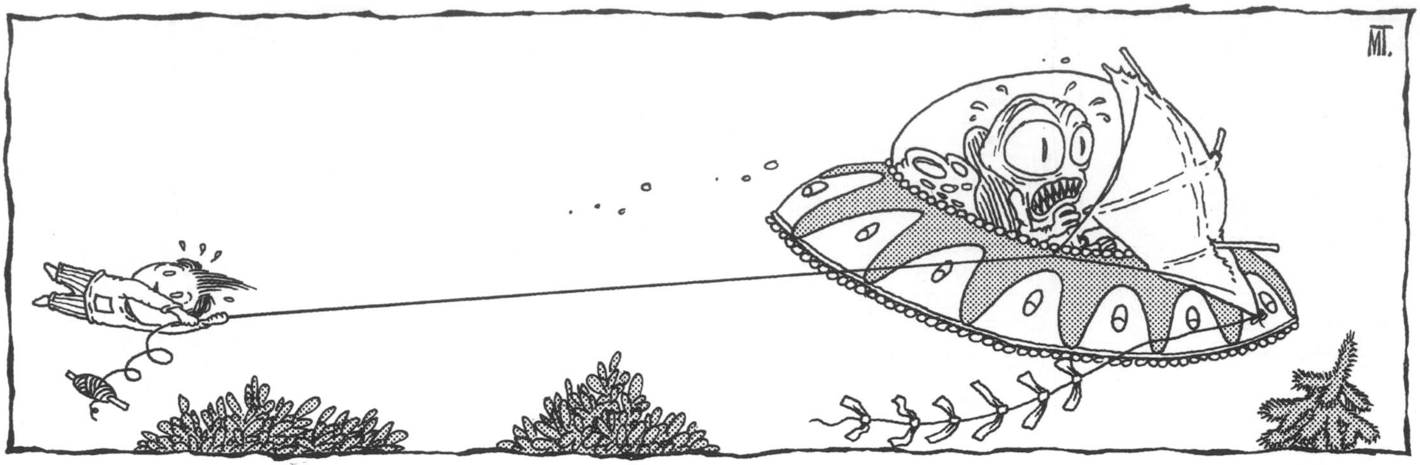

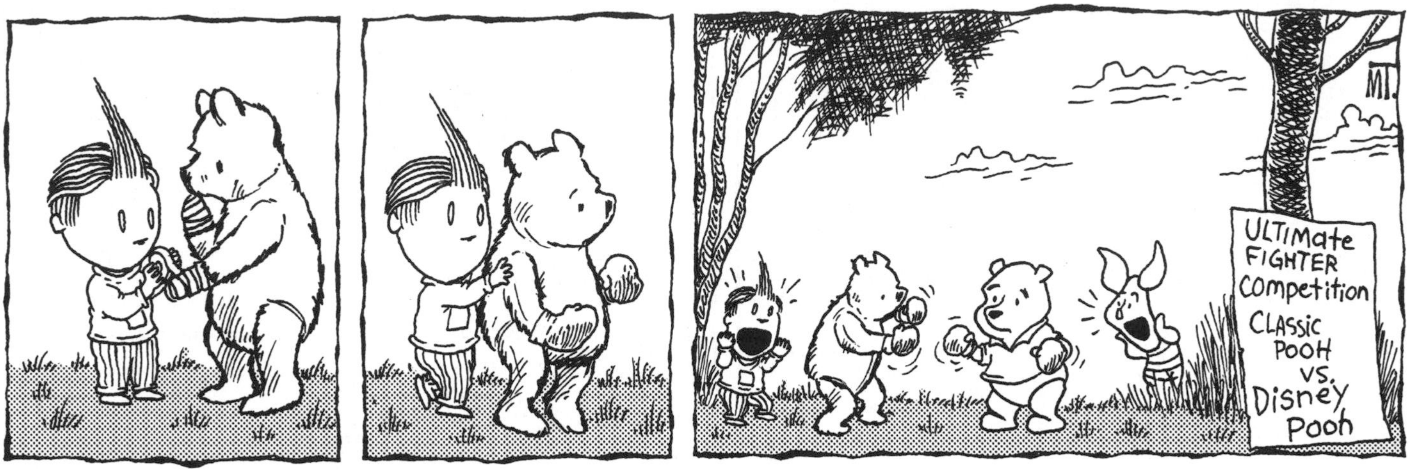
ULTIMATE FIGHTER Competition
CLASSIC POOH VS. Disney Pooh

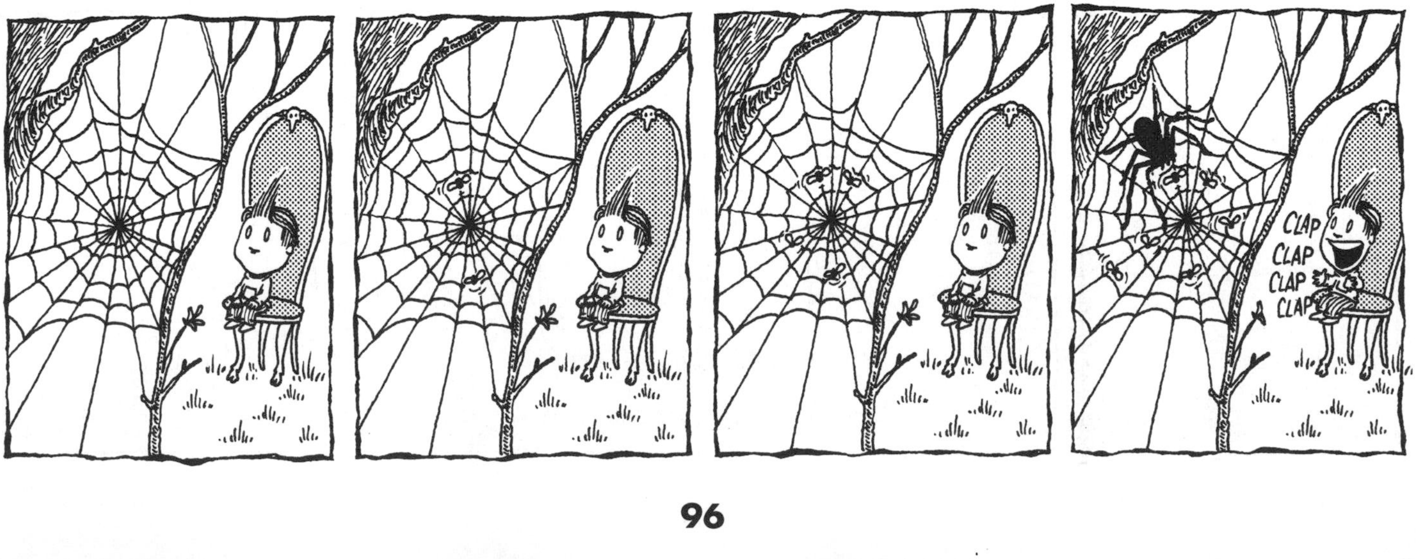
CLAP
CLAP
CLAP
CLAP

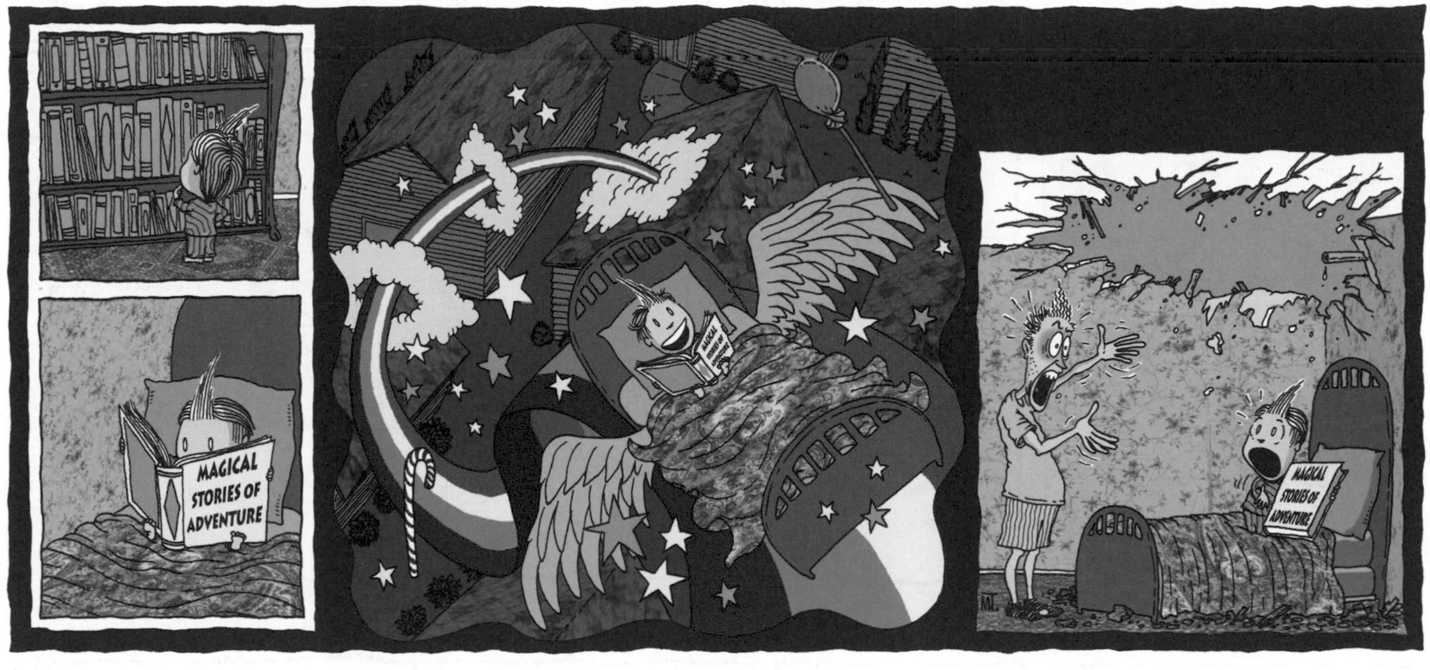
MAGICAL
STORIES OF
ADVENTURE
MAGICAL
STORIES OF
ADVENTURE

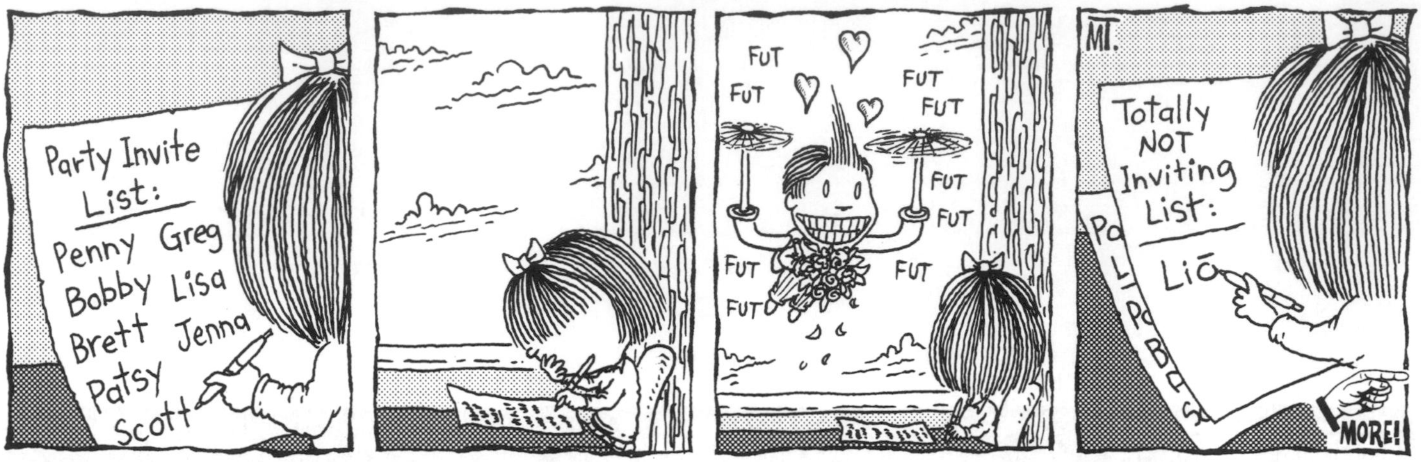
Party Invite List:
Penny Greg
Bobby Lisa
Brett Jenna
Patsy
Scott
FUT FUT FUT FUT FUT FUT FUT FUT FUT FUT
MT.
Totally NOT Inviting List:
Li
MORE!

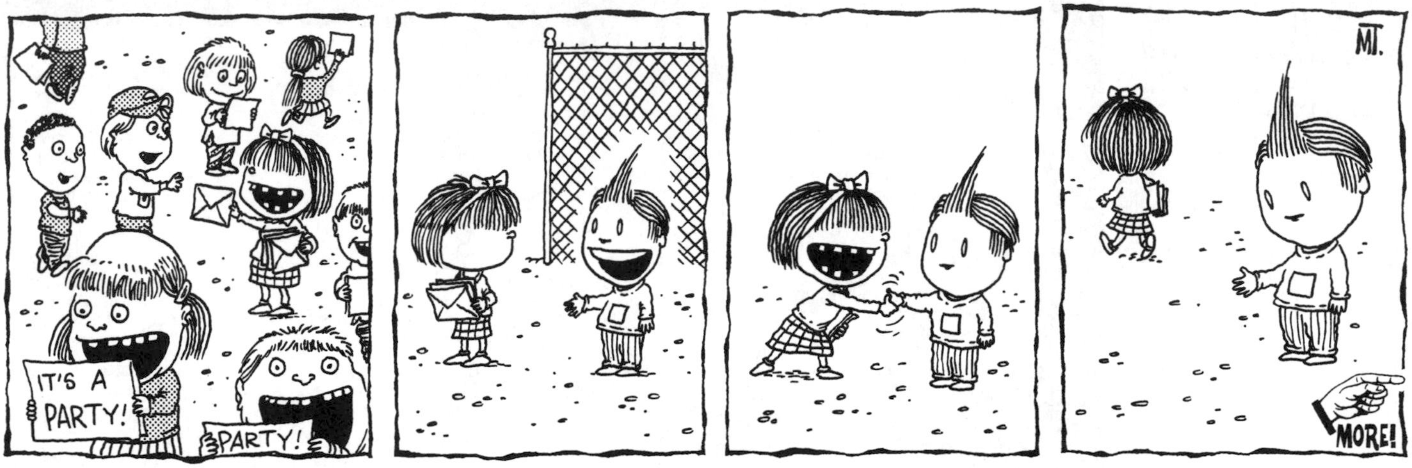
IT'S A PARTY!
PARTY!
MT.
MORE!

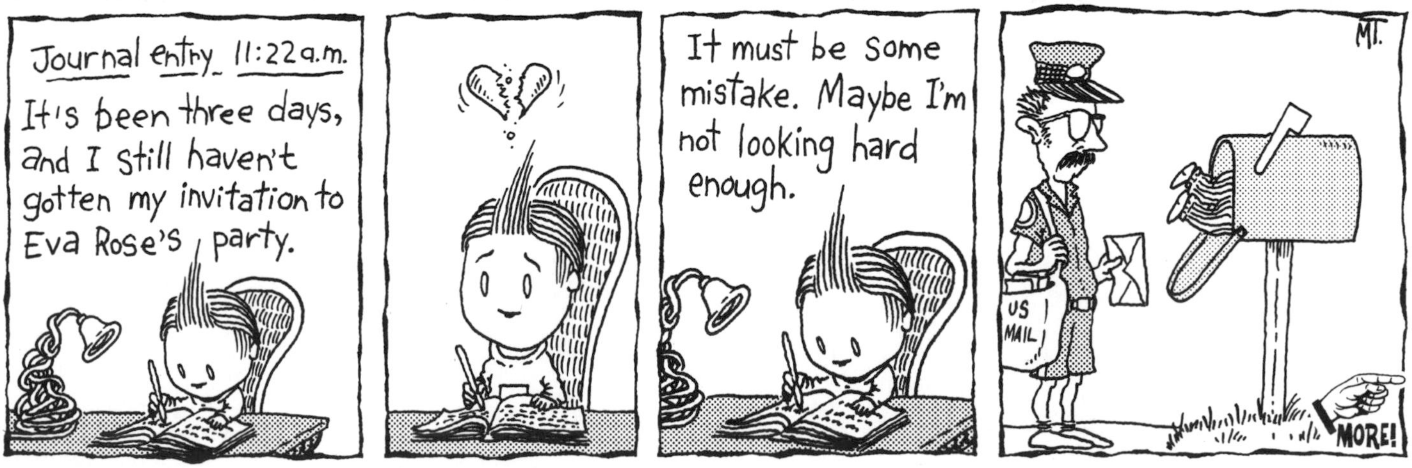
Journal entry 11:22 a.m.
It's been three days, and I still haven't gotten my invitation to Eva Rose's party.
It must be some mistake. Maybe I'm not looking hard enough.
MT.
US MAIL
MORE!

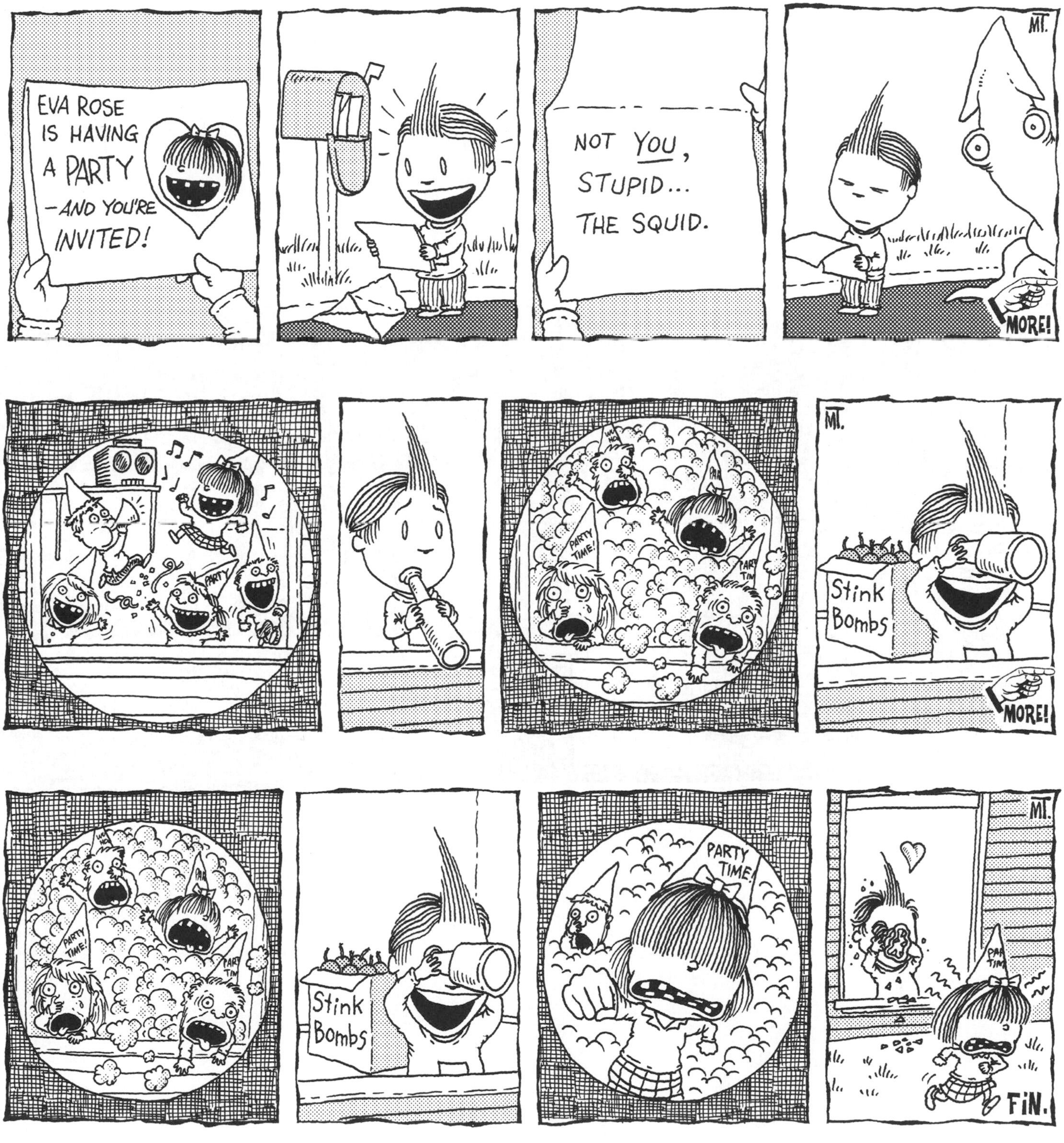
EVA ROSE IS HAVING A PARTY
—AND YOU'RE INVITED!
NOT YOU, STUPID... THE SQUID.
MT.
MORE!
PARTY
PARTY TIME!
Stink Bombs
MT.
MORE!
PARTY TIME!
Stink Bombs
PARTY TIME!
MT.
FIN.

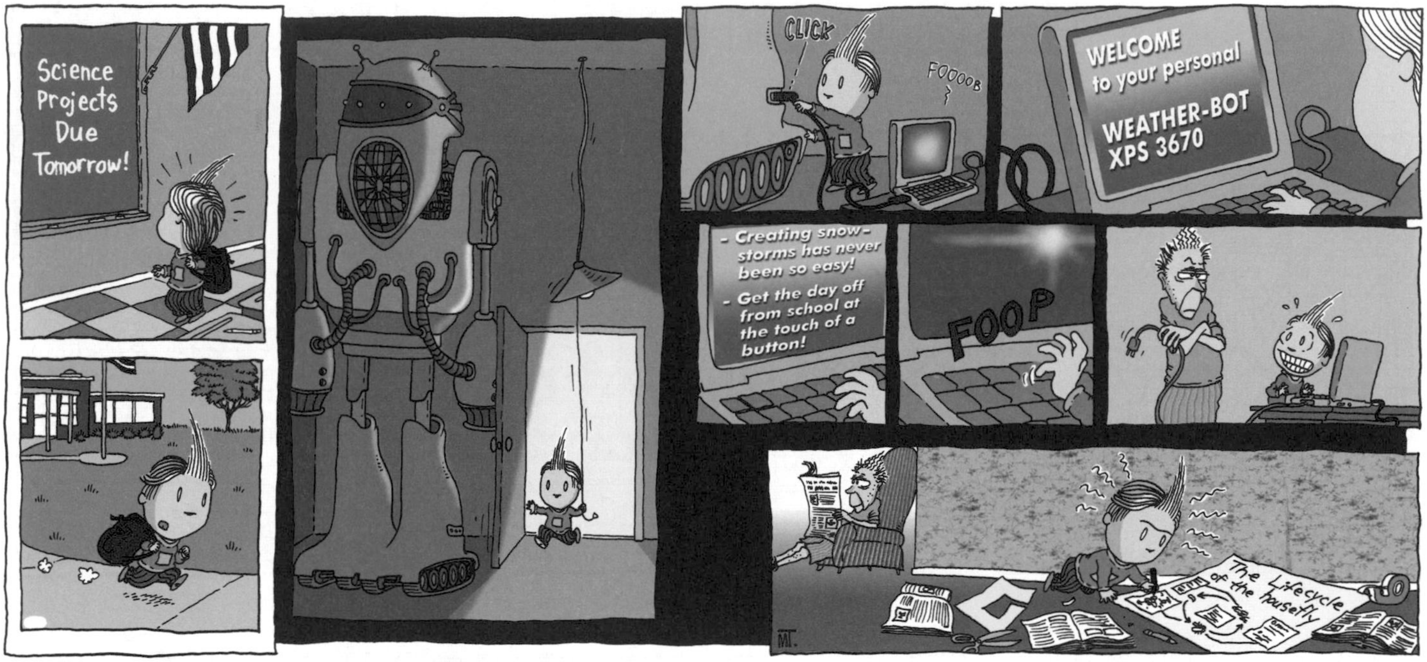
Science Projects Due Tomorrow!
CLICK
FOOOOB
WELCOME
to your personal
WEATHER-BOT
XPS 3670
- Creating snow-storms has never been so easy!
- Get the day off from school at the touch of a button!
FOOP
The Lifecycle of the housefly

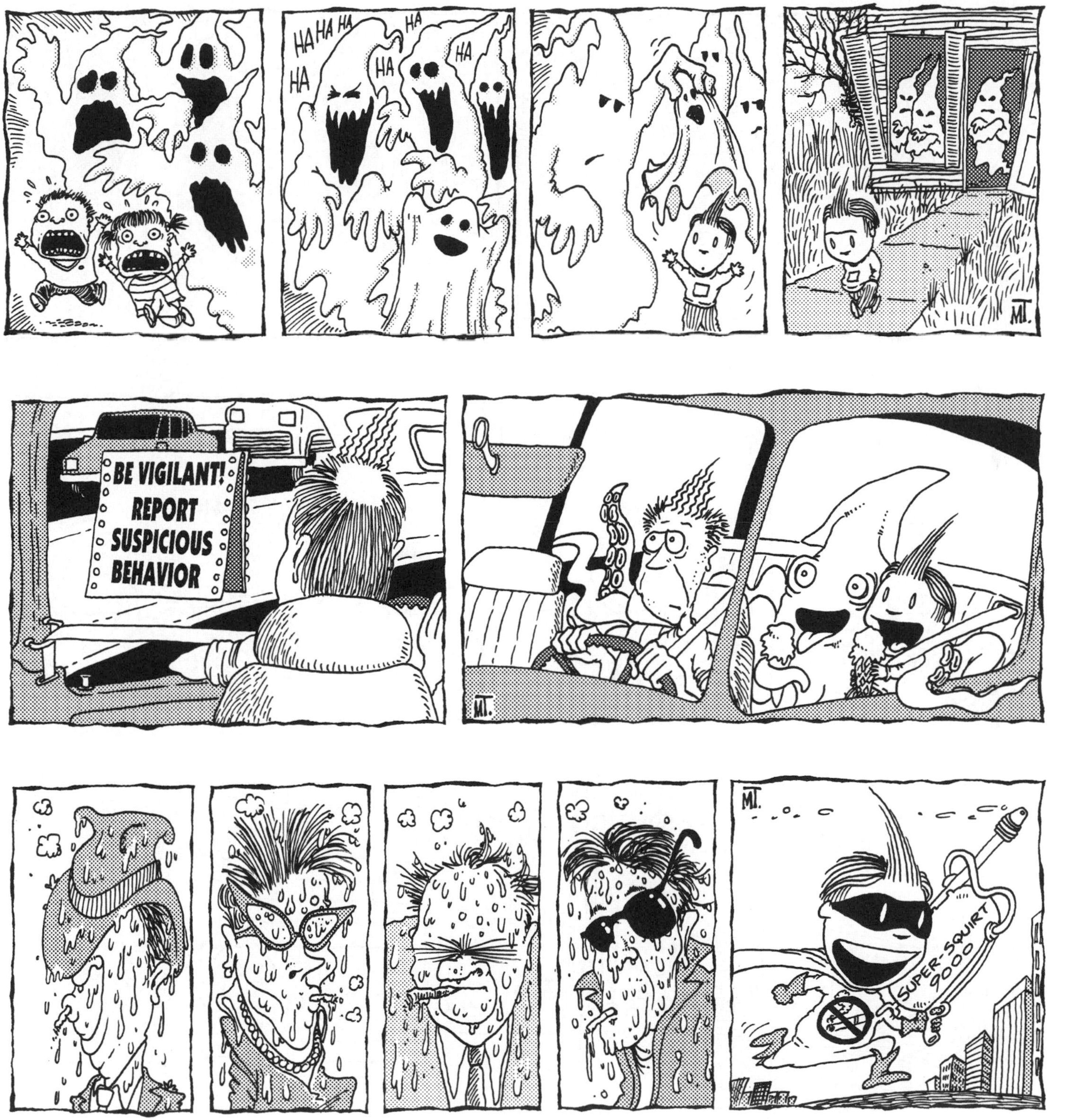
HA HA HA
HA
HA
HA
HA
BE VIGILANT! REPORT SUSPICIOUS BEHAVIOR
SUPER-SQUIRT 9000

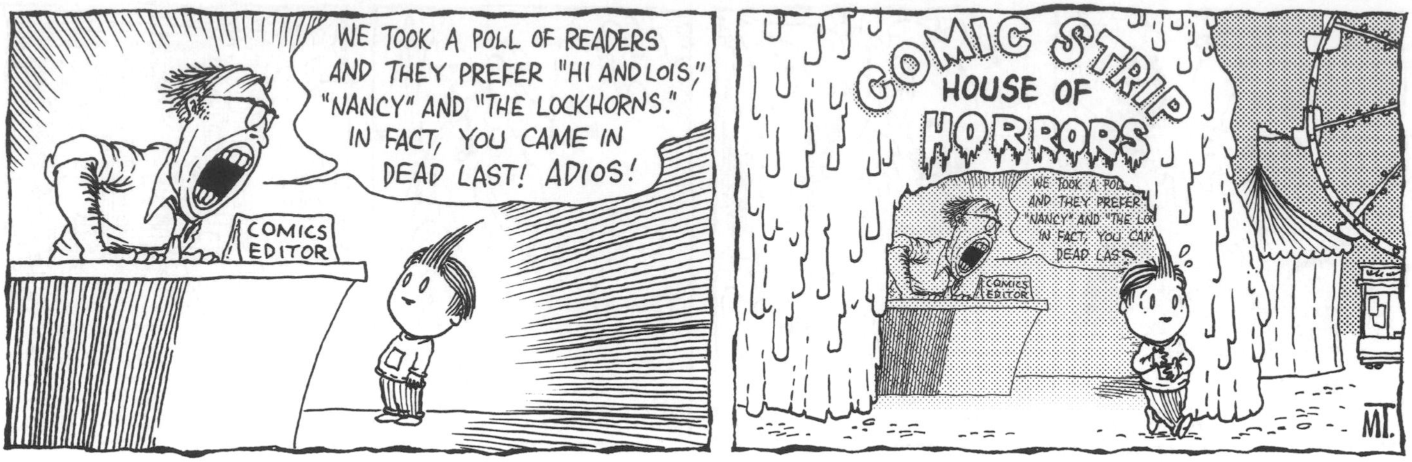
WE TOOK A POLL OF READERS AND THEY PREFER "HI AND LOIS," "NANCY" AND "THE LOCKHORNS." IN FACT, YOU CAME IN DEAD LAST! ADIOS!
COMICS EDITOR
COMIC STRIP
HOUSE OF
HORRORS
MT.

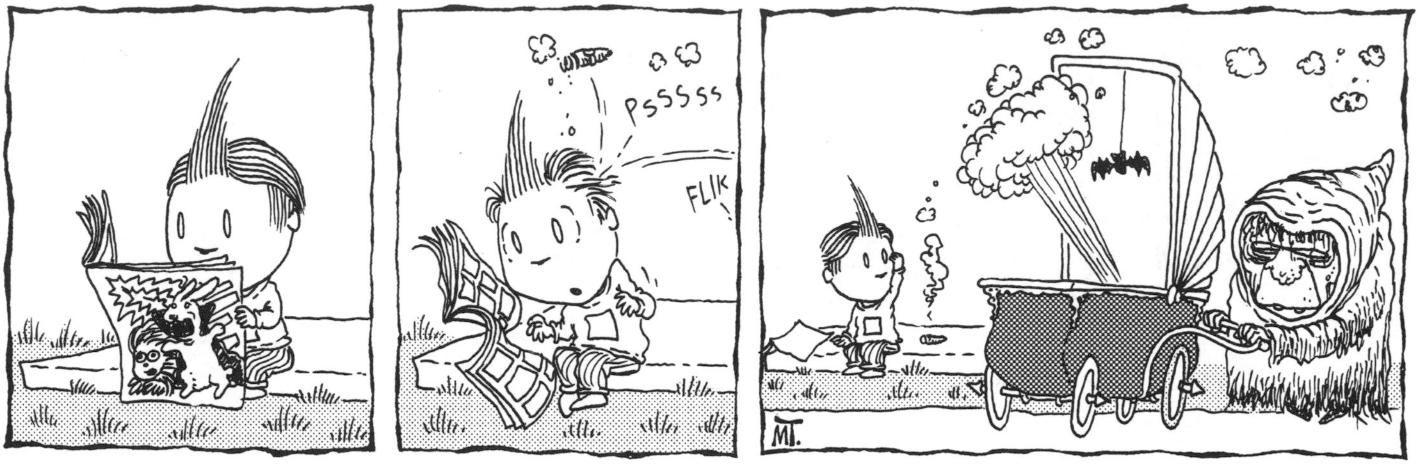
PSSSSS
FLIK
MT.

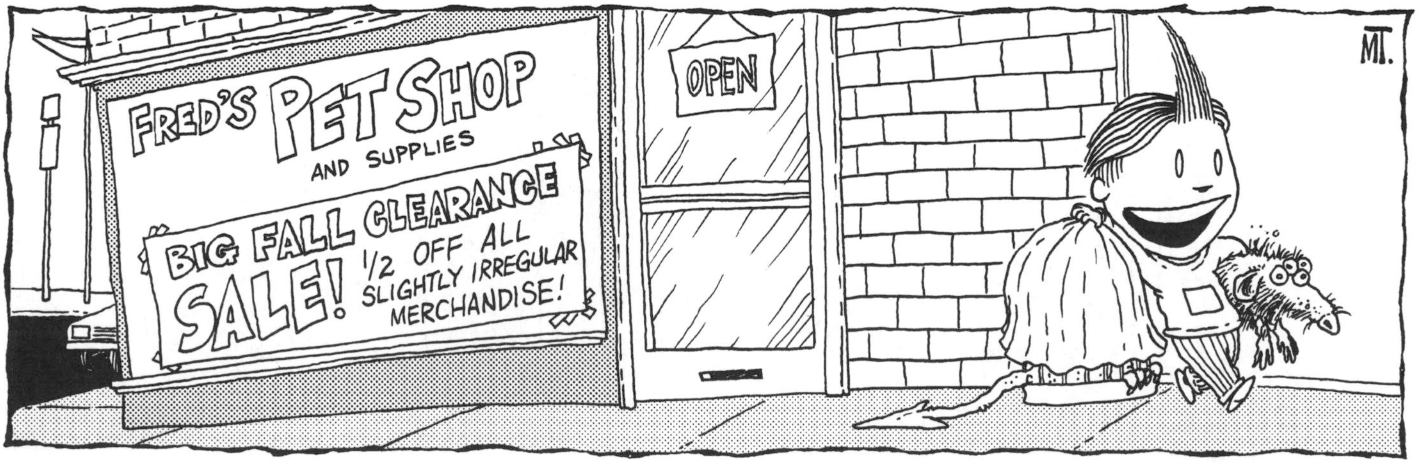
FRED'S PET SHOP
AND SUPPLIES
BIG FALL CLEARANCE SALE! 1/2 OFF ALL SLIGHTLY IRREGULAR MERCHANDISE!
OPEN
MT.

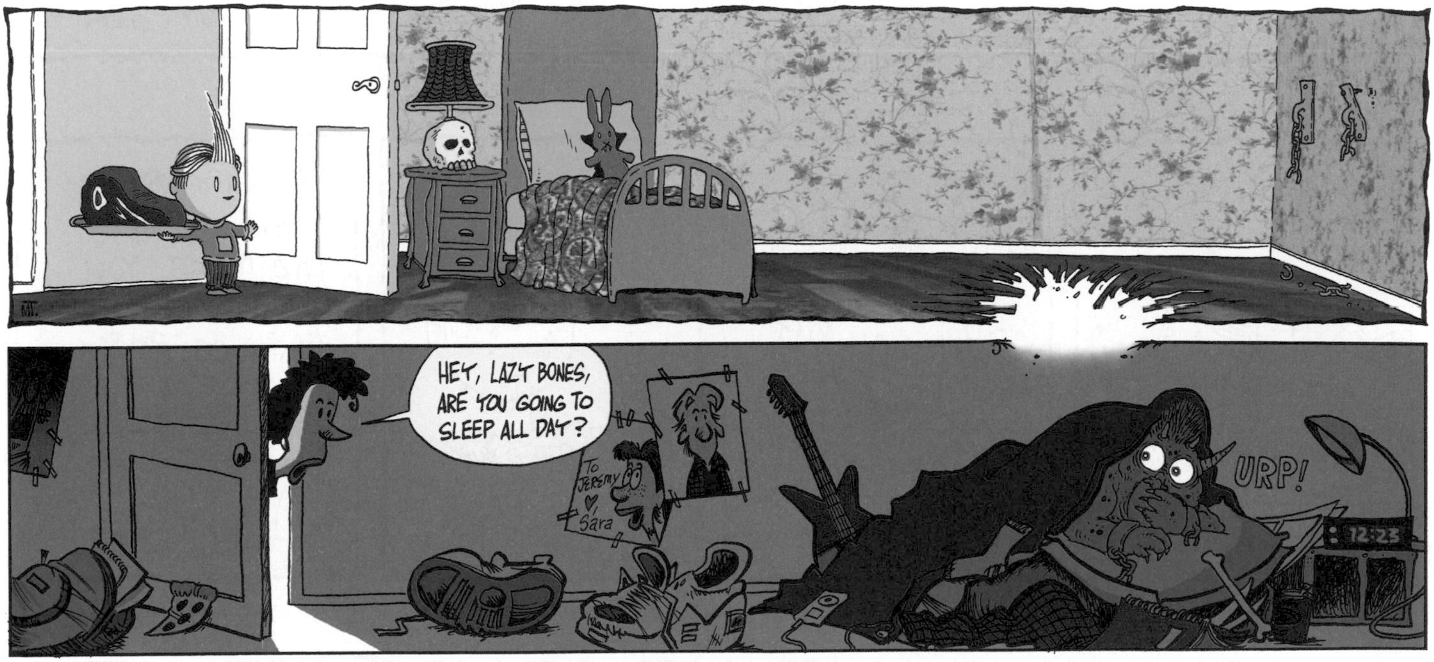
HEY, LAZY BONES, ARE YOU GOING TO SLEEP ALL DAY?
To JEREMY ♥ Sara
URP!
12:23

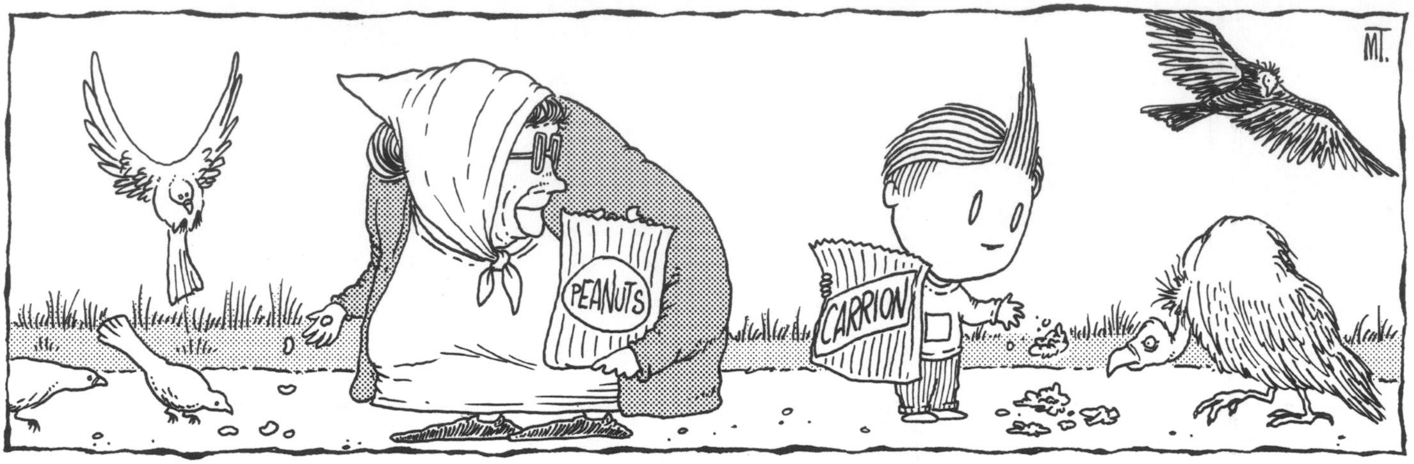
MT.
PEANUTS
CARRION

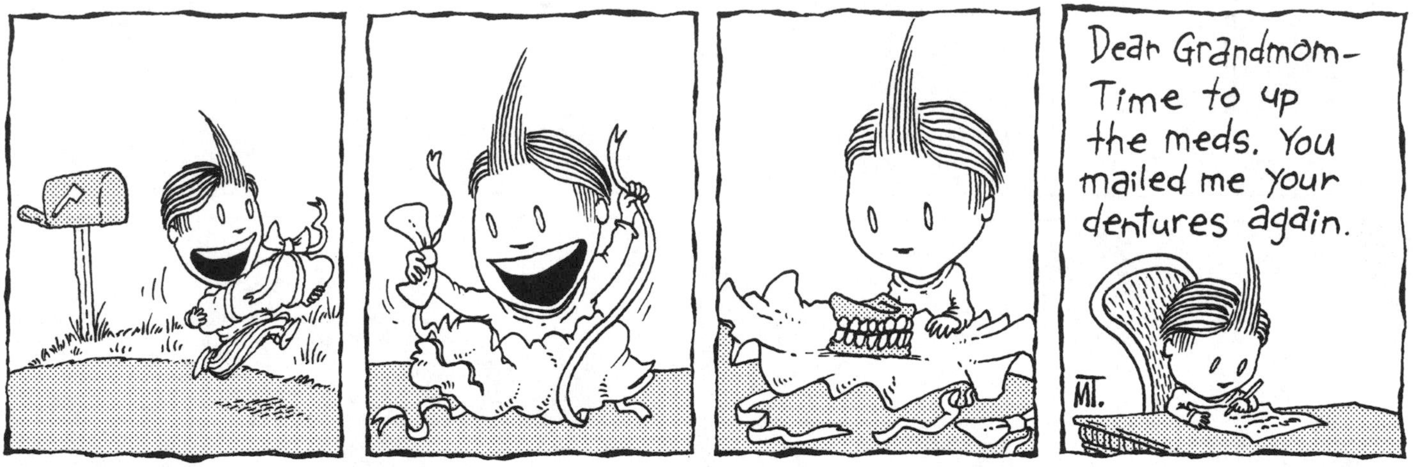
Dear Grandmom-
Time to up the meds. You mailed me your dentures again.
MT.

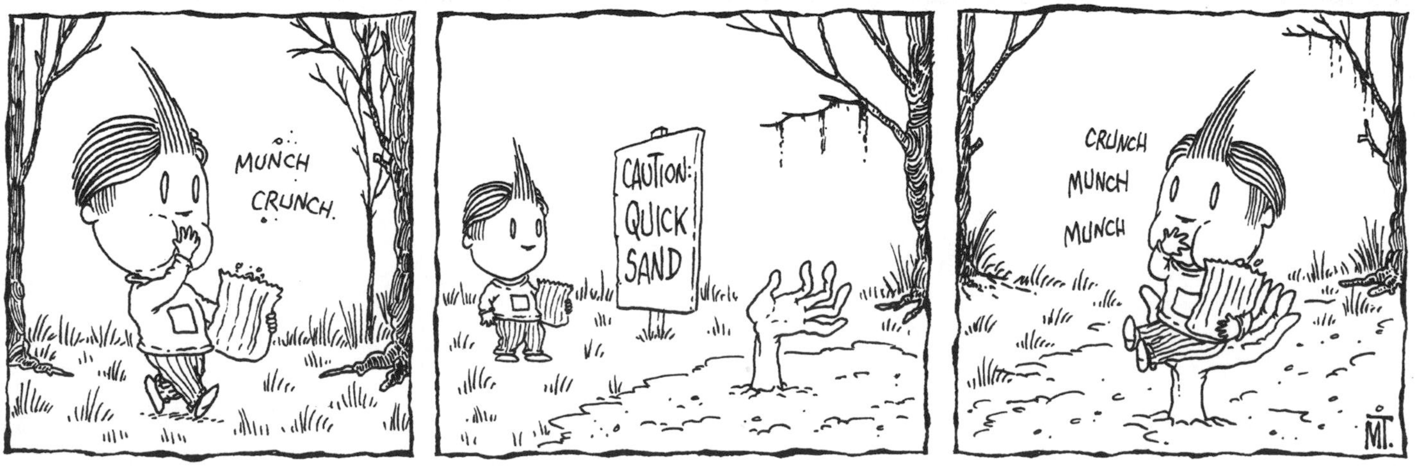
MUNCH
CRUNCH.
CAUTION: QUICK SAND
CRUNCH
MUNCH
MUNCH
MT.

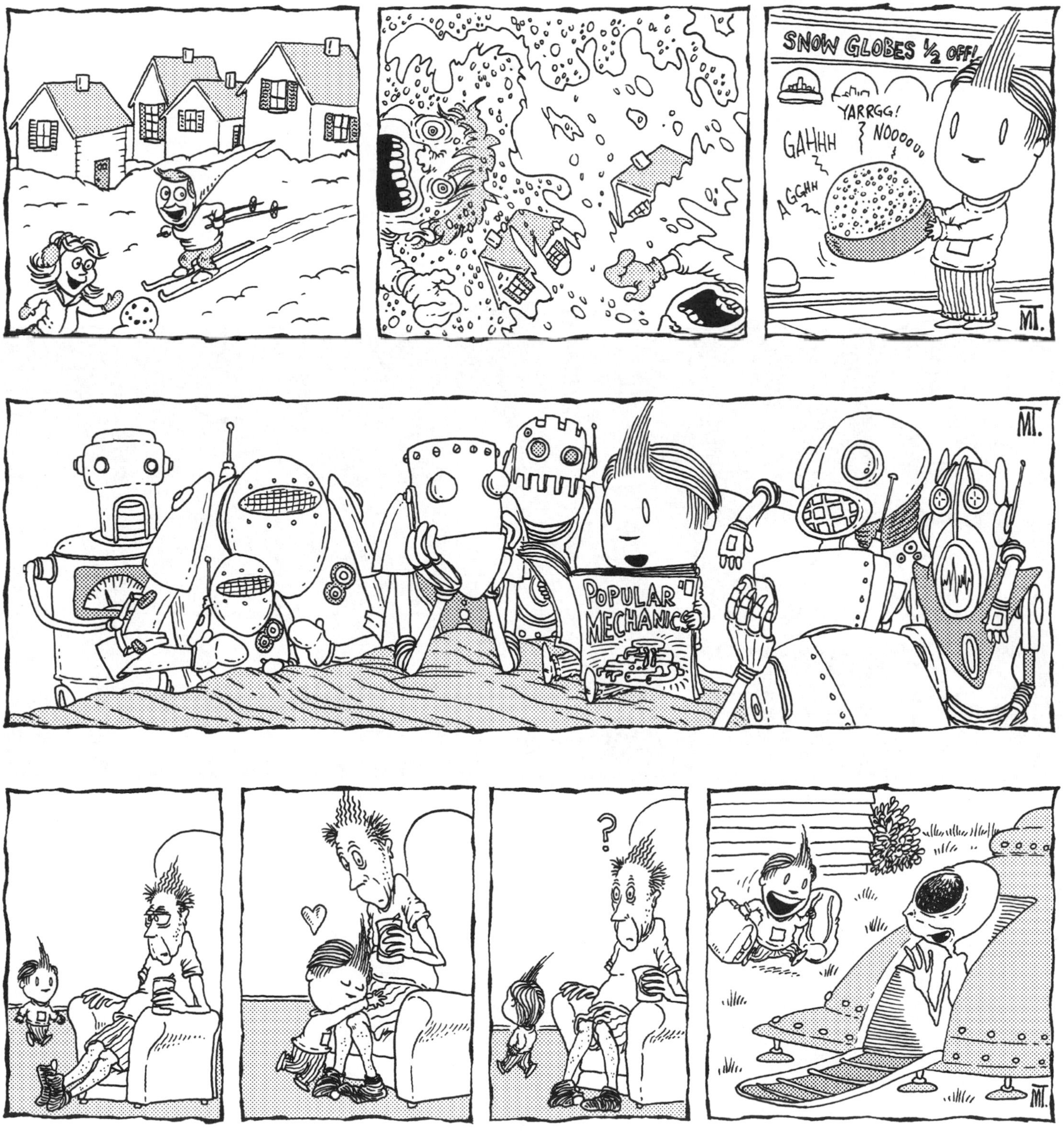
SNOW GLOBES ½ OFF!
YARRGG!
GAHHH
NOOOooo
AGGHH
MT.
MT.
POPULAR MECHANICS
?
MT.

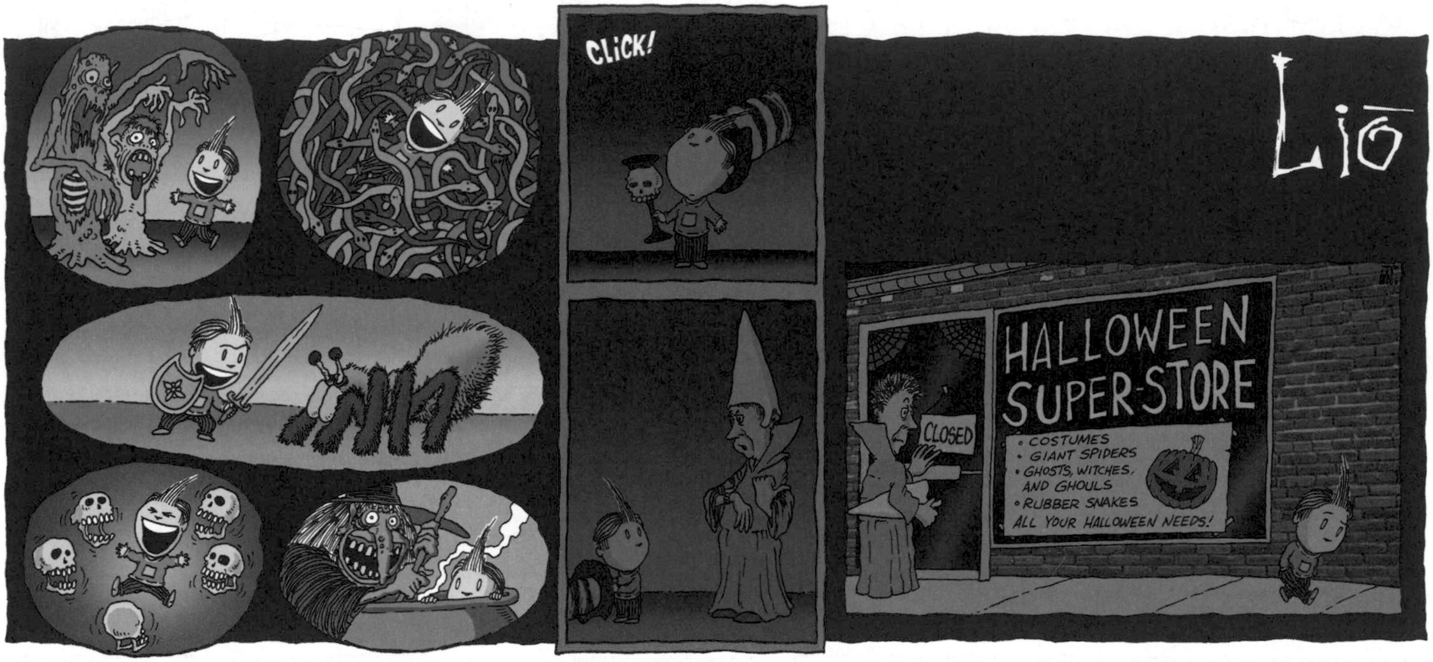
CLICK!
Lio
HALLOWEEN SUPER-STORE
CLOSED
• COSTUMES
• GIANT SPIDERS
• GHOSTS, WITCHES, AND GHOULS
• RUBBER SNAKES
ALL YOUR HALLOWEEN NEEDS!

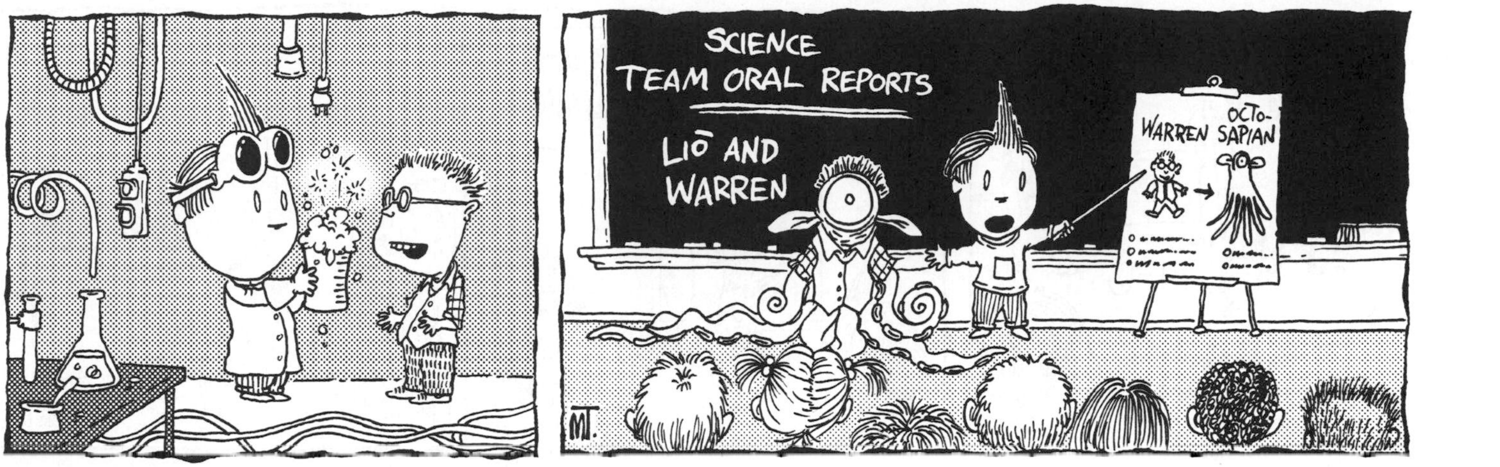
SCIENCE
TEAM ORAL REPORTS
LIŌ AND WARREN
WARREN
OCTO-SAPIAN

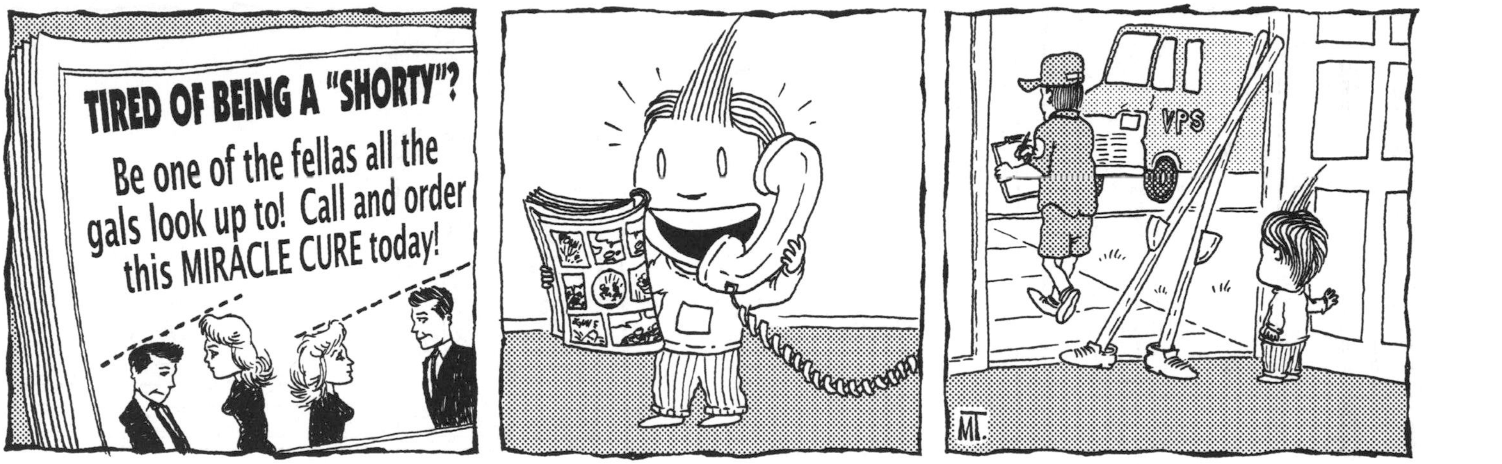
TIRED OF BEING A "SHORTY"?
Be one of the fellas all the gals look up to! Call and order this MIRACLE CURE today!
VPS

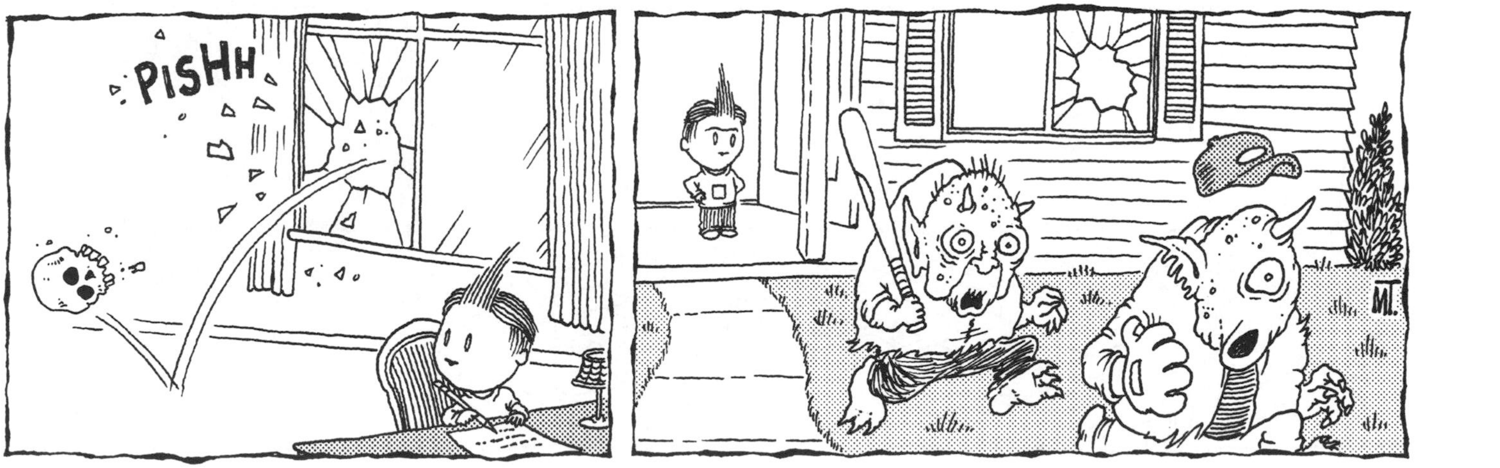
PISHH

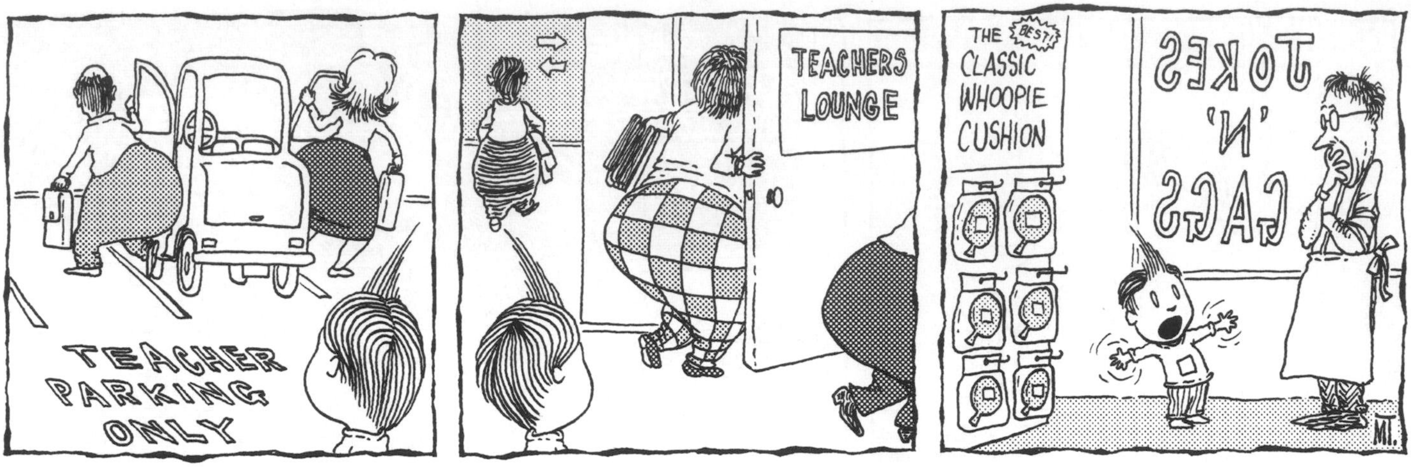
TEACHER PARKING ONLY
TEACHERS LOUNGE
THE BEST! CLASSIC WHOOPIE CUSHION
JOKES 'N' GAGS
MT.

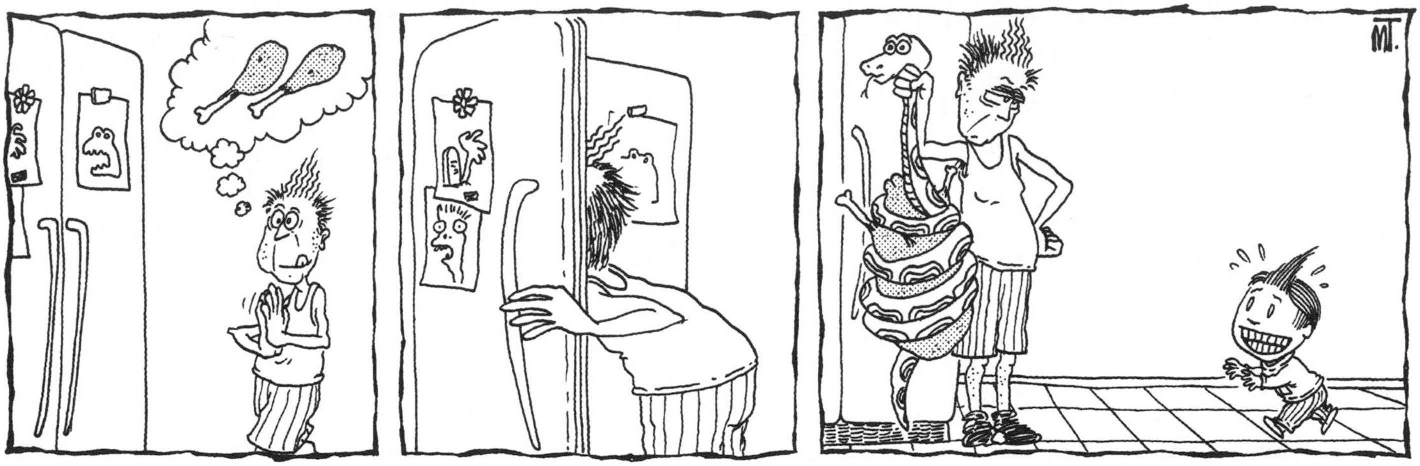
MT.

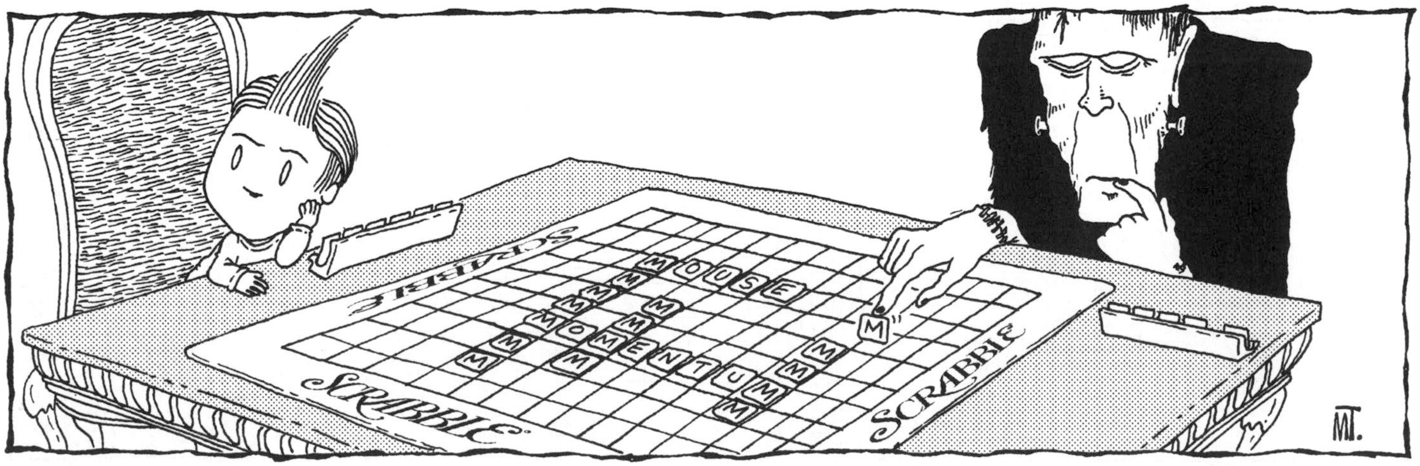
SCRABBLE
SCRABBLE
SCRABBLE
SCRABBLE
MOUSE
MOMENTUM
MT.

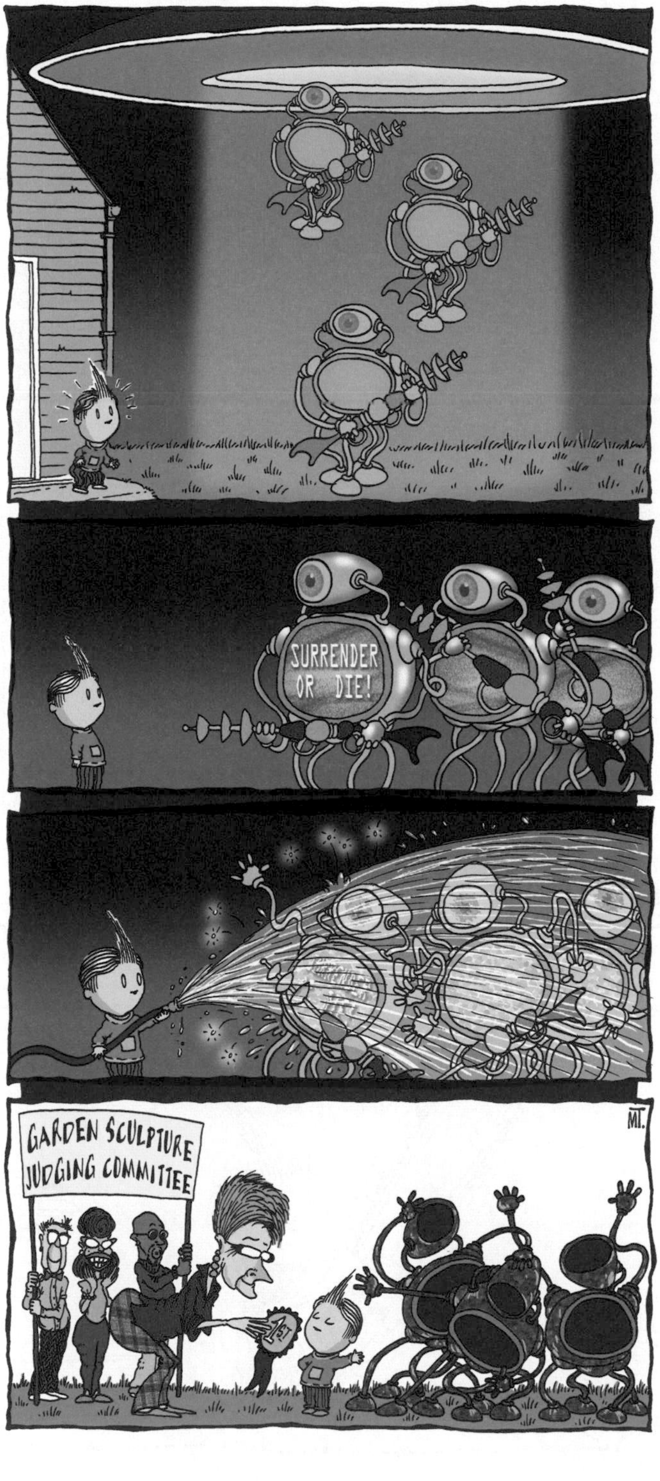
SURRENDER OR DIE!
GARDEN SCULPTURE JUDGING COMMITTEE
MT.

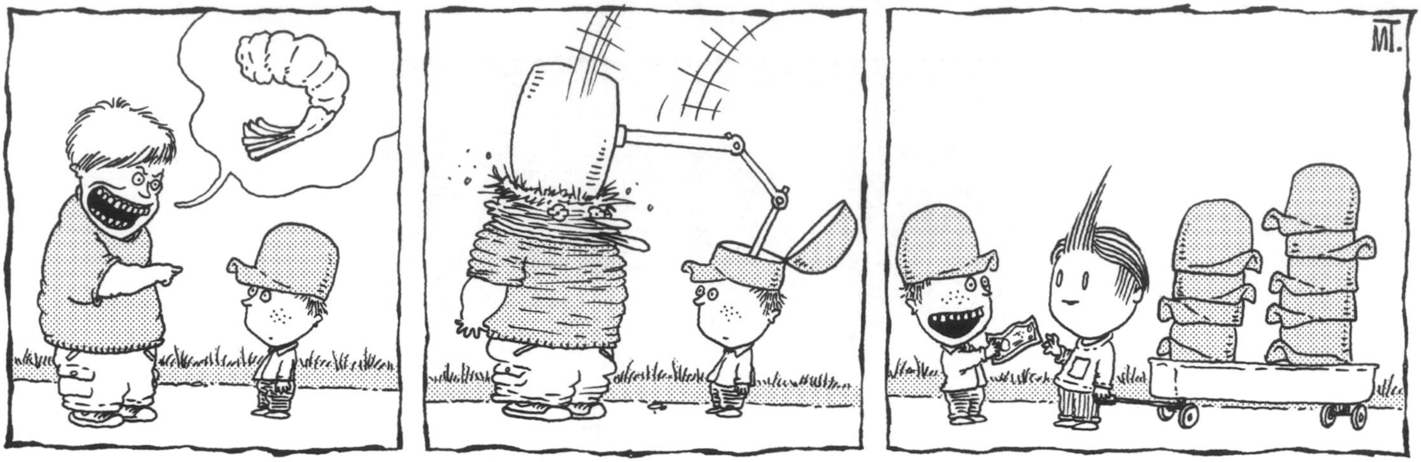

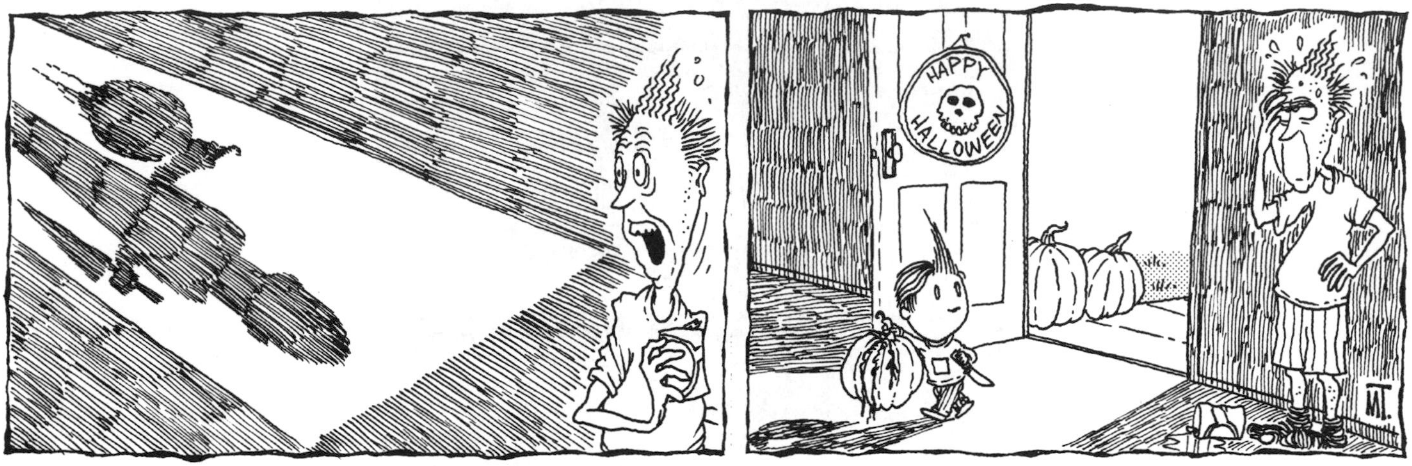
HAPPY HALLOWEEN

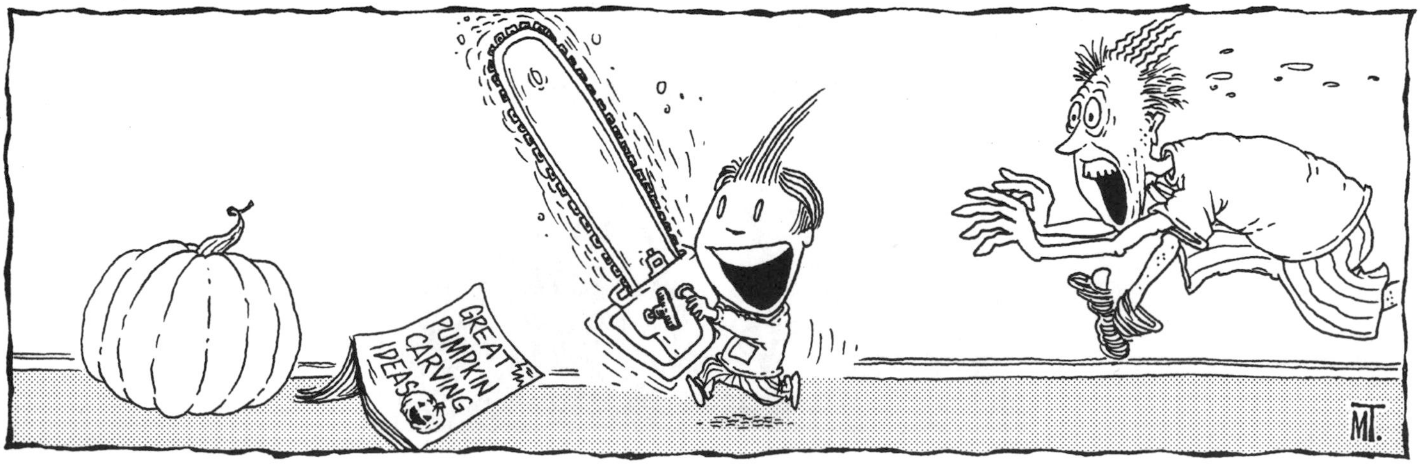
GREAT PUMPKIN CARVING IDEAS

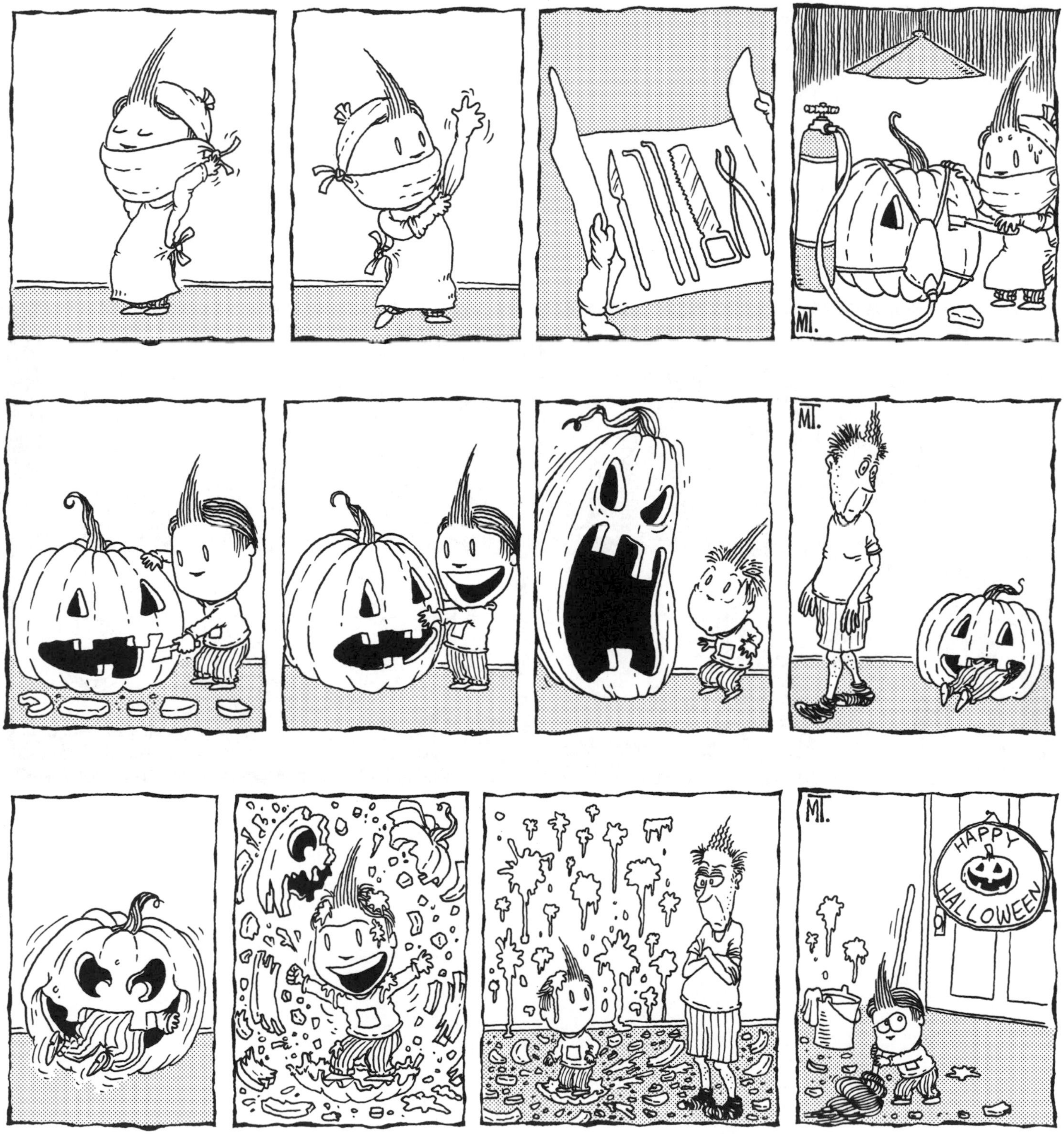
MT.
MT.
MT.
HAPPY HALLOWEEN

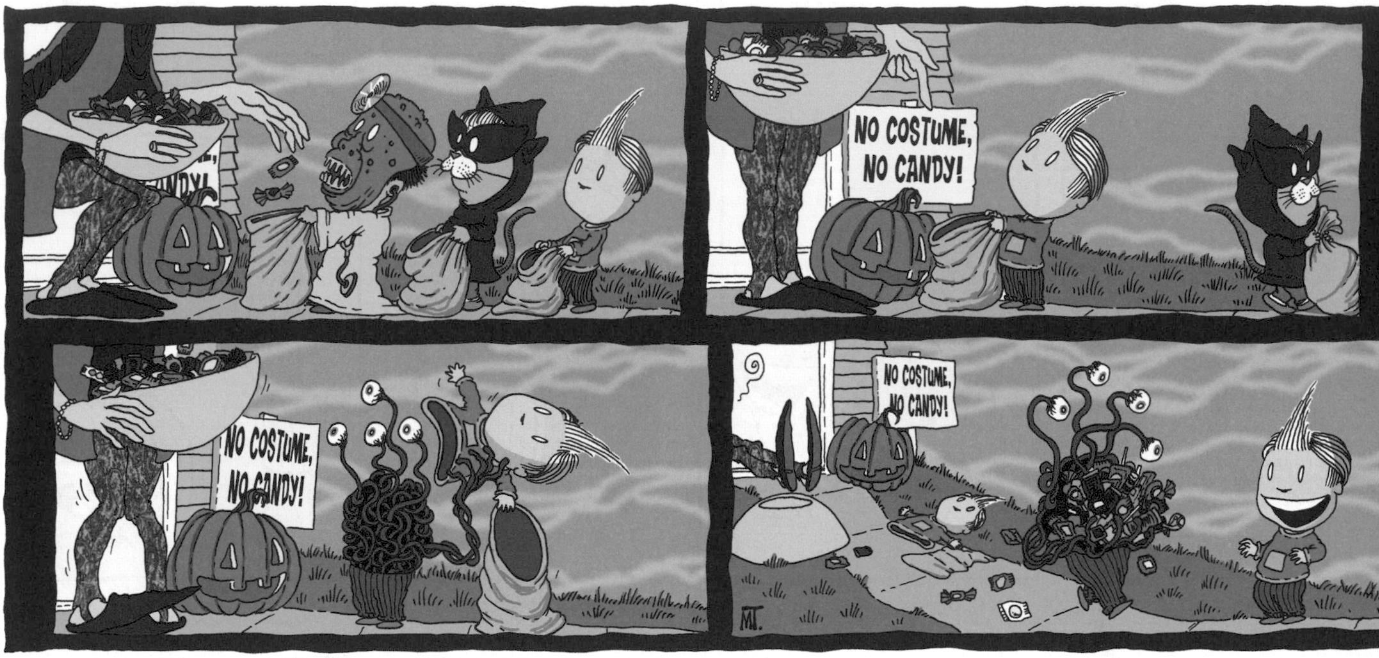
NO COSTUME,
NO CANDY!
NO COSTUME,
NO CANDY!
NO COSTUME,
NO CANDY!
NO COSTUME,
NO CANDY!
MT.

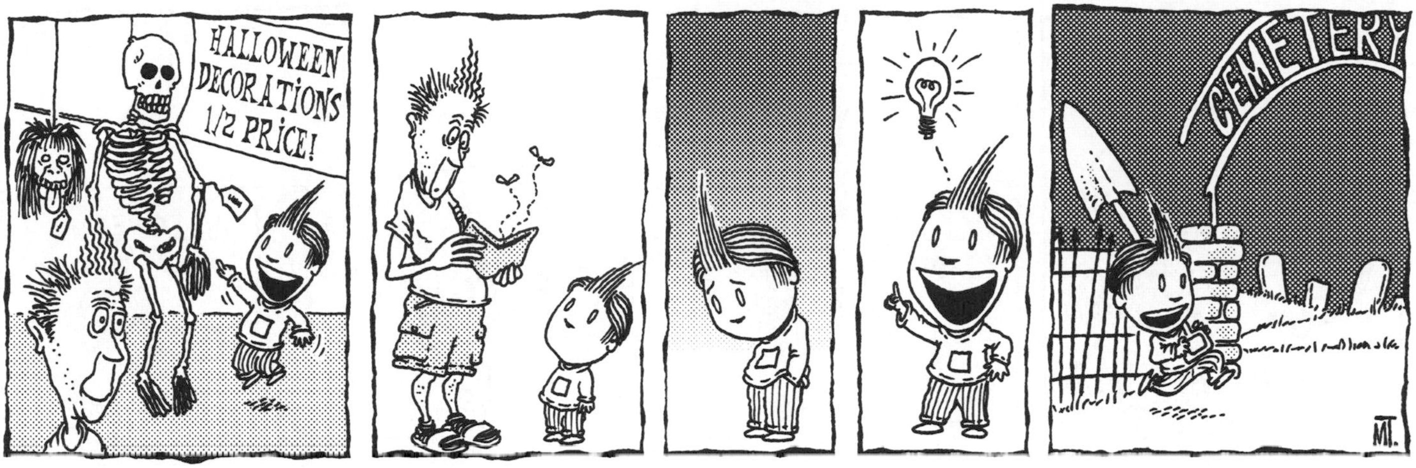
HALLOWEEN DECORATIONS 1/2 PRICE!
CEMETERY

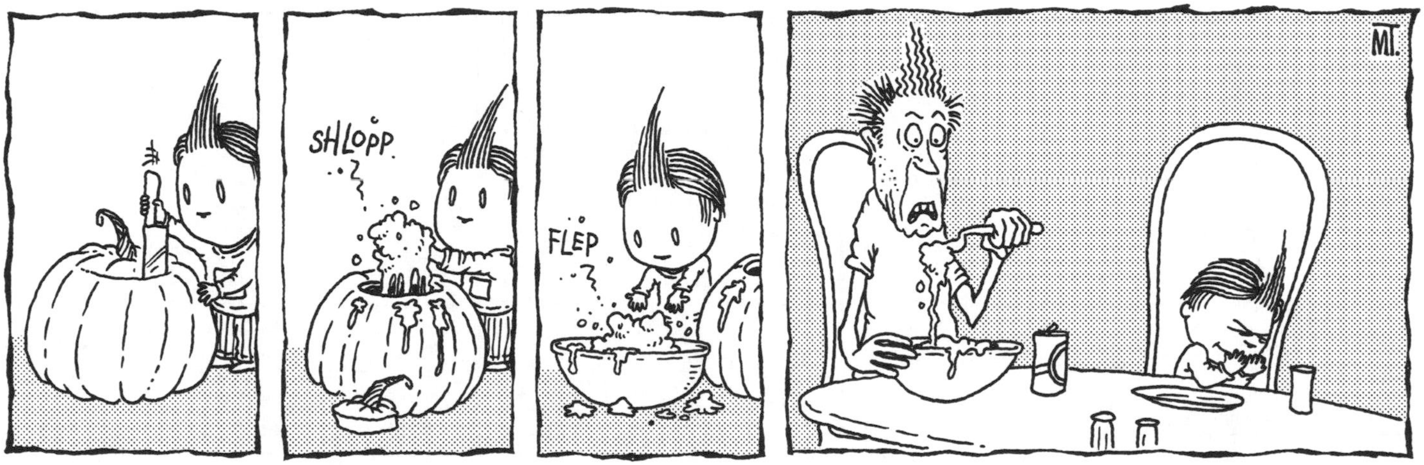
SHLOPP
FLEP

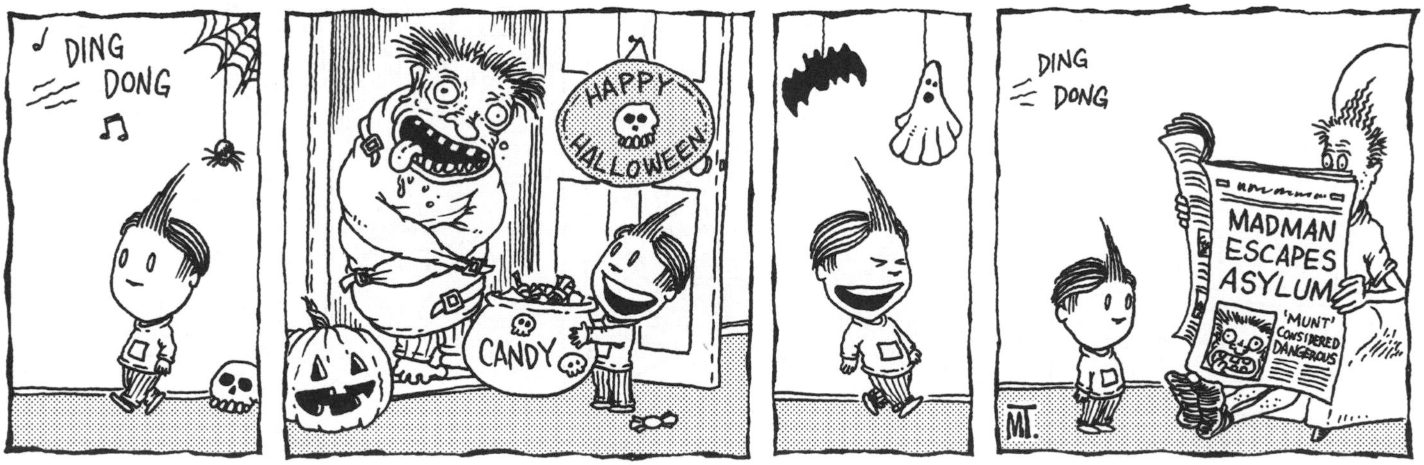
DING DONG
HAPPY HALLOWEEN
CANDY
DING DONG
MADMAN ESCAPES ASYLUM
'MUNT' CONSIDERED DANGEROUS

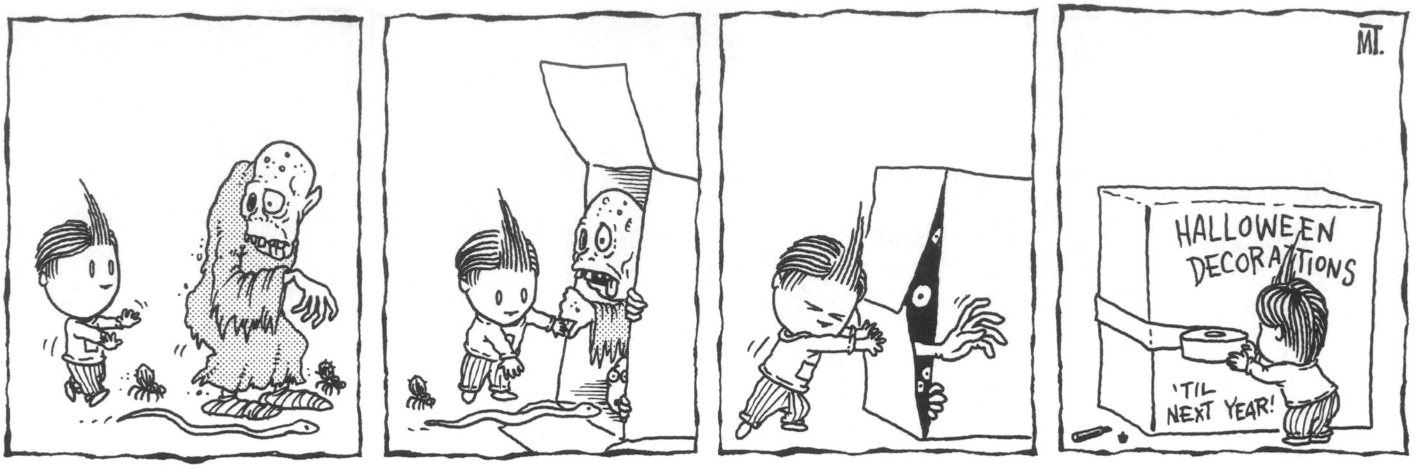
HALLOWEEN DECORATIONS
'TIL NEXT YEAR!

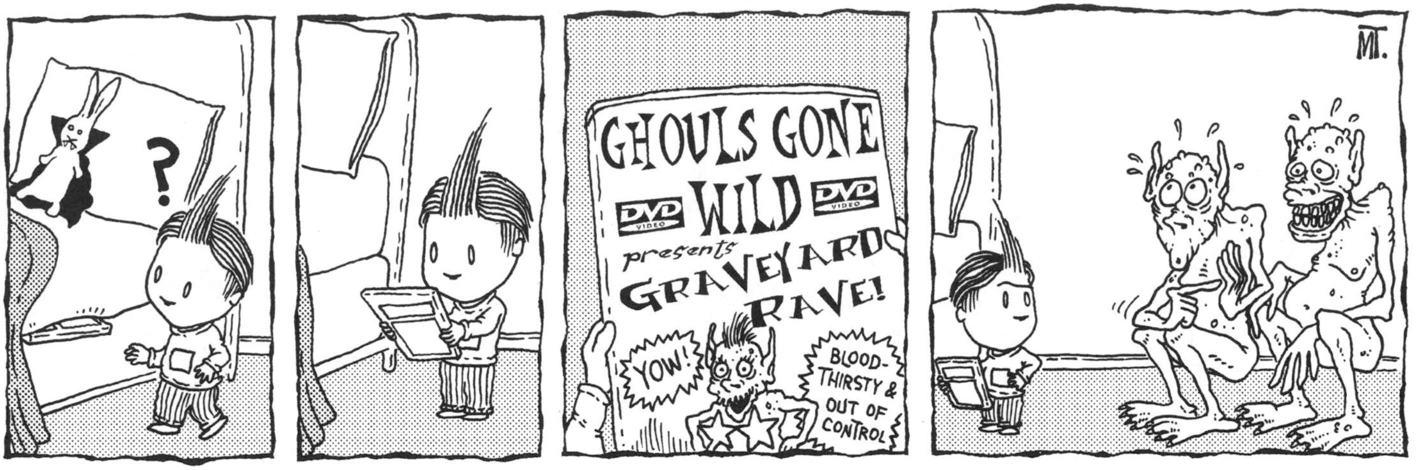
?
GHOULS GONE WILD
DVD VIDEO
presents GRAVEYARD RAVE!
YOW!
BLOOD-THIRSTY & OUT OF CONTROL

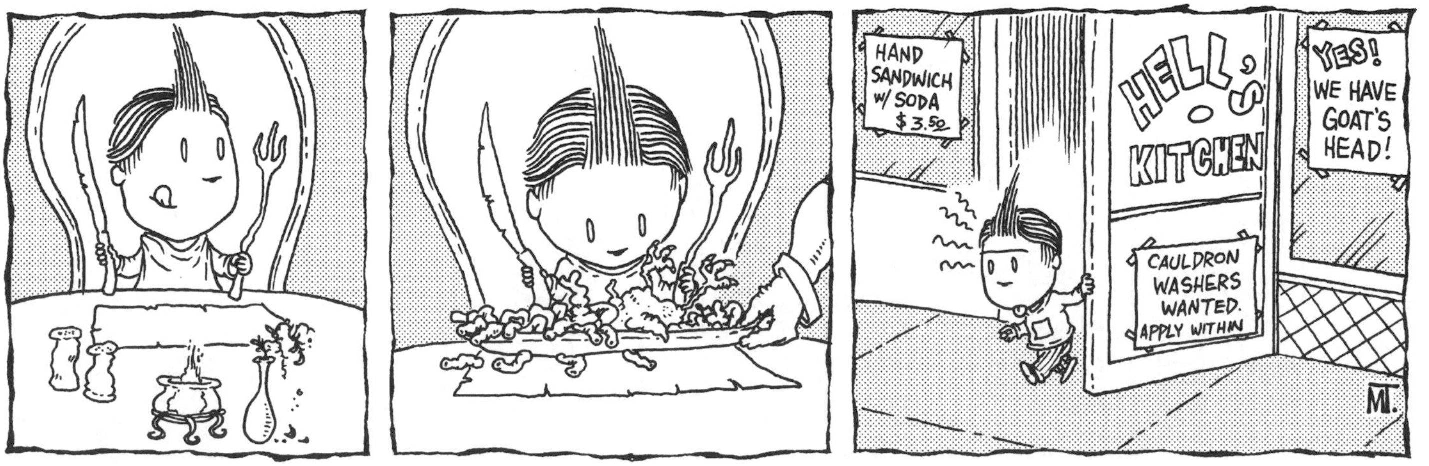
HAND SANDWICH w/ SODA $3.50
HELL'S KITCHEN
YES! WE HAVE GOAT'S HEAD!
CAULDRON WASHERS WANTED. APPLY WITHIN

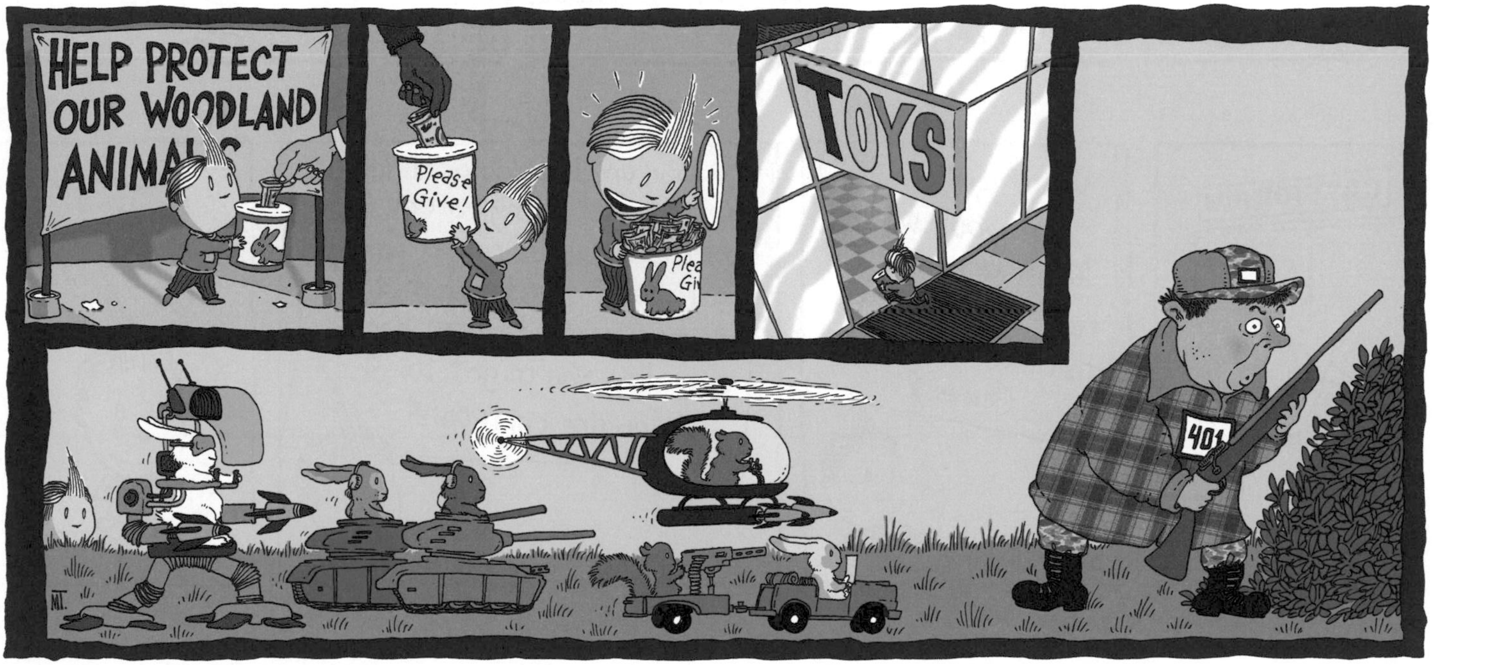
HELP PROTECT
OUR WOODLAND
ANIMALS
Please
Give!
Please
Give
TOYS
401
MT.

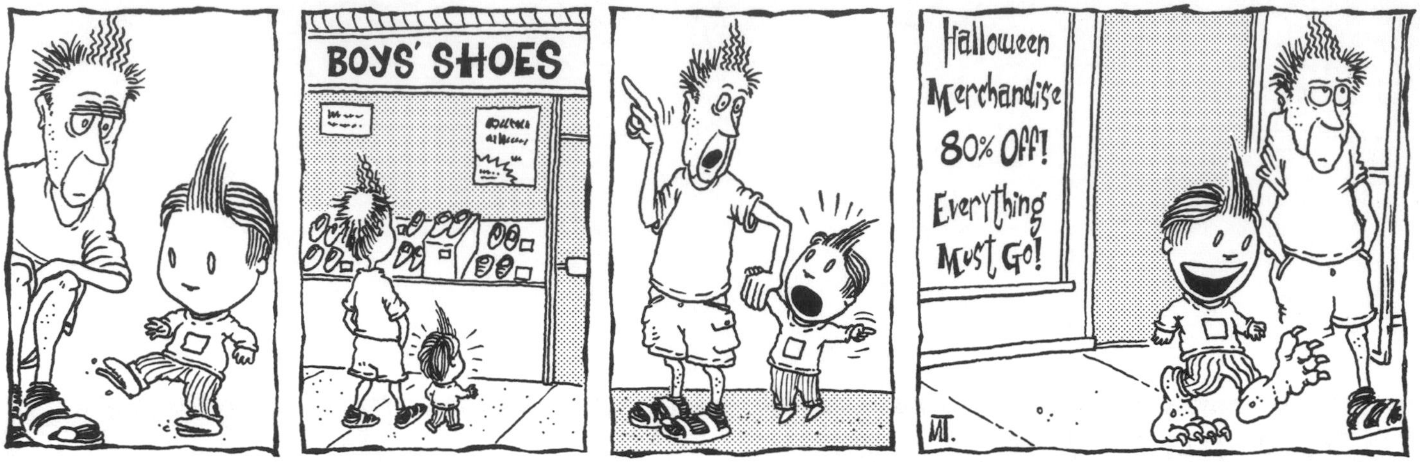
BOYS' SHOES
Halloween Merchandise 80% OFF! Everything Must Go!
MT.

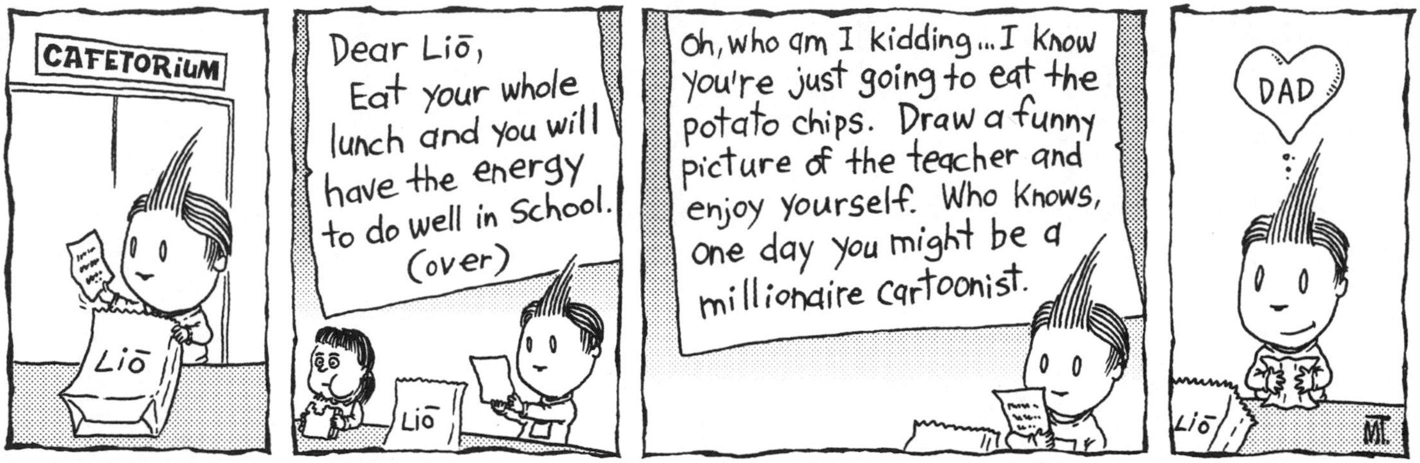
CAFETORIUM
Liō
Dear Liō,
Eat your whole lunch and you will have the energy to do well in School.
(over)
Liō
Oh, who am I kidding... I know you're just going to eat the potato chips. Draw a funny picture of the teacher and enjoy yourself. Who knows, one day you might be a millionaire cartoonist.
DAD
Liō
MT.

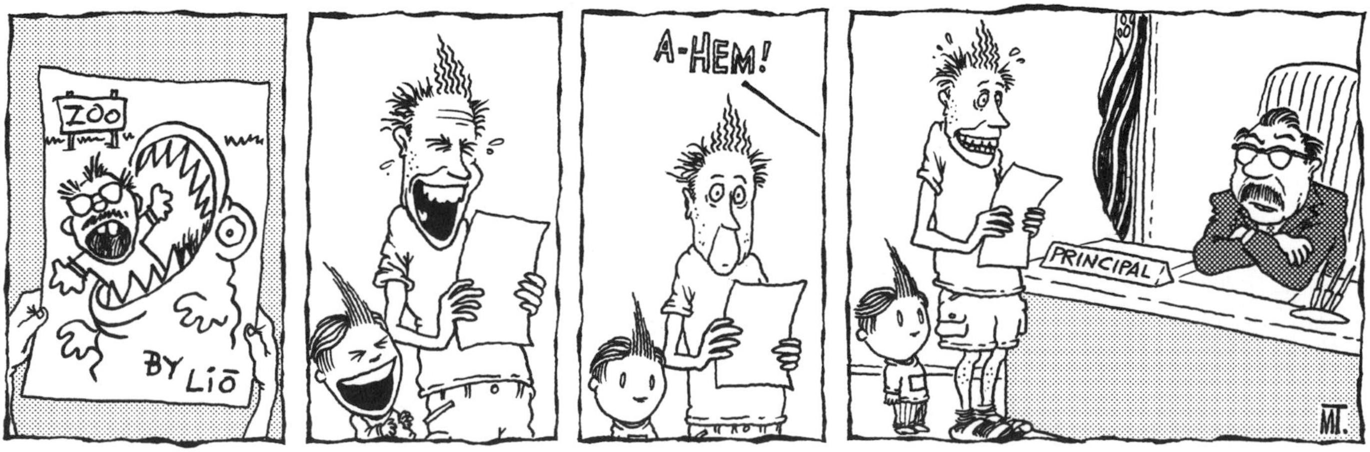
ZOO
BY Liō
A-HEM!
PRINCIPAL
MT.

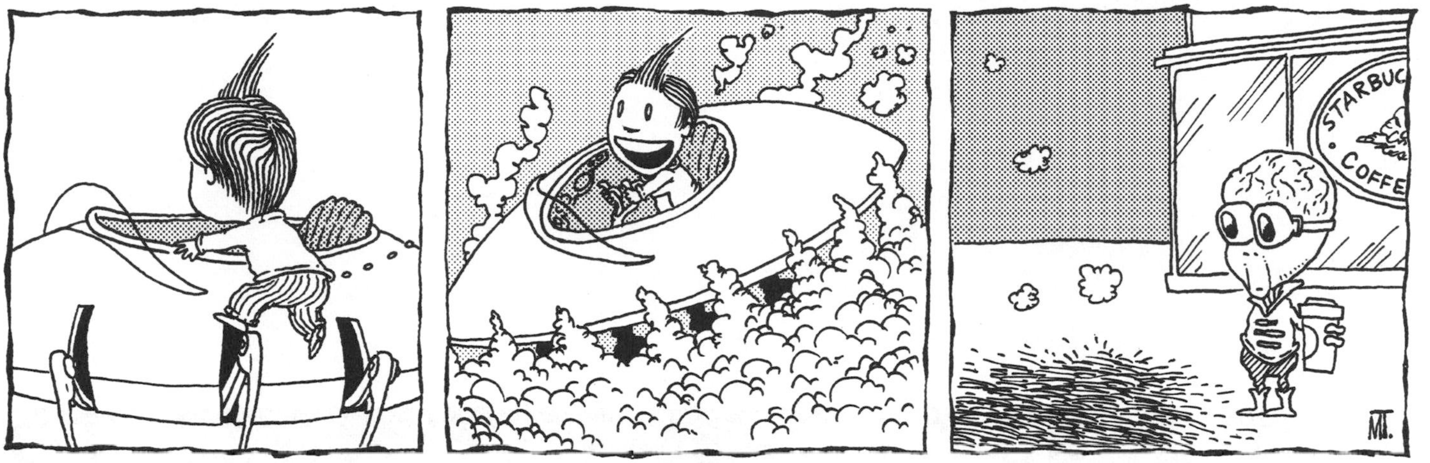
STARBUC
COFFE
MT.

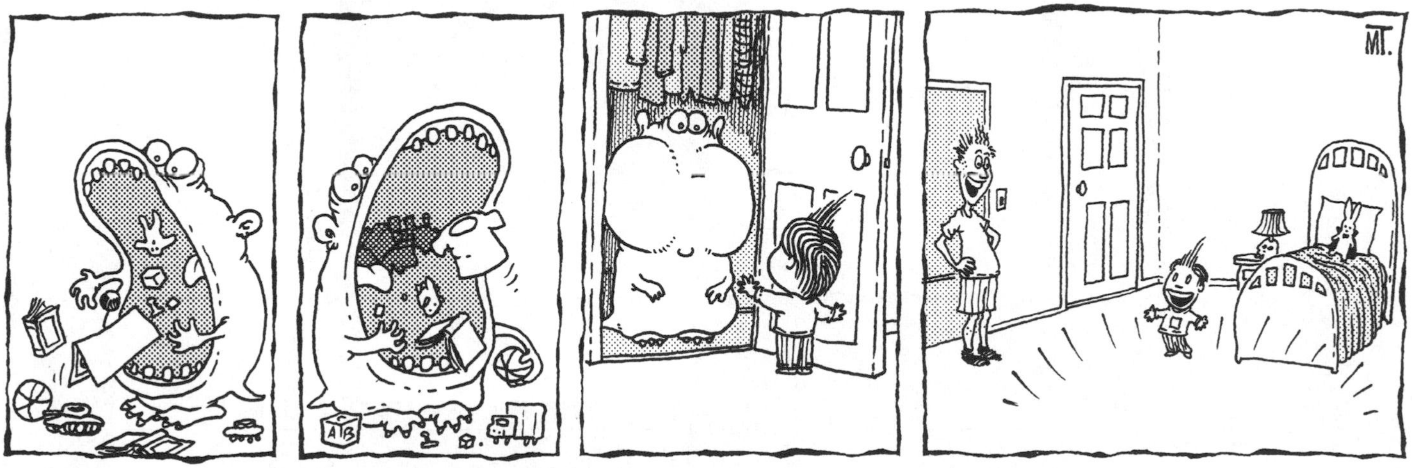
MT.

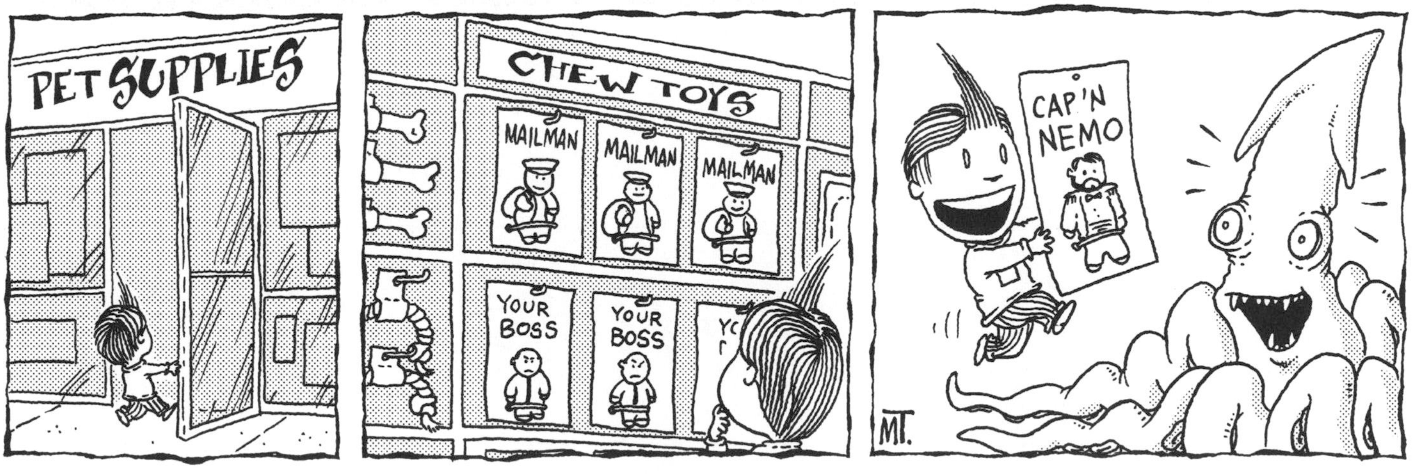
PET SUPPLIES
CHEW TOYS
MAILMAN
MAILMAN
MAILMAN
YOUR BOSS
YOUR BOSS
CAP'N NEMO
MT.

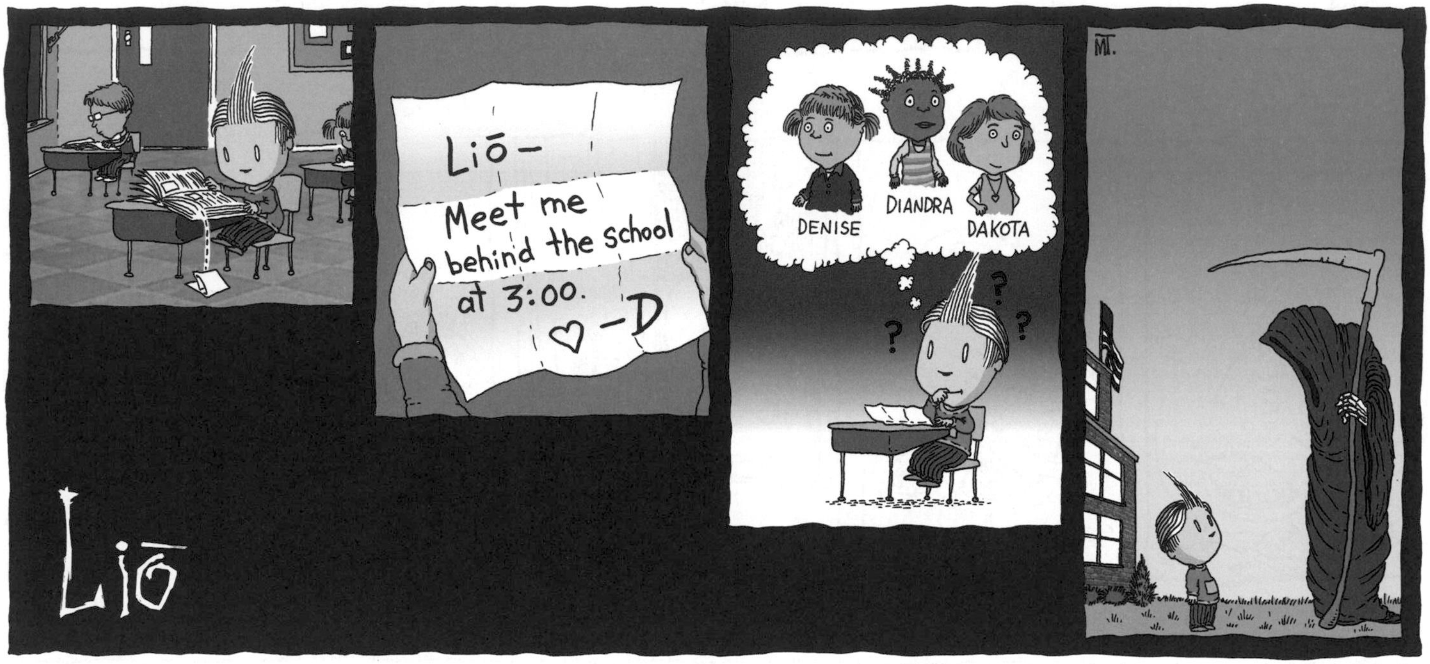
Liō-
Meet me behind the school at 3:00.
♡ -D
DENISE
DIANDRA
DAKOTA
?
?
?
MT.
Liō

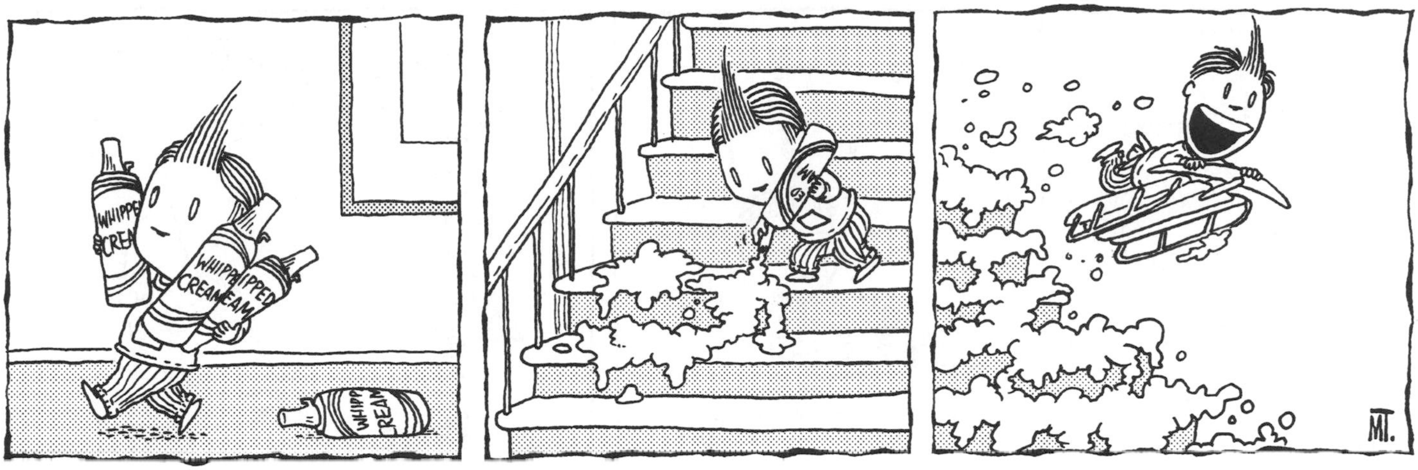
WHIPPED CREAM
WHIPPED CREAM
WHIPPED CREAM
WHIPPED CREAM
MT.

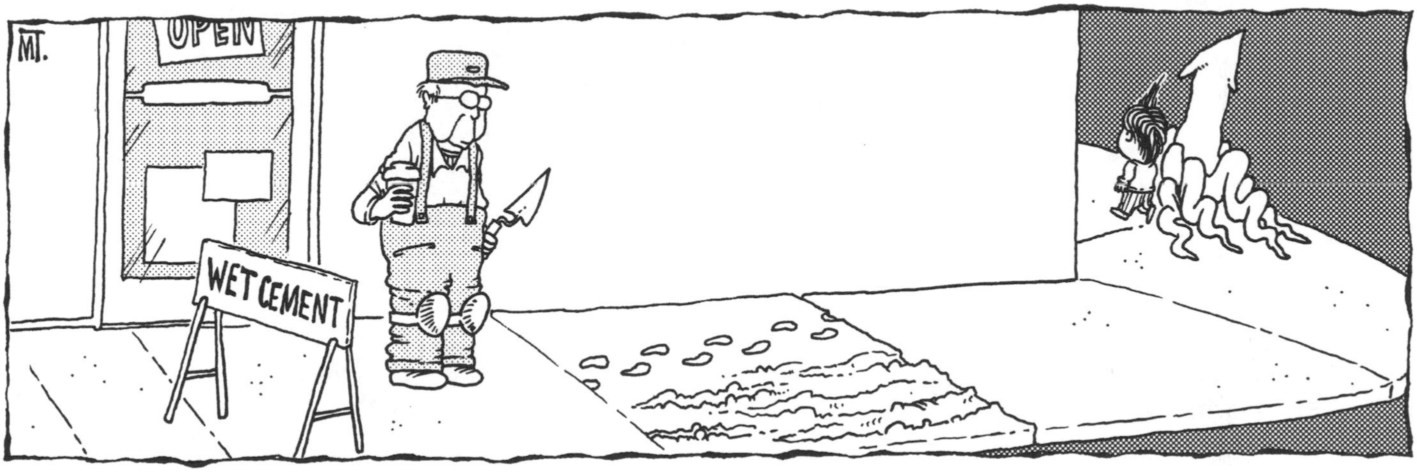
MT.
OPEN
WET CEMENT

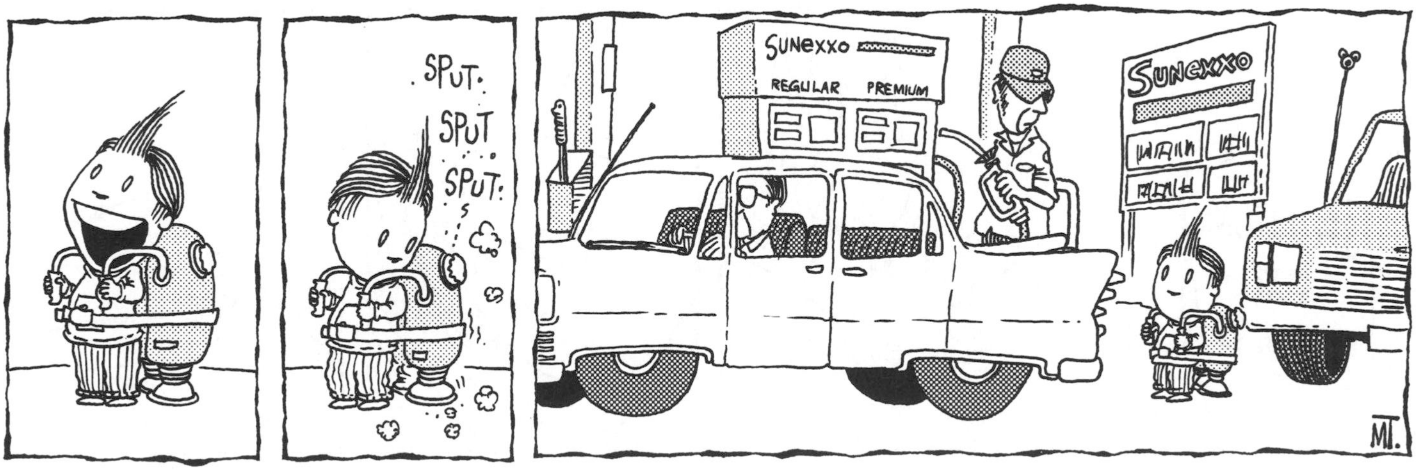
SPUT.
SPUT
SPUT.
SUNEXXO
REGULAR PREMIUM
SUNEXXO
MT.

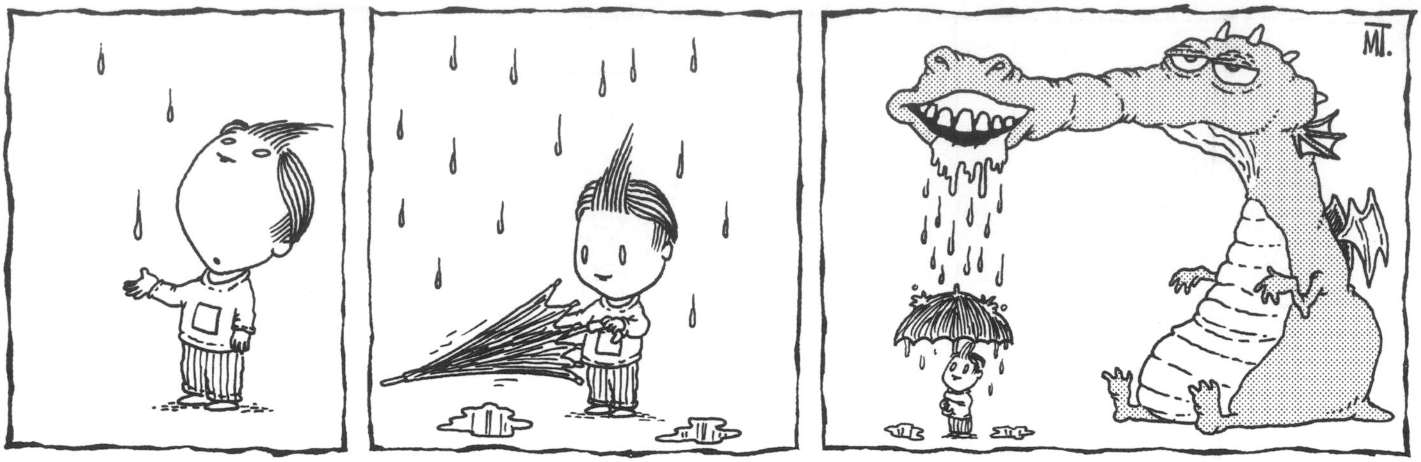

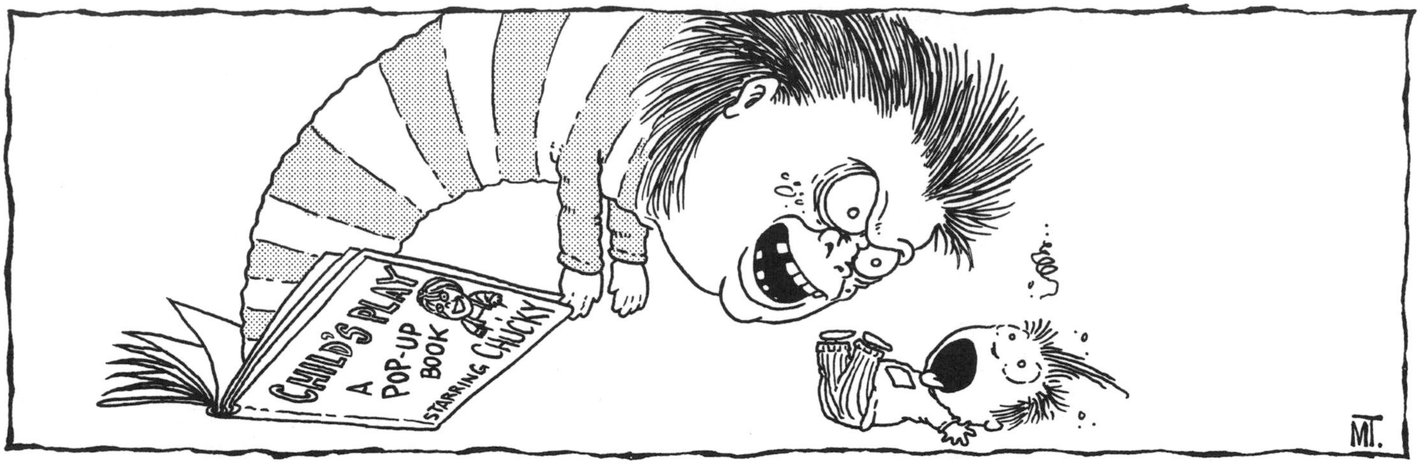
CHILD'S PLAY
A POP-UP BOOK
STARRING CHUCKY

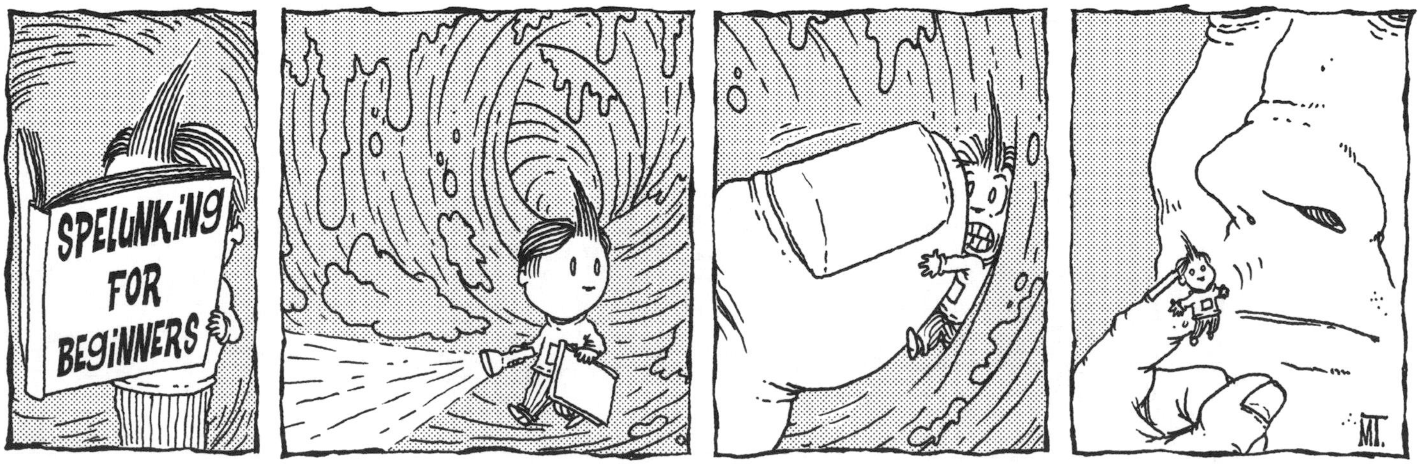
SPELUNKING FOR BEGINNERS

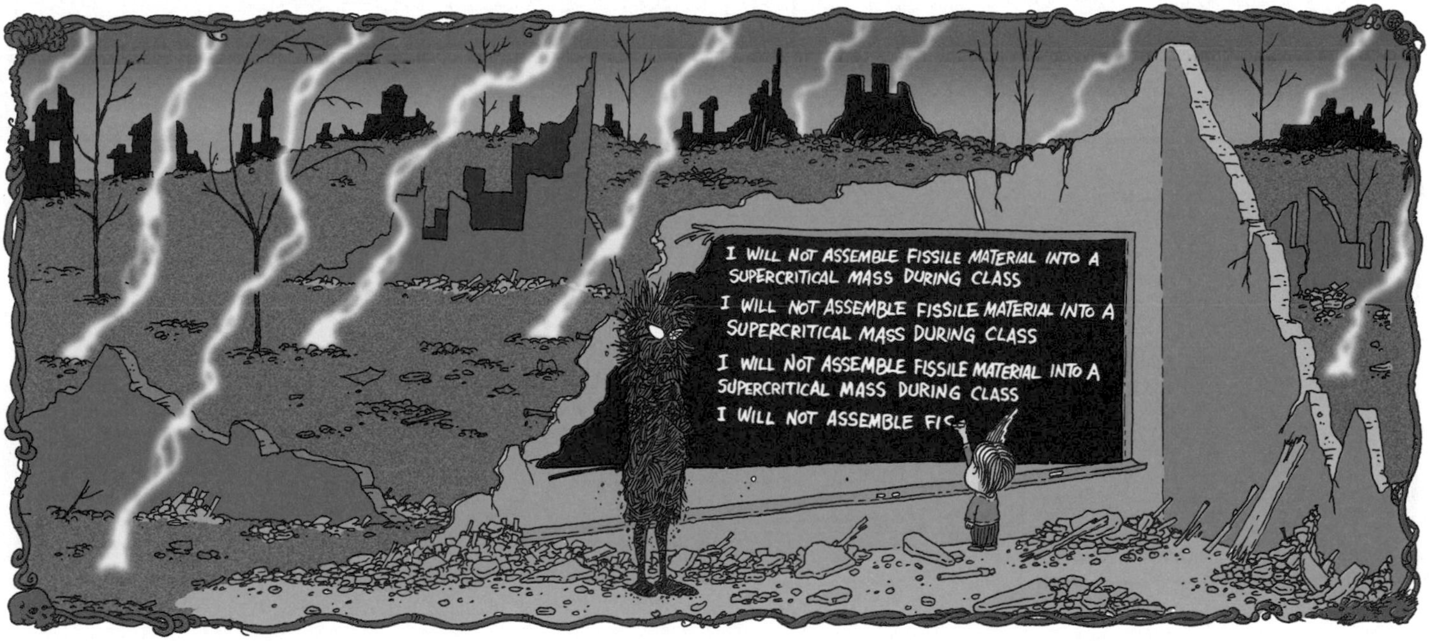
I WILL NOT ASSEMBLE FISSILE MATERIAL INTO A SUPERCRITICAL MASS DURING CLASS
I WILL NOT ASSEMBLE FISSILE MATERIAL INTO A SUPERCRITICAL MASS DURING CLASS
I WILL NOT ASSEMBLE FISSILE MATERIAL INTO A SUPERCRITICAL MASS DURING CLASS
I WILL NOT ASSEMBLE FIS

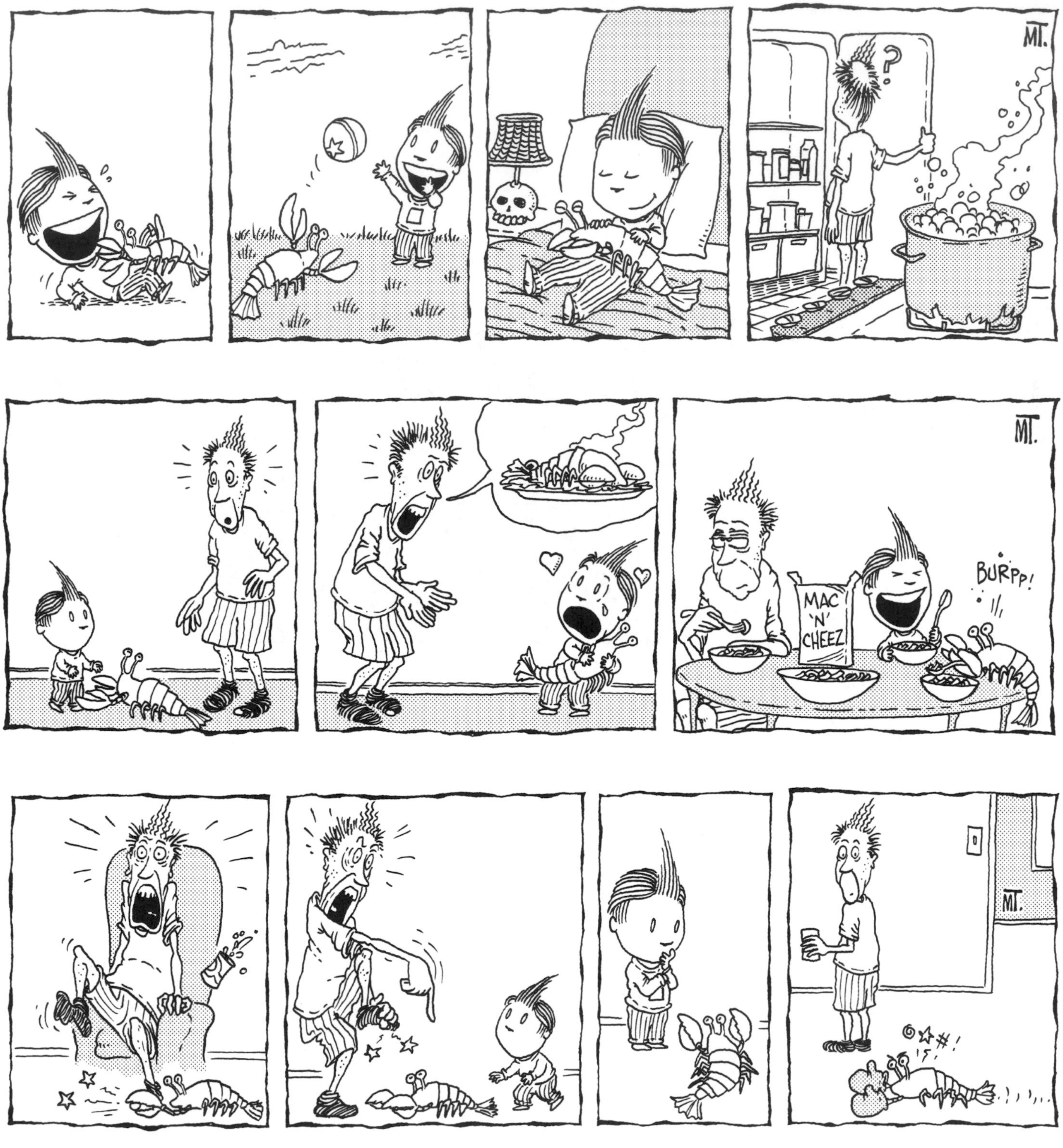
MT.
?
MT.
MAC 'N' CHEEZ
BURPP!
MT.

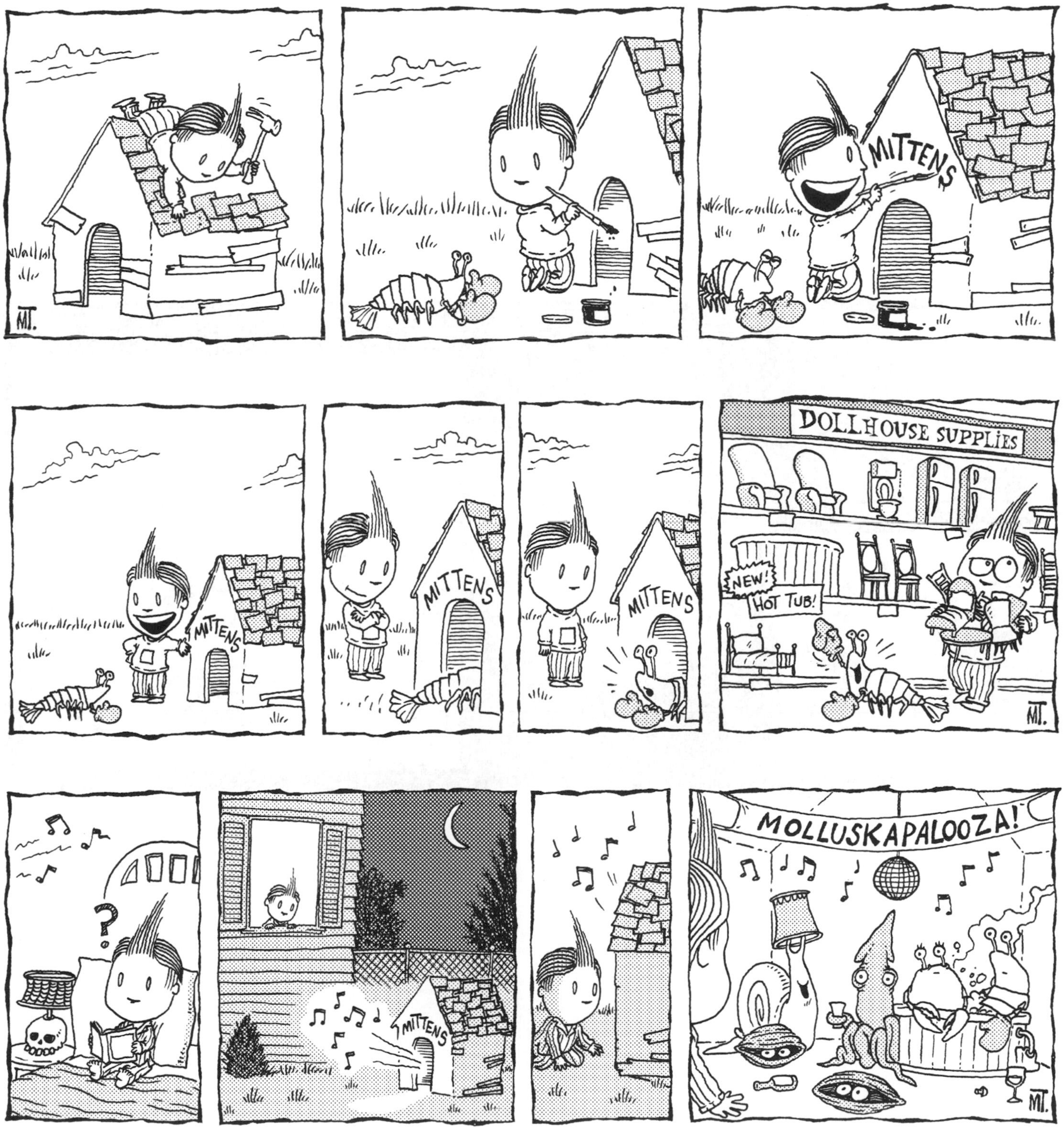
MT.
MITTENS
MITTENS
MITTENS
MITTENS
DOLLHOUSE SUPPLIES
NEW!
HOT TUB!
MT.
?
MITTENS
MOLLUSKAPALOOZA!
MT.

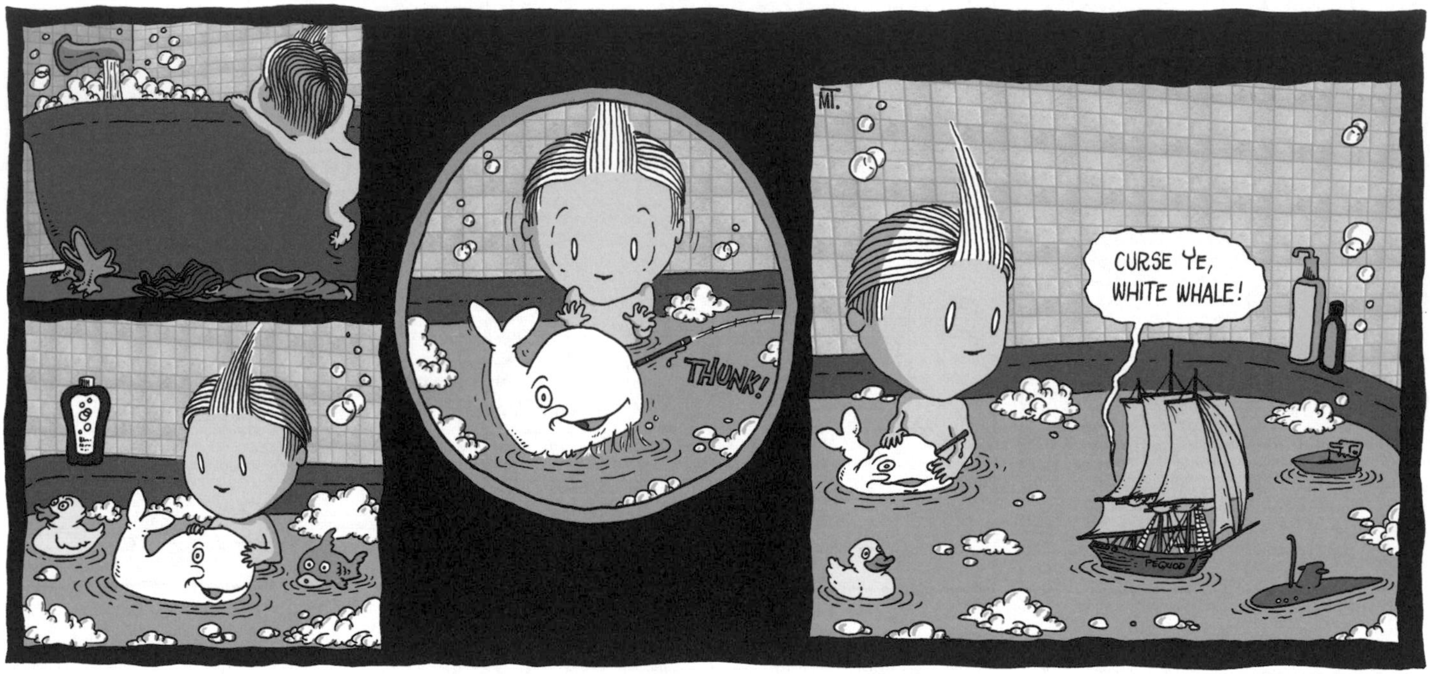
THUNK!
CURSE YE,
WHITE WHALE!
PEQUOD

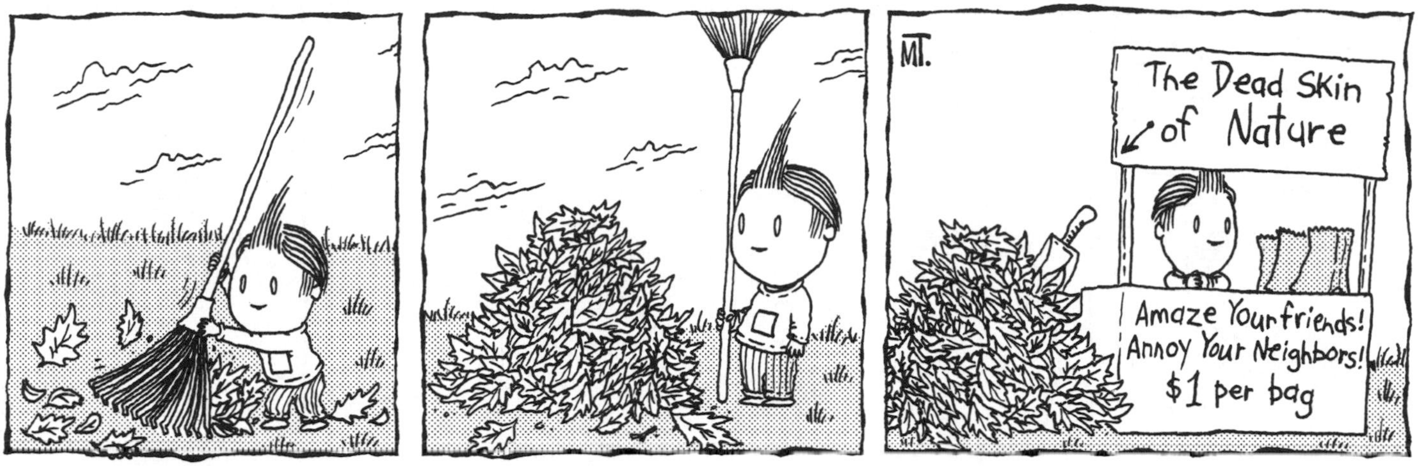
MT.
The Dead Skin of Nature
Amaze Your friends! Annoy Your Neighbors! $1 per bag

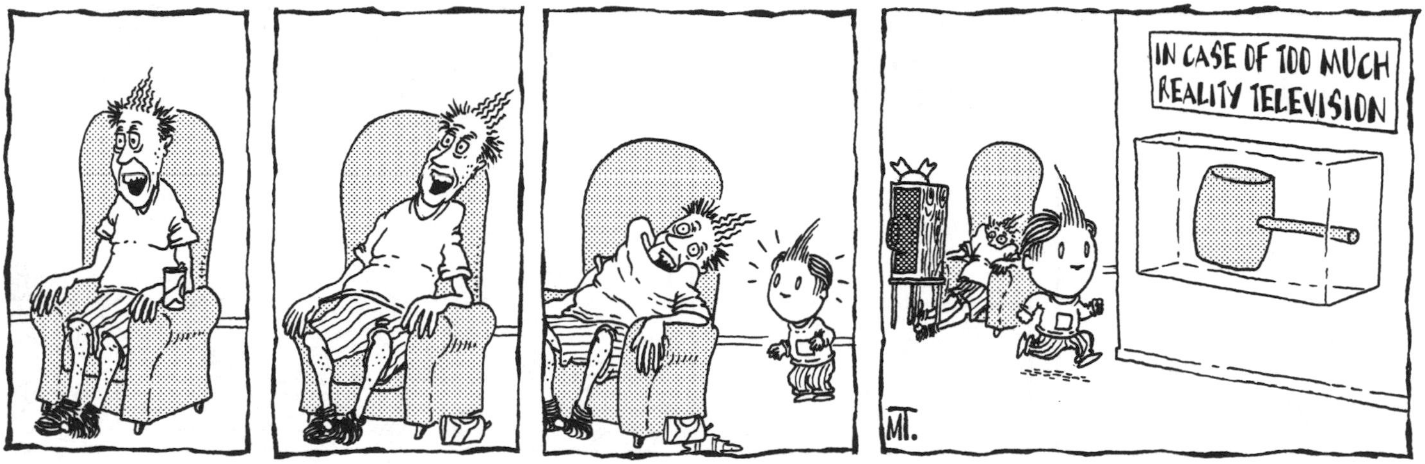
IN CASE OF TOO MUCH REALITY TELEVISION
MT.

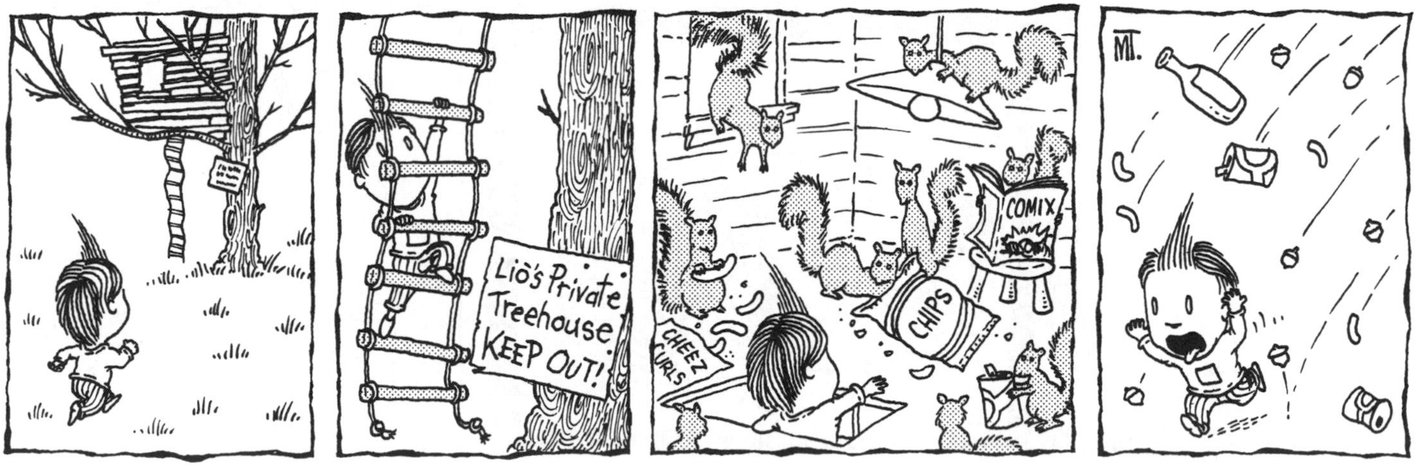
Lio's Private Treehouse KEEP OUT!
CHEEZ CURLS
CHIPS
COMIX
MT.

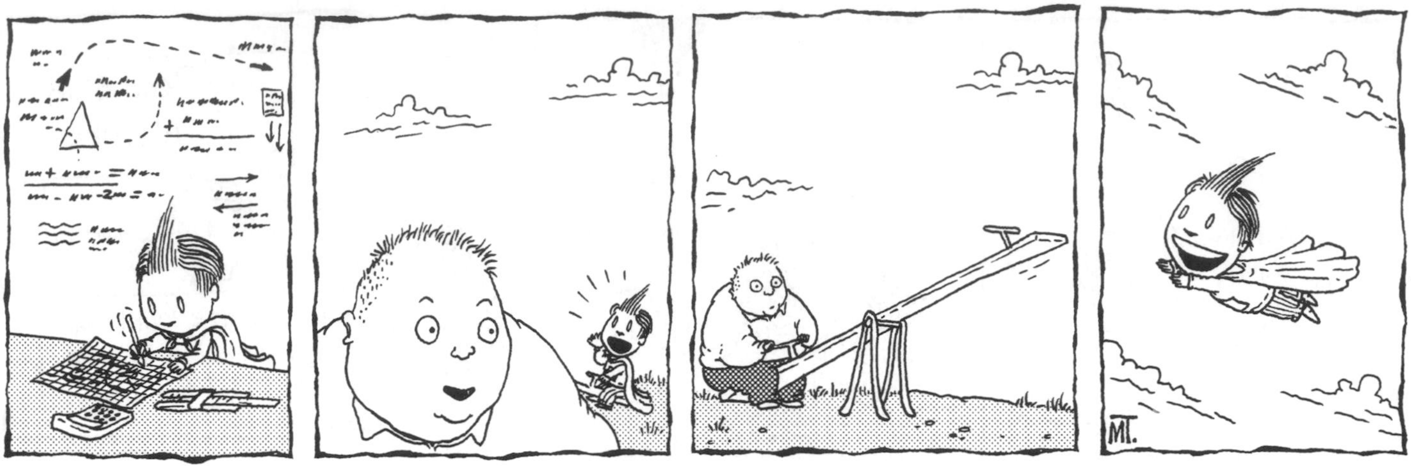

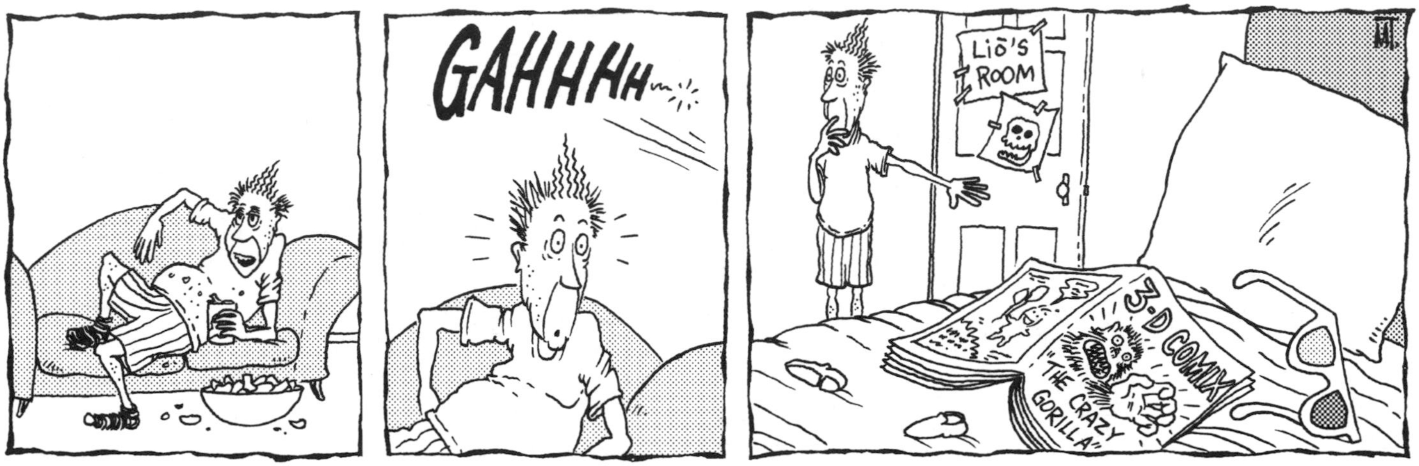
GAHHHH
LIO'S ROOM
3-D COMIX
"THE CRAZY GORILLA"

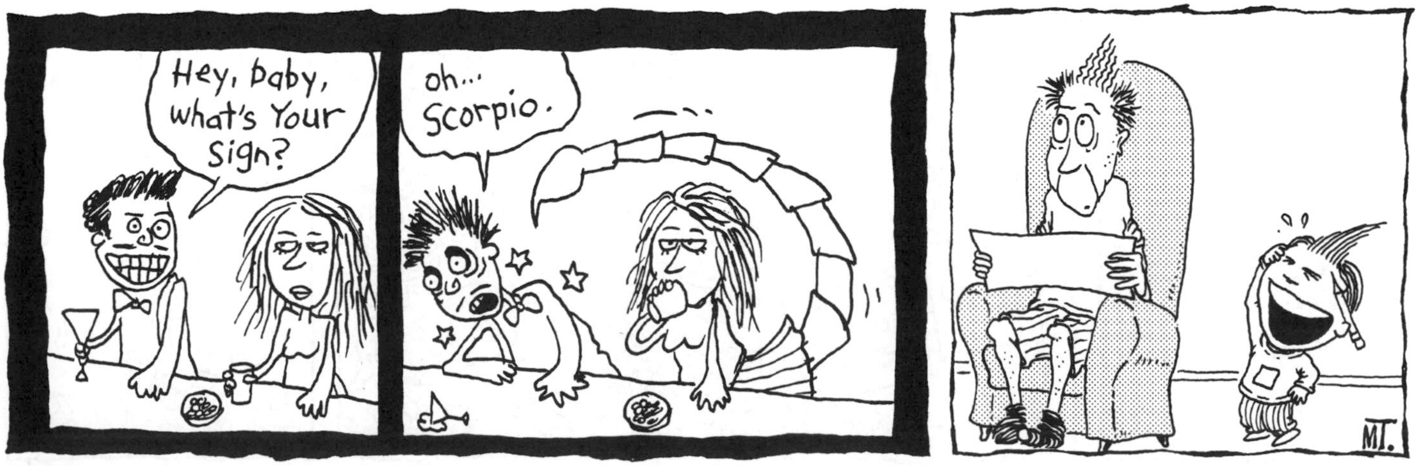
Hey, baby, what's Your Sign?
oh... Scorpio.

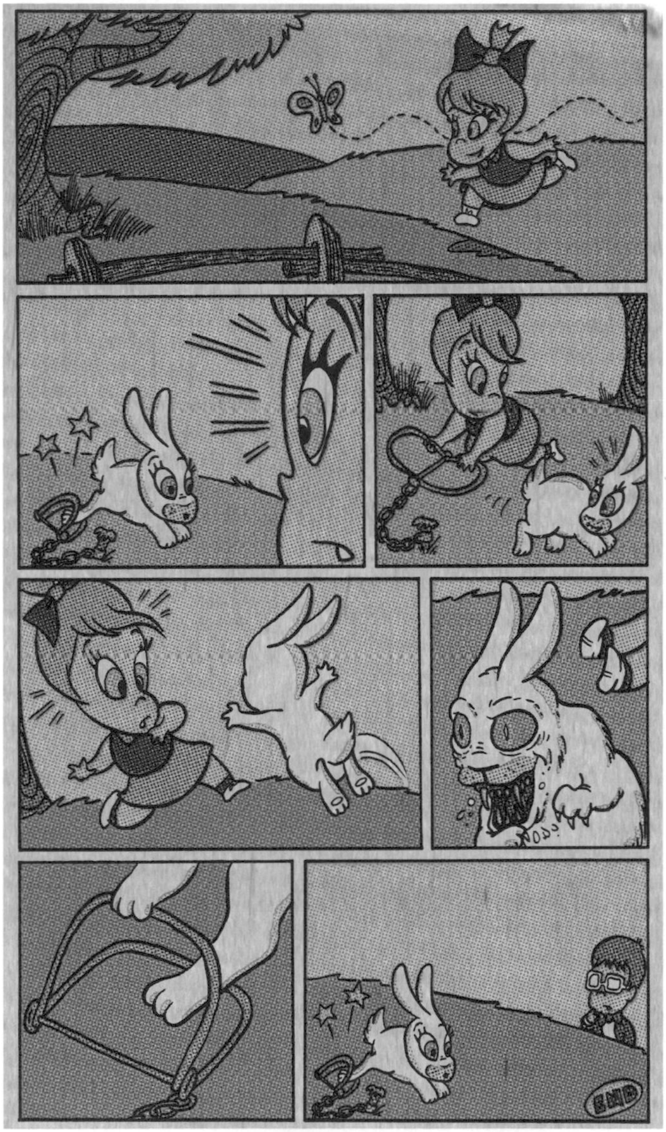
END

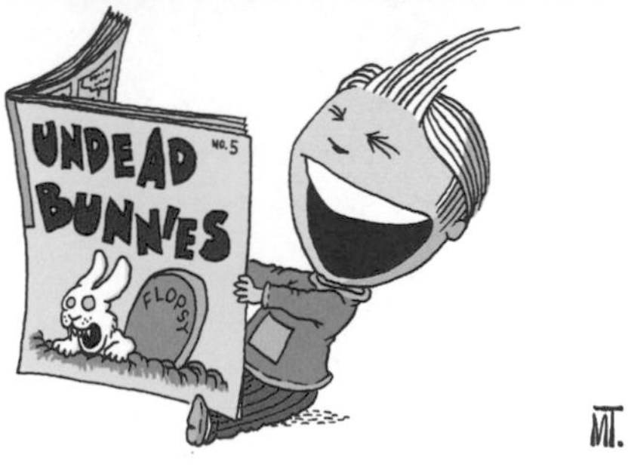
UNDEAD
No. 5
BUNNIES
FLOPSY
MT.